# THE BEST SHORT PLAYS 1983

# THE
# BEST
# SHORT
# PLAYS *1983*

*edited and with an introduction by*
RAMON DELGADO

*Best Short Plays Series*

*Chilton Book Company*
*Radnor, Pennsylvania*

Copyright © 1983 by Ramon Delgado
All Rights Reserved
Published in Radnor, Pennsylvania 19089, by Chilton Book Company
Library of Congress Catalog Card No. 38–8006
ISBN 0–8019–7296–5
ISSN 0067–6284
Manufactured in the United States of America

0008 - 83 - 083 - 1

*for Alan Denton*

# CONTENTS

# INTRODUCTION

At the time of this writing the 1981–82 theatre season has been over for several months, and the 1982–83 season has barely begun. The season concluded was termed "lackluster" by *New York Times* critic Frank Rich, "disappointing" by *Christian Science Monitor's* John Beaufort, and *Variety* headlined: "B'WAY SEASON LOOMS WORST IN YEARS, HIT SHOWS SCARCE, ATTENDANCE DOWN." Though box office grosses were higher, the increase was due to inflated ticket prices—$22.40 average versus about $19.00 in 1980–81. But significantly, attendance itself was off more than 500,000 admissions.

In such a difficult environment for theatre, what fate befell the less spectacular, sometime orphan—the one-act play? Perhaps surprisingly there was a dramatic increase in Off-Broadway, Off-Off-Broadway, and regional theatre productions of one-acts—in New York largely due to settlement of a contract dispute between playwrights and Actors Equity over Equity terms for showcase productions. Much to playwrights' satisfaction, the issue was resolved in their favor, and more new plays were made available than during the two years the issue had been in litigation.

The Ensemble Studio Theatre in Manhattan presented a four-part marathon of one-acts, the Actors Theatre of Louisville again presented both a festival of "Shorts" and their annual spring showcase of new full-length and short plays, particularly emphasizing the monologue form. On the West Coast, the New One-Act Theatre Ensemble in Los Angeles, actively produced short plays, and the San Anselmo Bay Area Play Festival submitted their fifth program of both long and short plays. In New England, Boston's American Premiere Stage initiated their offerings with a festival of one-acts. And in the

Mid-Atlantic region, the new Philadelphia Festival Theatre for New Plays presented an entire season of short plays. Many of the plays collected in this series in the last few years have had productions with one of these groups.

Even Broadway welcomed the short play with the successful transplant from Off-Broadway of Harvey Fierstein's *Torch Song Trilogy*, a four-hour trio of one-acts depicting the gay adventures of a female impersonator.

One of the most significant events to encourage fledgling playwrights has been the development of the Young Playwrights Festival Workshop Program sponsored by The Dramatists Guild. Student playwrights from age seven to eighteen submitted 732 scripts to the project. Ten of the best were produced by Manhattan's Circle Repertory Company in May of 1982, with excellent direction and performances—a fine showcase for impressive, young talent. Hopefully, we will be able to include one or more short plays from this annual event in future volumes of *Best Short Plays*.

The reader may note that occasionally the copyright date of a play in these collections is several years prior to the publication date of the volume. A word of explanation is in order. Often a playwright, particularly an unknown writer, may spend several years circulating a script and searching for production (which usually precedes publication). A glance at the prefaces to *The Color of Heat, Am I Blue*, and *Charlie the Chicken* in this volume will provide specific examples of the sometimes long road to recognition and publication.

Also, it may be noted that though the editor makes a conscious effort at the time of selection to include unpublished plays as at least half of the collection, frequently by the date of publication many of those plays also have been selected for publication by editors of acting editions for the amateur theatre market. When such decisions are made—even as galley pages of *Best Short Plays* are being proofread—this information is added to the copyright information, so readers wishing to pursue production may contact the controller of rights more easily.

It is encouraging to see theatre students reading, studying, and producing the plays from this series. At Montclair State College I have utilized the latest volume of *Best Short Plays* in a recently offered playwriting class to introduce students to current models of the one-act form and to familiarize them

with the range of thematic and topical concerns of their con-
temporaries. Students in my directing classes have selected
the majority of their final projects from plays in this series—
without pressure from their professor, I might add. And frequently scenes for acting classes are drawn from these plays.
Why the student enthusiasm? I believe it is because some of
the most imaginative, humorous, touching, and powerful
characters, situations, and ideas are skillfully compacted into
today's one-act plays.

While compiling the contents of this year's collection of *Best
Short Plays,* I received an invitation to appear on a panel ex-
amining "American Values in the Plays of Contemporary
Writers" for the 1982 convention of the American Theatre
Association. Reflecting on the plays selected for the last three
volumes, one might conclude that:

1. the materialism of the American Dream is dying, while
   the spiritual hopes remain: *The Pushcart Peddlers '81,
   Twirler '82, Rupert's Birthday '83;*
2. the nuclear family relationship is breaking up: *Reunion
   '81, Reflections in a Window '82, It Ain't the Heat, It's the
   Humility '83;*
3. sexual relationships are in a turmoil: *Never Tell Isobel '81,
   Chocolate Cake '82, The Color of Heat '83;*
4. social and religious institutions are threadbare or crum-
   bling: *Sister Mary Ignatius Explains It All For You '81, Today
   A Little Extra '82, Loss of Memory '83;*
5. there is a nostalgia for a seemingly simpler, more romantic time: *The Nightingale and Not the Lark '81, In Fire-
   works Lie Secret Codes '82, Confluence '83.*

As the plays in this series are the best representatives of the
scores considered for publication, they are a reliable barom-
eter of the concerns of our playwrights, who more often than
not are in the vanguard of a changing society.

RAMON DELGADO
*Montclair, New Jersey*

*Murray Schisgal*

# A NEED FOR
# BRUSSELS SPROUTS

# Murray Schisgal

Murray Schisgal—whose satirical cartoon *The Pushcart Peddlers* appeared in *The Best Short Plays 1981*—scores again with the delightful character comedy, *A Need for Brussels Sprouts*. The premiere directed by Arthur Storch at the John Drew Theatre in East Hampton, New York, in July 1981, starring Anne Jackson as the tough lady cop and Eli Wallach (her off-stage husband) as the lonely, down-at-the-heels actor cited for disturbing the peace, drew plaudits from reviewers. Morton Gottfried declared that Schisgal is "writing at his funniest, and there is no playwright funnier." Alvin Klein in the *New York Times* calls the play "Mr. Schisgal's truest, wisest work yet. . . . Mr. Schisgal has written an engaging, romantic and upbeat comedy of despair, and just as it seems that he is glumly closing the book on male-female relationships, the Wallachs glowingly open it right back up again." The play was revived at Syracuse Stage in Syracuse, New York, with a companion piece, *A Need for Less Expertise*, under the collective title *Twice Around the Park*. Another successful six-week run opened at the John F. Kennedy Center in Washington in August, 1982, again starring the Wallachs.

Three months later Broadway greeted the production with Walter Kerr—long a Schisgal fan—glowing: ". . . you tend to lean forward, rooting for the next chuckle or boff to come in the nick of time and for that nice Wallach couple to put it all together again. I mean put together their special lunatic universe in which nothing is merrier than misery."

The whimsical events in the plays of Murray Schisgal are glittering reflections of his quixotic background. Before his writing supported him, he supported it with such odd jobs as setting pins in a bowling alley, playing saxophone and clarinet in a small band, pushing a hand truck in Manhattan's garment district and working as a dress hanger-upper in Klein's Department Store. Schisgal was a high school dropout, earning his diploma later in the U.S. Navy, where he became Radioman, Third Class. He attended the Brooklyn Conservatory of Music and Long Island University, received a law degree from Brooklyn Law School, a B.A. from the New School for Social Research, taught English at the James Fenimore Cooper Junior High School in East Harlem, and wrote sixty short stories and three and a half novels—all before the age of thirty-five.

The first productions of his plays suggest the luck of the enchanted. Having written five one-act plays while still employed as a teacher, he confidently quit the security of educating American youth and took off for Spain to continue his playwriting. On his way, he left the five short plays with The British Drama League in London, who immediately offered to produce *The Typists* and *The Tiger*—this in 1960—three years before they were presented in New York. Nevertheless, the plays were worth the wait and received both the Vernon Rice Award and the Outer Circle Award. His first commercial success, *Luv*, was also first produced in London in 1963; the premiere, a year before the play opened at the Booth Theatre in New York with Eli Wallach, Anne Jackson, and Alan Arkin, directed by Mike Nichols.

A steady flow of plays has bubbled forth from Mr. Schisgal's artesian well: a collection of one-acts, *Fragments, Windows and Other Plays* (published in 1965); *Jimmy Shine* (published in 1968); *Ducks and Lovers* (published in 1972); *The Chinese and Dr. Fish* (published in 1973); *All American Millionaire* (published in 1974); *All Over Town* (published in 1975); and *The Pushcart Peddlers* (first published in 1980).

# Characters:

LEON ROSE

MARGARET HEINZ

# Scene:

A living room in a West End Avenue apartment building. There is an entrance door on the right, downstage. A swinging kitchen door and a bedroom door in the left wall. In the rear wall a pair of windows; on the sills and on the floor, a group of houseplants. To the right of the windows, bookshelves.

The present tenant has still to unpack some cartons; framed photographs and posters are piled neatly around the room. By the front door, there is an antique coat rack with a goodly number of odd hats on it; there is an antique body-length mirror (or simply a wall mirror), left, rear; also a stereo unit. Downstage, center, a sofa, an ornate wooden armchair, a hassock, a Duncan Phyfe lamp table at right of sofa.

# Time:

Spring: late afternoon.

Before the curtain rises we hear someone singing Cavaradossi's aria from the opera Tosca with full orchestral accompaniment: "Quale Occhio Al Mondo Puo Star Di Paro."

# At Rise:

We see Leon Rose "singing," loudly, magnificently, along with recording, to his reflection in the mirror. He is wearing a once-elegant robe, an ascot, slippers, and a cavalier's plumed hat.

Leon moves downstage, "singing" with increased fervor. He places his foot on the hassock, raises his arms into the air. The doorbell rings several times, but Leon continues "singing," not hearing the doorbell. Then the sound of banging on the door. Finally Leon turns and moves to door.

LEON: (Shouts above music. Now we realize that he was merely miming the singer on the demo record) All right, all right, I'm

coming! I'm not deaf! You don't have to knock the door down!
Where's your common . . . (*He throws open door, takes a step back
as Policewoman Margaret Heinz, uniformed, no jacket, nightstick in
hand, enters. Leon faintly finishes sentence*) sense."
(*Margaret stares hard at Leon. She looks around apartment, swag-
gers with an almost masculine gait directly to stereo unit and shuts
it. She takes out her summons book, inserted in belt, gets ready to
write summons, moving downstage*)

LEON: (*Closes door; moves to her; nervously*) One . . . one second, Miss. I mean, Officer. Officer. I mean, Policewoman
Officer, that's what I mean. You're a Policewoman Officer,
am I correct?

MARGARET: (*Business-like; repressed anger*) Name.

LEON: Can't we talk? I mean, respectfully, with due respect, can't we talk before you write that ticket out? By the
way, I do not own a car. I do not drive a car, so if you're up
here because of a double-parked car, there is a terrible injustice being perpetrated, and I have always fought against
injustice, and that includes Fascism, Nazism, racism, and Communism!

MARGARET: (*Slight pause*) Do you give me your name, mister, or do I have to take you in?

LEON: May I ask, respectfully, what a tax-paying citizen is
being accused of in the privacy of his apartment when he does
not even own or drive a car?

MARGARET: You're in violation of a city anti-noise ordi-
nance for playing your phonograph too loudly. Does that
answer your question?

LEON: Not quite, because I know who put you up to this,
and now I'm getting mad; now I am definitely getting mad.
(*Drops hat on carton upstage of front door*) I recently moved into
this apartment, and I get along with all my neighbors except
for this crazy old hag upstairs. Every time I sneeze, she starts
banging on the ceiling and hitting the radiators with a frying
pan. She has to be a genuine crackpot.

MARGARET: Do you know the crazy old hag who lives upstairs?

LEON: No, I don't . . .

MARGARET: You're looking at her, mister. (*Shouts*) Name!

LEON: (*Answers quickly; hands at sides like a schoolboy*) Rose.
R-O-S-E. Leon. L-E-O-N. Leon Rose.

MARGARET: (*Writing; to herself*) Leon Rose. Residence is . . .

LEON: One second, please. I . . . I owe you an apology, Miss, I mean, Officer. Officer. I sincerely apologize. The truth is that I had no logical way of knowing that you were that crazy old hag who . . . (*Realizes he's ruined it; thin voice*) Would you by any chance care for a glass of Perrier water with a wedge of lime?

MARGARET: (*Writing; to herself*) Residence is 925 West End Avenue . . .

LEON: Wait. Hold it. Let's.not act precipitously. I have a single question to ask you: how much is that ticket going to cost me?

MARGARET: It's a summons, not a ticket. The fine is a hundred dollars.

LEON: A hundred dollars? For playing my phonograph too loudly? This is ridiculous. This is highway robbery. How much would it cost me if I screamed at the top of my lungs? Like this. (*He does so*)

MARGARET: It'll . . .

LEON: And how much would it cost me if I screamed at the top of my lungs and I jumped up and down and I clapped my hands? How much would this cost me? (*He does so, a mad little screaming dance*)

MARGARET: It'll cost you a hundred dollars for each violation.

LEON: It was an example! I was merely giving you an example!

MARGARET: Look, Mr. Rose, I just finished a twelve-hour tour of duty. I made three arrests, gave out fifteen parking tickets, nine summonses, and I chased a nude man from 56th Street to 44th Street where I lost him in a moviehouse that was showing *Mary Poppins*. So don't give me a hard time, huh?

LEON: I wasn't . . .

MARGARET: All I want to do is get out of these clodhoppers and soak my bones in a hot tub of water.

LEON: I understand.

MARGARET: Do you understand? Do you know what it's like to be out there on those streets? Did you ever wear a uniform and try to break up a sidewalk crap game or collar a pimp in a massage parlor?

LEON: No. Not that I recall.

MARGARET: Did you ever get hassled by a punk or have a

can of garbage dumped on your head during an anti-war demonstration?

LEON: No. Not recently.

MARGARET: We're understaffed, undersupported, underpaid, and we still have to buy our own lousy bullets with our own lousy money!

LEON: Personally I think the police department is doing a wonderful job . . . wonderful.

MARGARET: Do you? Did you ever write to the mayor and ask him to give us a little extra consideration?

LEON: I was planning to do that this evening.

MARGARET: I bet you were.

LEON: I was. I was. Officer, I wouldn't be making such a to-do about a crummy hundred dollar fine, if you didn't catch me at a particularly awkward time vis-a-vis my cash flow.

MARGARET: Your what?

LEON: My financial situation. It normally isn't a problem with me, but I recently had to pay the landlord two month's rent in advance plus one month's rent security; I had to pay the moving people nine hundred dollars to carry my belongings from the East Side to the West Side . . . (*Indicates work done*) I had to pay to paint the apartment, wallpaper the bathroom, install a telephone, connect an . . . (*"Air conditioner" would have followed, but she interrupts*)

MARGARET: Mr. Rose, you can explain that to the judge. Just let me finish . . .

LEON: I insist that attention must be paid! After all, we are neighbors. That's what neighbors are for. To help one another. To stick together. To be friends.

MARGARET: So you want to be friends.

LEON: Yes, I do. If neighbors can't be friends, there's no hope for civilization. We might as well pack our suitcase and move back to the dark ages.

MARGARET: Some people should pack their suitcases so some other people can have some peace and quiet! Where do you get off playing your phonograph so loudly? Do you think I like banging on the ceiling? Do you think I have nothing else to do when I get home from work?

LEON: I can explain . . .

MARGARET: I've been living in this building for seven years. For seven years I didn't hear a sound from this apartment. There was a nice elderly woman living here and she knew what it was to be considerate of other people. She died, poor woman . . .

LEON: She died? In this apartment?

MARGARET: That's right. She was . . .

LEON: What room did she die in?

MARGARET: In the bedroom.

LEON: In my bedroom?

MARGARET: There was a big brass bed in there.

LEON: That's my big brass bed. The landlord sold it to me for a hundred and thirty dollars.

MARGARET: That was her bed. She was so quiet nobody knew she was dead for more than a week.

LEON: This is strange. This is very strange. Every time I get into that big brass bed I have the creepiest sensation that someone is laying next to me.

MARGARET: Is that why you play your phonograph so loudly in the middle of the night?

LEON: No, no, I can explain.

MARGARET: Go ahead. Explain. I'm listening.

LEON: I am an actor, Officer, a trained, professional actor. I'm preparing for an audition that requires I pantomime an opera singer. And when I'm preparing for an audition, I lose all sense of everything else. I lose myself in my work.

MARGARET: And that's why you're getting a summons. I have two kids up there, Mr. Rose, two kids who go to school. Do you know that since you moved in my daughter can't study and her face has broken out with acne pimples? Do you know my son was sent home from school because when everybody was standing and singing "God Bless America," he was sitting and sleeping?

LEON: No, I . . .

MARGARET: Why don't you lower that thing when I bang on your ceiling?

LEON: I didn't realize . . .

MARGARET: Last night was the last straw. Where's your dog? Do you know he was barking until one o'clock in the morning?

LEON: In that regard you're incorrect, Officer. I do not own a dog. I did own a dog. I bought him after my East Side apartment was burglarized the second time. But the third time they burglarized it, they took the dog with them. This is the dog you heard. (*He moves to stereo unit, pushes tape button. We hear a dog barking and growling viciously; shuts stereo*) I put on this tape whenever I leave. It doesn't do that much good. I was burglarized four times in my East Side apartment. Besides my dog, they took my television set, my cameras, my Betamax, my silverware, my blender, my Cuisinart. . . . Anything that wasn't nailed down, they took. They wiped me out. The fourth time they broke in there wasn't anything to take so they left me a book of food stamps.

MARGARET:   That still doesn't excuse your playing that thing until one o'clock when my kids are trying to get some sleep.

LEON:   I agree. It was thoughtless of me. I give you my word it won't happen in the future. I'm sure as a police officer you can sympathize with the plight of your everyday citizen.

MARGARET:   We sympathize, but we have half as many officers on the force as we need. Half. How can we do the job if we don't have the personnel?

LEON:   I'm not criticizing. You guys are doing everything humanly possible. I know it's a jungle out there.

MARGARET:   A jungle, is what it is. The minute we collar one bum, two bums take his place. And do you think the bum we collar goes to jail? Oh, no. Not on your life. The judge pats him on the back, gives him a speech, and in an hour he's on the street again.

LEON:   I know. I know that for a fact. I read about this prostitute that a judge took home with him because she had no place to stay for the night.

MARGARET:   You think that's something? I once brought in a prostitute and the judge married her!

LEON:   No-o-o.

MARGARET:   I'm telling you he married her! They're living in Oyster Bay now. They have a house, a car, a sailboat, a swimming pool. . . . That hooker's living a better life than I am!

LEON:   Disgusting.

MARGARET:   It's worse than disgusting. Did you ever visit one of those minimum security prisons?

LEON:   I was planning to do that this summer.

MARGARET:   They're not prisons; they're country clubs. With each meal the prisoners get a menu and they can select what they want to eat from a variety of choices.

LEON:   Do you know what I had for lunch today? A hard Kaiser roll and a slice of baloney.

MARGARET: During the day they play baseball, volleyball, tennis, golf, or they can go horseback riding.

LEON: I havén't been on a horse since the Korean War.

MARGARET: In the evening they have concerts or Las Vegas entertainment and they sleep in separate bedrooms with no bars on the windows.

LEON: How do you like that. Do you know I have bars on my bedroom window?

MARGARET: I couldn't sleep if I didn't have bars on my bedroom window.

LEON: We have to have bars and the criminals don't have to have bars.

MARGARET: We're the ones in prison, not them.

LEON: What we should do is change places. We'd be a lot safer and a lot happier living in those prisons of theirs.

MARGARET: You can't get into those prisons. They're so popular they have a five-year-waiting list!

LEON: What a sad, sad commentary on the state of our society.

MARGARET: It makes me sick just to think about it.

LEON: Look, Officer, now that we're better acquainted, let me introduce myself to you, properly. (*Extends hand*) Leon Rose, your neighbor, and I hope, in the future, your friend.

MARGARET: (*Shakes his hand*) Margaret Heinz.

LEON: Why don't you sit down? Relax. Can I get you anything?

MARGARET: (*Sits on sofa; removes cap and wipes sweatband with handkerchief*) It has been a long day for me. I wouldn't mind a beer if you have one.

LEON: Absolutely. (*Moving to kitchen*) One ice-cold beer coming up for my upstairs neighbor. (*Offstage*) How old are your children?

MARGARET: I have a girl fourteen and a boy eleven.

LEON: (*Offstage*) It must be difficult for you, having a full-time job and raising two children. What does your husband do?

MARGARET: He's dead.

LEON: (*Offstage*) That is difficult.

MARGARET: It was more difficult when he was alive. (*To herself*) The lying, sneaky bastard.

LEON: (*Enters, carrying a tray with a beer can and glass on it*)

Is it all right if I call you Margaret? I don't like being formal. Especially with a neighbor.

MARGARET: I don't usually get this kind of treatment when I write out a summons. You're not trying to bribe me are you?

LEON: Why do you even think such a thing? Drink up. It's imported. From China.

(*Margaret takes can from tray, ignoring the glass. She pulls off tab, puts the can to her mouth and drinks—beer can be drained in present—without removing can from her mouth. Leon puts tray aside*)

LEON: I'm surprised the name Leon Rose doesn't mean anything to you. I assume you're not much of a theater goer. Anyone who attends the theater with any regularity would certainly be familiar with . . . (*He turns to see that the can is still glued to her mouth. His eyes widen; his voice falters*) . . . the name . . . Leon Rose . . .

(*Whistles to pass the time, moving about; then*)

Do you . . . go to the theater . . . with any . . . regularity?

(*At last Margaret removes the empty can from her mouth; wipes her mouth with shirt sleeve*)

LEON: Can I get you anything else, Margaret? A six-pack, perhaps?

MARGARET: No, thanks. It's not bad, Chinese beer.

LEON: It's not. (*She unwittingly crushes beer can and hands it to him*)

LEON: (*Reacts*) It goes extremely well with a T-bone steak and baked potatoes.

MARGARET: I'll have to try it sometime.

LEON: I'm surprised you haven't seen me perform any-where, Margaret. I've been in dozens of plays. (*He crosses into kitchen to get rid of tray and beer can*) Broadway. Off Broadway, regional theatre, stock, guest artist . . .

MARGARET: What plays have you been in?

LEON: (*Enters*) Oh, I've done so many I can't keep track. As a matter of fact, this chair is from *Another Part of the Forest*.

MARGARET: When I was a kid I was kind of interested in acting.

LEON: You were?

MARGARET: In high school I took a course in it and I'd go to the movies every chance I . . . Wait a minute. I recognize you. (*Rises*)

LEON: (*Beaming*) Well, I . . .

MARGARET: You do a TV commercial. It's for a cat food, isn't it? What's the name of that cat food? Tabby Chow? Kitty Tidbits? Pussy Grub! That's it! You're the meow-meow man on the Pussy Grub commercial.

LEON: (*Piqued*) What difference does it make. That's not my work! I'm an actor!

MARGARET: You are famous . . .

LEON: Actors do all sorts of things to . . . supplement their incomes. It's quite acceptable nowadays.

MARGARET: Do you know you're the only celebrity living in this building?

LEON: I am?

MARGARET: The only one. It's a weird feeling. I can't wait to tell my kids that the meow-meow man is living underneath them.

(*A car horn is heard. Margaret moves to window*)

MARGARET: If they come down, would you give them your autograph?

LEON: It would be my pleasure.

MARGARET: Thanks. (*Opens window; leans out and shouts*) Hey, you, you! (*Horn stops*) Cut that noise out down there! Cut it out or I'm pulling you in! (*She slams window shut, moves to sofa, pulling up her pants, pulling down on crotch*) I'm really sorry I have to give you this summons.

LEON: Margaret, you don't *have* to give me a summons, do you?

MARGARET: I already wrote your name and address, and once I do that . . .

LEON: Can't you erase it? (*Moves to desk in rear where he picks up very small bottle*) I have some excellent correction fluid. It doesn't leave a trace. No one has to know. (*He removes cap from bottle*)

MARGARET: My record's clean in the department. I don't like messing with it. You can plead guilty with an excuse. Maybe the judge'll take into consideration . . . (*Sits on sofa; puts on cap*)

LEON: Margie, it's not only the money. It's not. It's . . . the principle. I mean, paying for more tennis courts for prisoners. That's what's upsetting me. (*Returns bottle to desk*) But whatever happens, I'm glad we're becoming friends. (*Turns on charm*) I didn't know I had such an attractive upstairs neighbor. There's something very exciting about a woman in a policeman's uniform: (*Sits beside her*) the way her small, soft face shines and glows at the top of her blue shirt; the way her billowy hair curls around her little pink ears when she's wearing her cap; the way she carries a gun on her hip, emphasizing the full roundness of her plump buttocks. I find it very, very, very exciting. (*He puts his arm around the back of the sofa, behind Margaret*)

MARGARET:  (*Glances at his arm*) Do you?

LEON:  I do. You're a beautiful woman, Margie. You're like a combination of Goldie Hawn and Ethel Barrymore.

MARGARET:  Who was Ethel Barrymore?

LEON:  She was an incredible actress, with a magnificent stage presence.

MARGARET:  I remind you of her?

LEON:  (*Nods*) Your eyes in particular. They have the same regal majesty, the same irrepressible passion burning in them.

MARGARET:  What would your wife say if she walked in now?

LEON:  She probably wouldn't say anything. But I'd probably faint. She's been dead for eight years.

MARGARET:  Were you married long?

LEON:  No, no. I've been an extremely fortunate man. I've been married three times and they were all short marriages. In fact my first marriage was so short it ended before the honeymoon ended. (*He breaks into a laugh*)

MARGARET:  You think that's funny, huh?

LEON:  What's that?

MARGARET:  I don't think that's funny! I think that's sick, real sick! Oh, you're a sly one, you are. Coming on so strong, so sweet, so lovey-dovey. Maybe you can pull that stuff on some dumb sixteen-year-old kid, but not on me, mister! (*Rises; pulls Leon to his feet, pushes him to wall, right*) Get on your feet! On your feet! Up against the wall! Move it! Move it!

LEON:  (*Does so; utterly confused if not frightened*) Wha'-wha' . . . Margie, wha'-wha' . . .

MARGARET:  Get your hands behind your back. Spread your legs! Wider! Wider! (*Kicks them apart*) I heard about you actors and what you do for kicks. I know all about it. (*She runs her hand down his chest, his legs, up between his legs, inadvertently hitting his privates*)

LEON:  (*Jumps up*) Ooops!

MARGARET: Stand still! Stand still! (*She runs her hand up between his legs again, again hitting him in the privates*)

LEON: (*Jumps up*) Oooops! Oooops!

MARGARET: I got a whiff of something the minute I walked in. What is it? Pot? Grass? You were smoking a joint, weren't you?

LEON: (*Turns to her; hands on wall*) No, no. Chicken. I mean, I have a pot of chicken curry simmering on the gas range. It's for my dinner!

MARGARET: (*Moves to the kitchen*) We'll see about that!

LEON: (*Moves away from wall*) Margaret, what got into you? We were having such a pleasant conversation. Why are you . . . ?

MARGARET: (*After looking in kitchen*) Let me tell you a couple of things about your upstairs neighbor you don't know, mister. I've been used and abused by men like you for as long as I can remember. When I think of how dumb I was, how innocent, how trusting . . . I get so damn angry I just wanna plug holes into every slimy, deceiving, two-legged male in this city!

LEON: (*Sits in armchair*) Let's . . . Let's be calm now, Margie. Your record's clean. You don't want to spoil your record, do you?

MARGARET: I didn't start out dreaming of being a cop; that wasn't my dream. You men put me into this uniform; you put this gun on my hip, and you showed me what to do with it, so don't get smart with me, Leon, I'm warning you.

LEON: No, no. I wouldn't.

MARGARET: I've got more damn anger in me than I can handle. To get this job I hada lift and carry a seventy-five pound dummy up and down a couple of flights of stairs; I hada take courses in boxing and wrestling; I hada learn how to swing a nightstick and put away six-foot apes. (*Wagging nightstick*) But for the sake of my kids I try my damndest to control the anger.

LEON: You sound like a wonderful mother.

MARGARET: I met their father when I was sixteen, sixteen, what did I know? I believed him. I believed every stinking lie he told me. He was on the force. Every day when I got out of school he'd be standing in the middle of the street, directing traffic, a tall, strong, handsome Irishman with a smile that was pure blarney.

LEON:   I don't recall if I told you, Margie, but I'm not Irish. I'm not. I hope you understand . . .

MARGARET:   You talk when I tell you to talk, got it?

LEON:   Yes, Ma'm. Absolutely.

MARGARET:   Timmy. Timmy the Great, that's what we kids called him. When he saw me, he held up his hand to stop the traffic and he waved me across. I felt like a Queen in a fairy tale. I'd say hello and he'd give me a grape lollypop. The rat knew I was crazy for grape lollypops.

LEON:   I used to love the ones with the Tootsie-roll centers. Did you ever . . . ? (*Raises hand*) That's it. Not another word. (*He "locks" his mouth with an imaginary key, tosses imaginary key away*)

MARGARET:   The day I graduated high school we were married. I was so dumb that I thought being married to somebody was something special. It wasn't special. It wasn't anything. He'd come in and out of the apartment as if it was a Chinese laundry, to drop off and pick up his shirts. That's when we had sex . . . when he was changing his shirts. He probably figured he was half undressed anyway, what did he have to lose? But after the second kid was born, he stopped coming in to change his shirt. That ended our sex life. That wasn't the worst thing. He started calling me Mommy.

LEON:   Mommy?

MARGARET:   Mommy. But I didn't complain. I didn't nag him. My reward was that he ran off with a cheerleader from my old high school. After I got my divorce . . .

LEON:   Now I'm getting mad. That rat! That sick, degenerate rat! If I were you, Margie, I'd go after him and I'd . . . (*Seeing that Margaret is displeased again by his interruption, he looks around floor, picks up imaginary key, "locks" his mouth and tosses away key, over his shoulder*)

MARGARET:   After I got my divorce, I had a drawerful of bills and two kids to support. I didn't have a job. I didn't have experience. I went from employment agency to employment agency; I answered ads in the newspapers; I did everything until at last . . .

LEON:   You got a job?

MARGARET:   I got a job.

LEON:   What job did you get?

MARGARET:   I was a raccoon.

LEON:   A raccoon?

MARGARET:   Didn't you ever hear of the raccoons?

LEON:   I heard of them. But I didn't know they could get jobs in the city.

MARGARET:   Raccoons are cocktail waitresses. In the Hotel Geneva on 56th Street.

LEON:   Oh. Cocktail waitresses. You'll have to excuse me. I've been out of touch . . .

MARGARET:   It was a dynamite job. I wore long, black stockings and a mini-skirt with a low-cut blouse that went down to here, you know, very sharp; and I had a cap on my head with furry raccoon ears and a furry little raccoon tail. (*Turns and points to indicate to him*)

LEON:   You must have been one terrific looking raccoon.

MARGARET:   Not bad, if I say so myself. I really liked working there. I had an opportunity for advancement and could have been Head Raccoon which pays twice what a waitress gets. What happened was the manager started hassling me, bugging me for a date, using his hands, that kind of thing. I could have handled him, but he had a mouth like a cesspool.

LEON:   Why didn't you complain to the owners?

MARGARET:   Don't think I didn't. Forget it. You men are expert at covering for each other. I had a quit. I had no choice. That's when I met the other slimy skunk.

LEON:   Heinz?

MARGARET:   Transit Officer Henry Heinz. Oh, he was a smooth one, he was. Dapper, dimple-chinned Henry Heinz. Did I tell you he died?

LEON:   Yes, you did. I recall distinctly . . .

MARGARET:   (*Moves to window*) He didn't die. But to me he's dead. Just like the other one. Just like all men are dead to me. Dead . . . Dead . . . Dead . . . (*She glances out window, throws it open; leans out and shouts*) Hey, mister, double-park that car, and I'm coming down and giving you a ticket! Did you hear me? Move it! Move it! (*Sound of car screeching off. Margaret slams window shut, pulls up her pants, pulls down on crotch of pants*)

MARGARET:   Soon after I got on the force, Henry Heinz decided he had enough of patrolling the subways. He said he wanted to be a lawyer. Would sweetie-pie give him a hand until he finished law school? Sweetie-pie, the jerk, gave him everything he asked for because she was a giving person, a giving and trusting wifey-mousey who still believed that marriage was giving and trusting. Eventually I found out he wasn't going to law school. He was using my money to pay rent for another apartment and he was keeping his hooker there. Can you believe it? Taking food from the mouths of my kids to support his hooker? Oh, I got rid of him fast enough.

LEON: Margie, all men aren't the same. Some men . . .

MARGARET: You're wrong on that score. All men are the same. All men are sneaky, lying, yellow, hypocritical, two-legged, selfish animals! (*She takes nightstick and bangs it on the table*)

LEON: (*Jumps up, moves to table and examines it; aghast*) What did you do? Look what you did to my Duncan Phyfe! I used a whole can of Lemon Pledge waxing it this morning. You ruined it. You . . .

MARGARET: All men aren't the same, huh? Some men are good and some are bad, is that what you were gonna say, Leon?

LEON: I was. I was also going to say that there are some men who are decent and trustworthy and generous.

MARGARET: Where are they?

LEON: Who?

MARGARET: The men you're talking about.

LEON: They're around. If you look, you'll find them.

MARGARET: They wouldn't be in this room, would they?

LEON: It's possible.

MARGARET: Okay. I'll give you a chance to prove it. Let's hear about your three marriages. Go ahead. Let's see how decent and trustworthy you were with your three wives.

LEON: This is silly. What are we having, a trial?

MARGARET: (*Carries table; sits on sofa*) That's what it is, neighbor. A trial. I'll be the judge. You're the defendant.

LEON: You can forget it, Margaret. I'm not participating in . . .

MARGARET: (*Places summons book on table*) I noticed you piled boxes and cartons in front of the fire-exit in the hall. I really don't want to give you another summons, Leon.

LEON: How did I get into this? I didn't leave my apartment today and already it's costing me two hundred dollars!

MARGARET: Court is now in session. The state versus Leon Rose for having three short marriages. The question is: did he use and abuse his wives? Did he act in a manner detrimental to the health and welfare of women? Is he a slimy rat like all the rest of them? Judge Heinz presides. You can begin with your first wife.

LEON:  I object.

MARGARET:  What's your objection?

LEON:  I object on the grounds of the Fifth Amendment.

MARGARET:  Objection overruled!

LEON:  I appeal.

MARGARET:  Appealed denied!

LEON:  I ask the court for a recess.

MARGARET:  On what grounds?

LEON:  (*Starts left*) On the grounds I have to make a peepee.

MARGARET:  Peepee denied!

LEON:  This is incredible.

MARGARET:  The court is waiting, Mr. Rose. Your first wife. Or do you want the judge to write out the two summonses charged against you.

LEON:  All right, all right. I'll do it. I'll do it. But there are going to be repercussions, I promise you. My first wife. She . . . She was a young girl. She was still in college. Her name was . . . Glenda Fogelman, that's her. I need no defense for that marriage, none whatsoever. There was a physical problem that destroyed it. On our honeymoon, I tried to, you know, consummate the relationship. But I couldn't do it. I couldn't. I don't like to go into intimate detail, but it seemed to me her privates were built peculiarly.

MARGARET:  Her privates were built peculiarly?

LEON:  That's right, your honor. There was something . . . How shall I express it discreetly, without offending the sensibilities of the court? In my opinion, there was something, let us say, anatomically screwed up down there.

MARGARET:  Are you saying that the marriage wasn't consummated, Mr. Rose?

LEON:  That's precisely what I'm saying. Try as I might, and try I did, day and night, night and day, I could not achieve what was required of me.

MARGARET:  But you were kind to her.

LEON:  No man could have been kinder. And I'm compelled to confess to the court that I never worked so hard in my life with such poor results.

MARGARET:  You didn't force her . . .

LEON:  Force her? The girl weighed a hundred and ninety pounds. I couldn't even force her to give me half the bed!

MARGARET: Go ahead, Mr. Rose.

LEON: It was dreadful; the worst honeymoon I ever had. The truth is we were both virgins. I woke up one morning and she was gone. Her parents had the marriage annulled.

MARGARET: She left you.

LEON: She did, your honor. I swear on my third wife's grave.

MARGARET: And your second wife? How were her privates?

LEON: Not bad. Not bad. But she was a sick woman. Mentally. She was a very sick woman.

MARGARET: How long was that marriage?

LEON: Seventeen months. We had a son. He teaches at Berkeley. I don't see him as much as I'd like to . . . That's how it is.

MARGARET: Did you at any time strike your second wife?

LEON: Strike her?

MARGARET: Hit her, punch her, knock her to the ground.

LEON: Your honor, I am appalled, appalled and astonished that such an accusation could be made in this courtroom. I have always fought against brutality and injustice, whether it was described as Facism, Nazism, Communism or . . .

MARGARET: Just answer the question, Mr. Rose.

LEON: No. I never laid a hand on her. Never. Oh, on occasion a light pat on the buttocks, but only done in the most playful manner. Barbara, that was her name. She was an actress, a terribly ambitious and competitive woman. While my career was growing, hers was shrinking. She couldn't tolerate my being more successful than she was. She turned into a mean, bitter woman, and she started drinking heavily.

MARGARET: How heavily?

LEON: Well, let me put it this way: she was the only wife I had who knew how to make a vodka salad dressing. And I heard from a very reliable source that in 1962 she was voted Miss Jack Daniels, by a chapter of Alcoholics Anonymous.

MARGARET: You did nothing to cause her to drink? You didn't cheat on her? You didn't go out with other women?

LEON: I did not! I worked. I paid the bills. I gave her a home. I didn't fool around. What did I do? You tell me what I did?

MARGARET: Your third wife?

LEON:   I don't like this, Margie. I'm not finding it amusing
or . . . (*Gives it up*) I had it with college girls and ambitious
actresses. I said to myself, if I ever marry again, it would be
to a single, devoted, uncomplicated woman. My third wife was
an American Indian.

MARGARET:   From the West?

LEON:   No, from East Hampton. She was a Shinnecock.
Evidently, I don't have much judgment when it comes to
women. Nothing I did could satisfy her. I wasn't rich enough,
famous enough, sexy enough . . . One day she withdrew all
our savings and ran off with a real estate salesman. (*Firmly*)
There's another piece of evidence that's relevant here. Last
night I had a date with a woman I hadn't seen in over twenty
years. We were supposed to have a gourmet dinner in her
apartment, that she had spent all week preparing. While I
was eating a rather too spicy leek soup, she crawled under
the table and started pulling on my pants. I'm eating leek
soup and she's pulling on my pants! I said, "Hold it, hold it
a second. The least you can do is let me finish my leek soup!"
But no, she couldn't wait. She wanted it, right away, that
instant, and not from a particular man, mind you, not from
a particular human being, but from a sex machine who merely
existed for her pleasure. I walked straight out and went to
the movies, alone; that's what I did last night. Listen, I learned
a thing or two myself. Relationships are too painful. I make
no pretense about it. I don't need women. I can do very well
without them.

MARGARET:   (*Rises; angrily*) *You* can! I get up every morning
and I get down on my knees and I thank sweet Jesus for
giving me the strength to live a life without men. Do you know
what it's like to feel clean and decent and free of you and
your kind?

LEON:   Not nearly as exhilarating as being free of you and
your kind! You don't make love to a woman any more. That's
over. That's in the past. Nowadays you have to service her.
You have to engage in foreplay, in titilation, in excitation, in
lubrication. After a while you don't know if you're a man in
bed with a woman or a mechanic working under an old sta-
tionwagon!

MARGARET:   If you can't stand the heat, mister, stay out of
the kitchen!

LEON: Listen, lady, I don't need the heat and I don't need the kitchen. It so happens that I personally don't believe there is such a thing as a woman's orgasm, how do you like that?

MARGARET: If a woman's dumb enough to go to bed with you, she wouldn't believe there's such a thing as a woman's orgasm either!

LEON: Funny. Funny. I think it's the biggest fraud ever perpetrated against civilization. Vaginal orgasm, clitoral orgasm, multiple orgasm, multiple, multiple, multiple orgasm . . . A man has to take a college course in gynecology just to know what the hell all the screaming is about!

MARGARET: Screaming? Women scream when they're in bed with you? What do you do, tie them in chains and pretend you're the meow-meow man on the Pussy Grub commercial?

LEON: Don't push me too far, Officer Heinz. I'll let you go so far, but beyond a point you're not going so far, I can guarantee you that!

MARGARET: I have the feeling, Mr. Rose, you can't deliver the cookies. You're not afraid of being impotent, are you?

LEON: Afraid? That's been my secret wish since I was eighteen! Fortunately I am mature enough so that I have control over my libido. If it's of any interest to you, I haven't had sex in thirteen months, and I'm in the best physical condition I've ever been in!

MARGARET: You think that's a big deal? I haven't had sex in nineteen months, and last April I ran twenty-six miles in the Boston Marathon!

LEON: (*Babyishly*) But you didn't win, did you?

MARGARET: (*Mimics him*) No, I didn't win. But I had to jump over the bodies of fifty men who were in the same best physical condition you're in!

LEON: You think you're so tough, don't you?

MARGARET: As tough as you are, mister!

LEON: You think so?

MARGARET: I know so.

LEON: All right. Give me your hand. Come on, give me your hand.

(*Leon assumes posture for an Indian arm-wrestling match. Margaret clasps his hand, places her foot next to his foot*)

LEON: We'll see how tough you are.

MARGARET: You shouldn't do this with me. I won the women's inter-departmental handwrestling championship three years in a row.

LEON: Save your energy, lady.

(*Straining, panting, they engage in a fierce tug-of-war with first one and the other tilting dangerously and almost losing the match. But suddenly Margaret jerks Leon over her foot and sends him flying into the wall or over the sofa. Leon jumps to his feet immediately, brushes off his clothes*)

LEON: One thing you should know about me. I am not a quitter. I don't quit. Let's see you pick me up in your arms. (*He squats in a sitting position*)

MARGARET: If you stand straight, I can lift you on my shoulder.

LEON: I'm not asking you to lift me on your shoulder. I'm asking you to pick me up in your arms. Like this. (*He picks her up and holds her so that she is seated in his arms*) Can you do this? Can you hold me in your arms like this?

MARGARET: I . . . couldn't. You're . . . too heavy for me.

LEON: You're not too heavy for me. I can hold you like this all night. You feel light and comfortable and . . . Margie?

MARGARET: (*Suddenly seductively*) Yes, Leon?

LEON: Margie?

MARGARET: Yes, yes, Leon?

LEON: You know, we . . . we've had this date with each other from the beginning.

(*Impulsively he kisses Margaret on the lips, either while holding her or after he puts her down*)

MARGARET: (*Flustered; moving away; stumbling*) That . . . That didn't happen. It didn't. It was a mistake. (*Picks up summons book from table; writes; officiously*) Apartment 4C. Zip code one-zero-zero . . .

LEON: You're still giving me a summons? (*Slight pause*) What about the trial? What was the verdict?

MARGARET: You presented some strong arguments, Leon. Maybe you're not like other men; maybe you are an exception.

LEON: Margie, you can't . . . I mean . . . We've had our ups and downs . . . I want to say something now. This is important. I . . . I have enormous respect and admiration for you. What you did, taking a job as a police officer and raising those children yourself. It's not easy. I know it's not. You have to be a very special person.

MARGARET:   Is that another line of yours?

LEON:   No, Margie, it isn't. I wasn't putting you on before. I do find you an extremely attractive woman, and despite my recent expenses. I wouldn't be going through all this just to avoid a hundred dollar fine. I told you, I'm a very successful actor. Do you have any idea how much I earned in 1958?

MARGARET:   Why did you move from the East Side to this building if you're so successful?

LEON:   In the theater it . . . it goes in cycles. You work day and night for a few years and then there's a period when . . . when there aren't any parts for you, or some producer has it in for you or . . . (*It's too painful for him to go on. He sits on sofa*)

MARGARET:   I'm sorry. I shouldn't have asked you.

LEON:   No, no, it's good for me to talk about it. Things are a little slow now, but that's the business.

MARGARET:   Maybe you'll get the job you're auditioning for, the opera singer.

LEON:   It's a commercial. For a non-fattening pizza pie made of soy beans.

MARGARET:   Who eats that stuff?

LEON:   Don't ask me. I only do commercials when I have nothing else going for me, professionally. Once in a while I do get to feeling very insecure. (*He returns table to where it was*)

MARGARET:   I know what that's like. I must be the most insecure person in the world.

LEON:   I never would have guessed that.

MARGARET:   I am. I really am. If I read they're cutting the budget or laying off civil service workers, I get so panicky . . . I wonder where the money's coming from to pay the rent and the bills and the . . .

LEON:   You don't have to worry about your job, Margie. You're a terrific police officer. They'd never discharge you. (*He leads her to sofa; they sit*)

MARGARET:   Weekends I take classes on how to operate a computer, in case . . .

LEON:   You see, you are special. Not one of my wives would have had the foresight to plan for an emergency.

MARGARET:   If you met my kids, you'd know why I did it. They're special.

LEON:   I'm sure they are. Margie, you're not in a hurry, are you?

MARGARET:   (*Shakes her head*) The kids are having dinner with their grandmother.

LEON:   Let's talk. You know, when you live alone, sometimes you like to talk to someone and when there's no one living with you, it becomes a little difficult.

MARGARET:   I understand that feeling. Often I kind of daydream, and I think . . . I shouldn't tell you. It's too crazy.

LEON:   No, please. I'd like to hear it.

MARGARET:   I think that God made a mistake in creating only a man and a woman; that it's too hard for us; that a man and a woman are too opposite in their natures. I think, wouldn't it be marvelous if there was a third something that a man and a woman could talk to and have a relationship with besides each other?

LEON:   What do you mean a third something?

MARGARET:   I said it was crazy. It's something, someone. It would be like we had another choice, another chance.

LEON:   You mean a third specie with intelligence and sex like we have?

MARGARET:   That's it. A different kind of human being . . . or a vegetable even.

LEON:   A vegetable?

MARGARET:   (*Nods enthusiastically*) A superior vegetable. Through evolution it could come from the same family as, say, carrots or brussels sprouts.

LEON:   Brussels sprouts?

MARGARET:   Why not? We don't know everything. Then a man and a woman would have something else to turn to. They wouldn't have to put up with each other all the time; there wouldn't have to be so much pain.

LEON:   (*Thoughtfully*) Another specie introduced into human society. A superior brussels sprouts.

MARGARET:   I have a wild imagination, don't I?

LEON:   It's not so wild. Now I'm going to tell you something incredible. I think I saw them.

MARGARET:   Who?

LEON:   The third specie. The superior brussels sprouts.

MARGARET:   Where did you see them?

LEON:   In the IRT subway. Last week. There were five or six of them. They got on the train at 34th Street and they marched off together, in a single file, at the Washington Square Station.

MARGARET: What did they look like?

LEON: They had green complexions, long arms and they were all wearing hats.

MARGARET: They sound like the Guardian Angels.

LEON: (*Laughing; not unkindly*) They probably were. Margie, I don't think God made a mistake. I think he made only a man and a woman, and we have to make the best of it.

MARGARET: That's too hard.

LEON: We *don't* have a choice, which is a good opening to ask you if you're going anywhere for dinner tonight.

MARGARET: I thought I'd soak in the tub, scramble some eggs . . .

LEON: I have a chicken curry on the gas range. I promise you it'll be delicious. Will you have dinner with me? I'd enjoy having your company.

MARGARET: Leon, I'm really tired.

LEON: All we'll do is have dinner, talk, watch a movie together on television . . .

MARGARET: (*Rises*) I'd like to, I would, but . . .

LEON: But what?

MARGARET: I don't think it's wise.

LEON: (*Rises*) As friends. It doesn't have to be more than that.

MARGARET: It gets scary for me.

LEON: What does?

MARGARET: Trusting somebody.

LEON: Does it have to be that way?

MARGARET: You yourself said relationships are too painful.

LEON: I haven't had much luck with them, that's for sure. I start out feeling so optimistic, so hopeful that . . . It'll be different.

MARGARET: And? And?

LEON: It's the same. Every time it's . . . the same.

MARGARET: It's not worth it. (*Puts on hat*) I do appreciate your asking.

LEON: You can't blame a guy for trying.

MARGARET: I'm glad you did.

LEON: It's a habit, I guess.

MARGARET: I thank you for your hospitality. (*She starts for door*)

LEON: Margie? (*She turns to him*)

LEON:   Didn't you forget something?

MARGARET:   Forget what?

LEON:   The summons.

MARGARET:   Oh. I'm sorry. I did forget. I really hate to . . .

LEON:   No, no. it's all right. You do your job. That's important. (*He takes the summons from her; puts it into bathrobe pocket*)

MARGARET:   You'll keep the volume down on the phonograph?

LEON:   You won't hear a sound from this apartment any more; not a sound.

MARGARET:   Thank you. (*Shakes his hand*) Goodnight, Leon.

LEON:   Goodnight . . . Miss.

(*They both smile at that, warmly. Margaret exits. Leon closes door, moves to phonograph, lowers volume. He puts cavalier's hat on his head, stands in front of the mirror and turns on phonograph. He starts to sing along with record of Cavaradossi's aria in Tosca. As he does so, a thought comes to him. He raises the volume of the phonograph, full blast, louder than at the start of the play. Singing along with record he moves downstage, stares up at the ceiling. He places his foot on armchair, removes hat and holds it over his head as he sings with all the passion in him, directing his attention to his upstairs neighbor. This may be the last attempt made by a man to win the favors of a woman*)

Lights fade

*Jennifer Johnston*

# ANDANTE UN POCO MOSSO

0008-083-83-1

# Jennifer Johnston

The highly acclaimed Irish novelist Jennifer Johnston, hailed by reviewer R.M. Seaton as "a new star in the Irish literary sky," returns to this series with the disturbing play *Andante un Poco Mosso*. Her poignant character study *The Nightingale and Not the Lark* appeared in *Best Short Plays 1981*. In her new play Ms. Johnston shatters the tranquility of a chamber music trio rehearsal with the violence of today's Belfast.

Ms. Johnston brings to her works for the theatre the same sensitivity found in her novels, *The Captain and the Kings* (1971), *The Gates* (1973), *How Many Miles to Babylon?* (1974), *Shadows on Our Skin* (1977), and *The Old Jest* (1980).

Turning her talents from novels to playwriting was a likely step for Ms. Johnston as she is the daughter of playwright and director Denis Johnston, author of the Irish comedy *The Old Lady Says "No"* (1929), staged at the Dublin Gate Theatre, and the drama *The Moon in the Yellow River* (1931), first performed at the Abby Theatre and subsequently in London and New York.

Ms. Johnston was born in Dublin and was educated there at Trinity College. She is married, has four children, and lives in Derry, Northern Ireland.

# Characters:

MAX, *piano*
STEVO, *violin*
KATE, *cello*
TONY
PATSY

*The action takes place in the living room of Max's little house, somewhere in Belfast. There is a window looking out onto the small garden that runs between the house and the street. A door also leads out into the garden, and there is an opening leading to a tiny kitchen. The furniture is sparse and strictly utilitarian. Bookshelves are filled with books and music scores, fairly messy, but the room is scrupulously clean. The one expensive item is a good upright piano. There is a sofa, past its best, but covered with a cheerful rug, the only bright colour in the room. It is an autumn evening, and warm, golden light comes through the window.*

*As the house lights go down and before the curtain rises, the last section of the first movement of Schubert's* Trio in B Major, Opus 99—*roughly from bar 290—can be heard. The quality of playing is remarkably good, sensitive, much better than average for amateurs. The curtain rises. Stevo and Kate are seated in front of their music stands, their backs to the audience. As the movement winds up, Max nods his head in approval. They finish. There are a few moments of silence as they relax.*

MAX:   It comes. It comes, my friends. It is not yet so good as Cortot, Thibaud, Casals, but I think we can say that it comes.
KATE:   Personally I thought it was terrific. I didn't know I was as good as that. What do you think Stevo?
MAX:   A little bit it comes.
KATE:   Listen to him. A little bit. The begrudger. It was great. D'you know I felt my cello was alive. Stevo?
MAX:   That is right. That is the way it should be.
KATE:   Stevo?
STEVO:   Yes. Oh, yes. Everything.
KATE:   What do you mean everything?
STEVO:   Everything you say is right. A hundred per cent right.

*(He gets up and walks over to the window. He stands looking out into the garden; the evening sun shining in his face)*

MAX:   He has his mind on other things. Far away things.

STEVO:   The garden's looking great.

MAX:   Sure. Sure, it is. *(He gets up and goes over to join Stevo at the window)* Look how dirty my nails are. I scrub and scrub, but I can't get the mud out of them. Unkempt peasant's hands.

STEVO:   I'd like a garden one day.

MAX:   In my country everyone had a garden, a flowerbed even, or a box. Maybe only a box on the window ledge. Everywhere there were flowers. Perhaps there still are. I like to think that. When you went for a day in the country, every little hut had its flowers. Marigolds. Round heads of bright orange marigolds. Everyone had that pride, that pleasure. But here, in the country, there are only weeds and mud. I often wonder why that is.

STEVO:   *(Almost automatically)* We're a subject race. Defeat and marigolds . . .

KATE:   Stevo!

MAX:   *(Laughs)* Maybe marigolds would make subjection a little easier to bear.

STEVO:   I . . .

KATE:   I'll make a cup of tea. *(She gets up and balances her cello against the chair carefully)* Wouldn't that be a good idea? Before we move on to the second movement?

MAX:   Yes. Tea would be good.

STEVO:   You have no marigolds. I recognise marigolds. My mother's just got weeds and mud in her garden. Eight-foot-high weeds. You can hardly see out of the window. There's not much to look at anyway, only everyone else's eight-foot-high weeds. What are those pink things by the wall?

MAX:   Nerines.

KATE:   I'll put the kettle on.

MAX:   There are chocolate biscuits in a red tin.

KATE:   Nyummy. *(She goes into the kitchen. Stevo moves away from the window)*

STEVO:   I'll have a pond, I think, with water lillies and gold fish. Shining, darting fish.

MAX:   You played good, Stevo.

STEVO:   "Well." It's "well," not "good."

MAX:   Yes. You'd think I'd know by now. After all these

years . . . a simple thing like that. You played well today. To be frightened sometimes makes people to play very well.

STEVO: (*Laughs*) I'm not frightened. Why should I be frightened? I just play well because I'm a genius.

MAX: I recognise fear. I have a good knowledge of fear.

STEVO: I want to play well on Saturday. I'm tense, that's what I am. They're always telling us these days we're all suffering from tension. I'm just another tense fiddler.

MAX: Don't worry about Saturday. We will all play good.

STEVO: "Well." I wouldn't want to blow it. I haven't played in front of people before. Not so that it mattered. Last time was at school. Then I had such confidence. I played the second movement from the *Double Violin Concerto* with a nutter from the Christian Brothers. He was about four foot ten and had black hair all over his arms. Right down to his finger tips. It was like playing with a gorilla . . . a very musical gorilla. (*Max laughs*) My mother always used to sit in the front row at those concerts. Nudge, nudge, she'd go at whoever was sitting beside her, that's my Stevo there with the fiddle. Nudge. I could see her at it. Played the fiddle before he could walk. She prays every night that I'll turn out to be West Belfast's answer to Jimmy Galway. I can see her sitting there in front of the box . . . all the neighbours in, my Auntie Cissie in her best clothes. Me and Jimmy there together. After you, Mr. Galway . . . no, no, no . . . after you, Mr. McMenamin. A toot on the flute and a twiddle on the fiddle, oh. "That's our Stevo," my mother would say, and Aunt Cissie would put down her glass and clap. That's her dream.

MAX: Will she be in the front row on Saturday?

STEVO: I don't know. I haven't . . . don't know.

MAX: You mustn't let her down.

STEVO: No. (*He wanders back to the window*)

MAX: What will you do, Stevo?

STEVO: Do?

MAX: With your life?

STEVO: Oh, that.

MAX: Already you have wasted too much time.

STEVO: Yes. I didn't know what I really wanted. I suffered from a lot of confusion.

MAX: Now you know?

STEVO: Yes. Do you think I'd have a chance of getting into an orchestra?

MAX: Here?

STEVO: No. Over there. I'm going to go over there.

MAX: But I always thought . . . You always said . . .

STEVO: You know nothing about me, Max.

MAX: I know you play the violin good.

STEVO: "Well." Do you really think so?

MAX: I know. I have been here many years now. Many, many years, many pupils. Always I say to myself, one day there will be one . . . You listen to them, watch them, help them, get angry, laugh. All those things and then one day there is someone . . . someone who is more than just . . .

STEVO: Just?

MAX: That girl, that Kate, she is O.K. I have many pupils who are O.K.

STEVO: Yes.

MAX: But you . . .

STEVO: I'm going on Sunday.

MAX: There is no need to be quite so . . .

STEVO: You really mean it? What you said?

MAX: I mean it. You must know yourself.

STEVO: How can you ever be sure?

MAX: There are some things about which you have to be sure.

KATE: (*Calling*) There's no milk. Not a drop. (*She comes in with a jug in her hand*) I think that awful cat must have been at it. It's empty, and the cat looks wildly guilty. (*She turns the empty jug upside down*) Will I run out and get some?

MAX: No. No. I will go.

KATE: Stevo . . . perhaps . . .

MAX: I will go.

KATE: We could drink it black.

(*Max takes his hat off a hook near the door and puts it on*)

MAX: A little air will do me good. A little five minutes of air.

(*He goes out*)

KATE: You might have gone. What's up with you at all? You're so sour. You should have gone and saved poor, old Max the trouble.

STEVO: If you were so keen to save Max trouble, you could have gone yourself.

(*He looks out of the window*)

KATE: Stevo . . .

STEVO:   Mmmm?

KATE:   Where have you been? I rang and rang. I called round seven, last week. Your mother didn't know where you were. She said . . .

STEVO:   I don't have to be at home all the time, do I? I'm free, white, and twenty-one.

KATE:   You haven't been there at all. Nobody knew where you were. I thought you mightn't turn up today.

STEVO:   Here I am. Look, this is me. All in one piece, and my fiddle on the chair.

KATE:   Your mother was worried. She couldn't think what had happened to you.

STEVO:   Why don't we practise? The trio. La, la, la—le—la. You know. Employ ourselves gainfully.

KATE:   I'm making the tea.

STEVO:   Then make the tea La, la, la, laa—le—la—la.

KATE:   I looked everywhere. You never turned up for any of your classes. Not even Davey . . .

STEVO:   Look . . . what is this? I don't have to answer to you for anything . . . or to anyone else either. You're as bad as my mother, for God's sake. "Mind yourself Stevo. Where were you, Stevo? Where are you going, Stevo? What time did you come in, Stevo? I law awake half the night listening for you, Stevo." You went to Davey's?

KATE:   Yes. Tuesday evening. I thought you might be there. All the lads were there. They . . . None of them knew where you were. None of . . . I was afraid . . .

STEVO:   Afraid of what?

KATE:   Afraid you mightn't turn up on Saturday.

STEVO:   (Laughs) I wouldn't do a thing like that on the old fella. You should know that.

KATE:   You never know what people will do. Sometimes you're not very reliable, you know.

(The kettle whistles)

STEVO:   Ouch. Whoever invented those gadgets should have been shot. Go and make that tea, there's a good girl. We've a lot of work to do.

KATE:   (Going toward the kitchen) Would you phone your mother anyway? Tell her you're all right.

STEVO:   I'll phone her in my own good time. (He picks up the violin and begins to play the beginning of the Trio) What did Davey have to say?

KATE: (*From kitchen*) What?

STEVO: Davey's . . . who did you see? What did they say?

KATE: (*Coming in with a tray of cups*) He said you were to give him a ring. For certain. I was to tell you that if I saw you. You were to . . . you'll do that, won't you? And ring your mother too.

STEVO: And what did you say?

KATE: Well, not much really. I . . . ah . . . told him about Saturday. He seemed interested in that. He . . . I was surprised he didn't know.

STEVO: Why should he know?

KATE: You're such good friends. I'd have thought you'd have told him a thing like that.

STEVO: We had other interests in common. He wouldn't know Brahms from the Beatles. He probably wouldn't even know the Beatles, come to think of it.

(*Kate laughs uneasily. He plays again*)

KATE: There's something up, isn't there? I'd do what I could to help you, if you'd let me. (*She goes out and comes back with the tea pot*) You've changed. You used to talk to me.

STEVO: We used to chat . . . and play music. You're a nice girl. I like you. Music is all we have in common. Take your cello there, and let's play. That's talking. The only talking there can be.

KATE: You have changed.

STEVO: No one changes. You find out things about yourself, discovery. Circumstances change, not people. Max is taking his time with the milk.

KATE: He's not young.

STEVO: No. (*He goes over to the window*)

KATE: What's so interesting out there? What are you looking for?

STEVO: Here he is now . . . looking like a question mark. He's the only person I know looks like a question mark. He ought to give that hat to a jumble sale.

KATE: My mother doesn't like Jews.

STEVO: Nobody likes Jews.

KATE: I often wonder why.

STEVO: I don't know. Maybe because they seem to be impossible to dispose of. Everyone's tried at some stage, and no one's succeeded. They have this infinite capacity for suffering which upsets people. After all . . .

KATE:   Ssssh.

(*Max comes in*)

MAX:   You need practice, my children, not to sit and gossip. We have not all the time in the world. There is the milk, Kate.

KATE:   I'll put it in a jug. (*She takes the milk and goes into the kitchen*)

MAX:   And put some in the bowl for my little Katya. I have been thinking as I walk back from the shop, we will next do one of Beethoven's trios. It popped into my head to sing there a while, to say I am next, Max. That will be good?

STEVO:   I won't be here. You'll have to find another fiddler.

MAX:   Ah, yes. That is so. Kate will mind.

STEVO:   Why should Kate mind?

MAX:   You are a very unobservant young man.

KATE:   (*Coming in*) Why do you say that to him?

MAX:   He cannot see what is before his nose.

KATE:   I'll pour out, will I? What's before his nose that he can't see?

MAX:   He sees only his fiddle. Now. That is the way he is now. Before he saw other things. Irrelevant things.

STEVO:   That's all I need to see.

MAX:   That depends, my friend, how you wish to pass your life. You have to work it out.

STEVO:   I have.

MAX:   Maybe if you are not careful you will end up like me. Alone. No achievement, only a short pattern of shrinking days in front of me. I am not being sorrowful, only giving you a warning.

STEVO:   Warning acknowledged.

KATE:   What on earth are you two going on about? Have a biscuit?

STEVO:   Thanks.

MAX:   Hasn't he told you?

KATE:   He tells me nothing.

STEVO:   Can I have some more sugar in my tea. Thanks. I like a lot. My mother says I'll have no teeth left by the time I'm forty. But what the hell. At least I don't play the flute.

KATE:   Anyway, what is it you haven't been telling me this time?

STEVO:   I'm going. That's all. Another emigrant scraping the mud of the motherland off my hob-nailed boots, wringing the salt tears from my snotty handkerchief as I climb the steps of the British Airways shuttle. I am going to become a . . .

KATE:   Be serious.

STEVO:   A statistic. I am being serious. I'm going on Sunday. I might even go on the last plane on Saturday.

KATE:   You're going to England?

STEVO:   That's the idea.

KATE:   After all you've said in the past. After . . . after all . . . Why?

STEVO:   What's there for me here?

KATE:   I never thought you'd do a thing like that.

STEVO:   I'm going to Annie. It's all arranged. She can put me up for a while. I've always got on with Annie. I have to work, Kate. I've left the decision far too long.

KATE:   But . . .

STEVO:   I can't work here. Too many things get between me and my music. I have to get out. Start clean. Even if I make a mess of the whole damn thing, I'll be able to say that I tried. After a lot of thought, time, pain, yes, real pain, I know what is important to me. That's all that matters now. I start new, clean from there.

KATE:   Is he crazy? I think he's crazy.

MAX:   He's just making life difficult for himself. Troublesome. He will be troublesome.

STEVO:   The very thing they used to say about me in school. Steven McMenamin is a troublesome pupil.

KATE:   Does your mother know?

STEVO:   Time enough for that.

KATE:   You ought to tell your mother. Go and see her before you leave. Anyway, you haven't explained where you've been the last couple of weeks.

STEVO:   Does no one want that biscuit? Keeping out of sight, if you really want to know.

KATE:   You've certainly done it most successfully I must say.

(*Max sits at the piano*)

MAX:   Andante un poco mosso.

KATE:   What have you been keeping out of sight for? Stevo, what have you been up to?

(*Max begins to play the beginning of the second movement*)

STEVO:   I've been up to nothing.

KATE:   Then why . . . ?

STEVO:   Davey's lot think I shopped Eamon. Now you know.

I just thought I'd be better off lying low. Keeping, as they say, a low profile.

KATE:  You never did a thing like that?

STEVO:  No. I never did a thing like that.

KATE:  Then why don't you tell them?

STEVO:  Because some people don't believe you when you tell the truth. They don't want to believe you. They don't bloody well understand. I don't want to be a hero any longer, but that doesn't mean I'm running away. I'm trying to face something in myself, not run away from it. I want to play the fiddle, and I don't care where I do it. Here, there, anywhere.

MAX:  Better than Jimmy Galway.

STEVO:  Aye. You could put it like that.

KATE:  But Eamon . . . he was shot by the British . . . I don't . . .

STEVO:  He was set up. Everyone knows that. But he wasn't set up by me. For God's sake, what do you think I am?

KATE:  I . . .

STEVO:  You needn't say a word.

MAX:  I think we should play music. It would be best. Second movement. Andante un poco mosso. Kate. Please, Kate. Ready. One and two and . . .

(He starts to play as before. Bar 3, Kate comes in with the melody. Stevo picks up his bow and waits)

MAX:  No. No, my child, it will not do. You have to concentrate. Put all things from your head except the music. Of all movements, this needs the great touch of love . . . feeling. Not just the sawing of the tree. You are sawing the tree. Now, again. From the top . . . And . . .

KATE:  Don't be such a bully, Max. How can I play? Haven't you been listening to him? You're as bad as he is.

MAX:  There is no point to listen to what does not concern you. We have a concert on Saturday. That is our concern now. We play therefore. If we do not play, we have no concert. It is simple. The people have buyed their tickets . . .

STEVO:  "Bought."

MAX:  . . . they will be expecting to hear . . . "Bought." All right then, bought. What do I do when you make your journey to England . . . become a person of fame. What then do I do with my English speaking? (Stevo laughs)

MAX:  Why you laugh?

STEVO:  You've been here thirty years, you damned old

cod. If you'd wanted to speak English properly, you'd have learnt it by now.

KATE:   You're always cracking jokes. Awful jokes.

STEVO:   You'd need to be. Just look around.

KATE:   I don't see anything to make me laugh.

MAX:   Andante un poco mosso.

KATE:   Particularly what you've just told me. What's funny about that? Go on . . . tell me. What's funny about that?

STEVO:   Its hilarious. Finally, after a couple of years of painful thinking I make the great decision of my life. I'm going to take off. Throw in my lot with Isaac Stern, Menuhin, Rostropovitch . . . foreigners to a man . . .

MAX:   Jimmy Galway.

KATE:   You're crazy when you talk like that.

STEVO:   Get out of this hole. I go and tell them. My pals, old school pals, streetcorner pals. Lookit, I say, my heroic stone throwing, petrol bombing, barricade-building days are over. No more plotting, heavy political speeches in community halls . . . Stevo McMenamin's . . .

KATE:   You'll never play the violin as well as Yehudi Menuhin.

STEVO:   . . . taking off. Going into orbit you might say. And what do they do? Do they congratulate me? Wish me luck in my insanity? Buy me a glass of stout? Not at all. They say I set up Eamon and put out a contract on me. If that's not hilarious, I don't know what is. She's not listening.

KATE:   This is not a hole.

STEVO:   It is a hole. A safe, deep, warm hole. It's too dark down here to see beyond the end of your nose. Safe, secure. You've nothing to lose but your kneecaps. We all believe we're so bloody important.

KATE:   You believed it too.

STEVO:   Aye. I did. I won't deny that. Come on . . . Max is right. We need to play. I stayed to play on Saturday, and I'm damned well going to play well . . . or "good" as Max would say. Can you give me a bed, Max, for the next two nights? Or a piece of floor? I've worn my welcome thin around the place.

MAX:   You can share the sofa with the cat. But I practise from six-thirty. I warn you that.

STEVO:   We'll do it together. Thanks. Thanks a lot, Max.

*(Max begins to play. Kate comes in bar 3. Stevo comes in bar 12. They play to bar 28. Max stops)*

MAX: No. No. Here you must come in singing. (*He sings a phrase*) Pianissimo. See. Then gently into the crescendo. You must forget everything except the meaning of the music. You must reach into it deep. It is more than just little marks on the page.

KATE: I just keep thinking of all the dreadful things you used to say about Eamon. You never liked him. He used to pull your leg about playing the fiddle. Everyone could see you hated him when he did that. And Annie. That trouble over . . .

STEVO: Just you leave Annie out of this.

KATE: Didn't Annie have to go to England over him. That's what everyone said.

MAX: My dear children . . .

KATE: It's no wonder they think you did it. I remember how you carried on when Annie went away.

STEVO: Annie is my sister. She's always been able to work out her own problems. She's never needed me to fight her battles for her. She's a great girl, Annie.

KATE: That's not what people were saying about her five years ago. Even you.

STEVO: No matter what I said about her five years ago. I was a kid five years ago.

KATE: She used to tear you apart for throwing stones at the soldiers. (*Max begins to play softly from bar 23*)

STEVO: Aye, and scrub my neck with the nail brush. If you haven't had your neck scrubbed with a nail brush you haven't lived. She was a nutter for cleanliness. She used to drive Mammy crazy. Always washing her clothes, her hair. There was never any hot water because Annie was always scrubbing something.

KATE: She never let you have fun.

STEVO: She sang like a bird. Remember her singing? Remember, Max, my sister Annie singing.

MAX: (*As he plays*) I remember her singing.

KATE: A wet blanket. I never could understand how she took up with Eamon. I couldn't think what he saw in her. None of us could. He liked a bit of fun.

STEVO: He got his bit of fun.

MAX: (*Stops playing*) This will not do, you know. You are friends. Friends since childhood days. You must trust.

KATE:   Trust. A fat lot of trusting he's been doing. Why didn't you tell me you were going? Where you were, instead of just disappearing off like that? You didn't trust me, did you? Why haven't you told your mother? Wait till she hears you're going to Annie. She'll be fit to be tied. You think of no one, only yourself.

STEVO:   Well at this moment my major worry is to get myself and my skin out of this city in one piece . . . and my fiddle. The more people you blow your mouth to, the more difficult the operation becomes. I would have sent you a postcard. And my mother. Maybe even Davey after six months or so. Just to show him there were no hard feelings. I don't have to answer for myself to anyone. Get that in your head. I haven't done anything wrong. I want space. A lot of space. I've a lot of work to do. Right, Max?

MAX:   A lot of work. I will write some letters for you . . . on your behalf. I have some high friends.

STEVO:   (*Laughing*) There you go again.

MAX:   (*After consideration*) Good-placed friends?

STEVO:   Why do I feel so happy when I'm with you, you old, foreign freak? Every bit of me feels happy. You'd better come with me. You and me and Annie and the kid. Maybe we could be happy forever, like in the fairy stories. How about it? Hunh?

MAX:   I have never looked for happiness. To be for some minutes without pain is the most one can ask.

KATE:   You make it sound like a crime to be happy.

MAX:   Maybe it is. Who can tell.

KATE:   What rubbish you talk. Most people are happy. My mam and dad . . . everyone I know, they're all quite happy. If it wasn't for the situation . . . that's the reason why . . . Don't smile like that. I'm going to be happy. I know I am. When this is over. I know what I want, and I'll get it. It's not much. I'm not a grabber. Just to be normal, live a normal life, have a bit of fun from time to time, nice friends, a home. Neither of you is normal. I used to think that Stevo was . . . just like all the rest of us. We've all done a few bad things in our time, but you settle down. Become . . . well . . . normal. Do normal things, like I said. It's difficult being young. They're always telling us that. It's true. Youth is a difficult . . . you know.

MAX:   No. I had no youth.

KATE: *(Laughs uneasily)* Oh come on.

MAX: Where I spent my youth, we grew up quick.

KATE: I . . .

MAX: Those who had the good fortune to grow up at all.

KATE: That was ages ago. Nothing's like that now.

MAX: Nothing really changes. Come, let us play. We go from the top. Andante un poco mosso.

KATE: Yes.

*(Max begins to play. Kate comes in. Stevo comes in. Bar 27, Max nods)*

MAX: Yes. Yes. Well. That is well.

*(About Bar 30 the door opens, and two men come in. At first the players do not notice them. They stand silently by the door for a few moments. One of them moves impatiently and Kate becomes aware of them. She stops playing)*

KATE: Mother of God, you gave me a fright.

MAX: What . . . ? *(He turns and sees them. Stevo also sees them, but continues to play for another few bars. Max gets up from the piano)*

MAX: Can I help you? Are you looking for me? I . . .

STEVO: No, Max. It's O.K. . . .

TONY: Aye. It's him we're looking for. Hi, Stevo. I hope you'll forgive us for barging in. The door was open, so we just . . .

PATSY: . . . came in, and there he is. Just like we were told he would be. How's Kate?

KATE: I'm . . .

TONY: We've searched the bloody city for you.

STEVO: I've been putting in a bit of work on the fiddle. You know how it is . . . If you're going to get any work done you have to keep . . .

TONY: Of course . . . putting in a bit of work on the fiddle.

PATSY: Six-thirty. That's what we were told. Come along at six-thirty.

KATE: I . . .

TONY: Davey was worried you might have skipped . . .

STEVO: As you can see, I haven't skipped. You can tell him. Calm his fears.

TONY: I think you should come and tell him yourself. He'd like to see you, that's the message.

PATSY: Six-thirty. That was what you told him, wasn't it, love?

KATE: I didn't mean any harm. Everyone was looking for you. I just said you might . . . might . . . That was all I said. I didn't mean . . .

PATSY: There's no harm in it at all. Davey just wants to see your man. That's all.

TONY: Sort a few things out.

STEVO: I'll pop along and see him later then. You can tell him that. We have this concert on Saturday, so I'm a bit pushed at the moment. I'll come when the concert's over.

TONY: I think he wants to see you now. I think he wanted to see you a fortnight ago.

STEVO: What's so urgent it can't wait till Saturday?

TONY: We're pals, Stevo. Don't give me a hard time. It's just a question of clearing something up. You know Davey. He likes to know what's what.

STEVO: I can't help him, I'm afraid.

PATSY: You weren't at the disco the other night. I was looking out for you.

TONY: Then come and tell him that.

PATSY: It was a great evening. Powerful. You shouldn'ta missed it. (*To Kate*) You holed up somewhere with your man then?

KATE: How dare you . . . you . . . you . . .

TONY: You're making things look bad for yourself, you know.

PATSY: Keep your hair on. I was only asking. No offence meant.

STEVO: Saturday evening, after the concert. I swear to God I'll come then. No messing.

MAX: We were rehearsing you know, when you interrupted us. The *Opus No. 99 in B flat* of Schubert. (*They all look at him in silence*) You know of Schubert? One of the great geniuses of the world. Some people wouldn't agree about his genius . . . his symphonies, they would say don't stand beside those of Beethoven. I wouldn't argue with them on that subject. But then you have to stop and think of his chamber music. His trios . . . quartets . . . quintets even. His lieder. Ah, my God, what a genius he was. He died young. It is a trio of his that we are playing on Saturday. A sublime work. Schubert.

Perhaps you would like tickets for the concert? There is also coming a young lieder singer from Germany. He will be for the first half of the programme. He is a young singer of good reputation. Well? Good?

STEVO: Good.

MAX: He was thirty-one when he died.

PATSY: (*Confused*) Who?

MAX: Schubert. Two years younger than Jesus Christ.

(*There is a long silence*)

TONY: We'll go now . . . won't we, Stevo?

KATE: Why don't you go away and leave him alone. He says he'll come on Saturday. Go and tell Davey that.

PATSY: Who's Hubert?

KATE: He'll promise to come on Saturday . . . won't you, Stevo?

MAX: Schubert. Franz Schubert.

STEVO: I'll promise nothing.

PATSY: I thought you said Hubert. I knew a fella once called Hubert. I just wondered . . . it's not a name you come across all that often.

KATE: Please be reasonable.

STEVO: Haven't you done enough harm already without any more interferring. Let's get this straight once and for all. I'm not going anywhere near Davey. You can tell him that. I have nothing to say to him.

TONY: He has something to say to you though.

STEVO: It will have to remain unsaid. I'll either talk to him on Saturday after the concert, or not at all.

TONY: I have orders . . . if it was up to me . . . you know, I'd . . . if it was up to me. Orders is . . . Ah, come on now, Stevo, Davey's a hard man. (*Stevo laughs*) That was always your problem . . . you laughed too much.

STEVO: Was?

TONY: We haven't seen you round for a long time.

STEVO: Davey's never had much sense of humour.

TONY: He likes you. He'd always want to give you the benefit of the doubt. That's what he said to me. He said, I'd want to give Stevo every chance. He did say that.

PATSY: He did and all. I heard him say that, so I did.

TONY: You weren't there. No one in their right mind would say anything important with you around.

PATSY: Now that's not a nice thing to say at all. You make

it sound as if I was thick or something. I heard him say that. Why would I tell a lie?

STEVO: Why indeed? Kate, why would he tell a lie?

KATE: Shut up.

PATSY: Don't let him get at you, love.

TONY: Come on, Stevo, on your feet. We haven't all night.

PATSY: There's some people get at you all the time. I said to Davey, I don't know why you send me out with Tony. He's always getting at me. I don't feel he has any respect for me at all.

STEVO: Why don't you go away and let us get on with our practising?

PATSY: You know why Davey sends me out with him?

KATE: No. I . . .

PATSY: I can shoot straight. That's why. So he can get at me all he likes, but he can't do without me.

KATE: Look here Patsy . . .

PATSY: He couldn't hit a double decker bus, so he couldn't if it was the only thing in Chichester Street.

TONY: I've had about all I can take from you.

PATSY: So what are you going to do about it . . . ? Hey? John Wayne. (*Patsy takes a gun out of his pocket. There is a reaction from the others*) You think you're the clever one, don't you?

KATE: Oh, God, he's got a gun . . .

STEVO: Now lookit here, Patsy, don't do anything foolish.

PATSY: If you think blasting a hole in that omadhaun is foolish . . .

TONY: Just you wait till Davey hears about this.

MAX: I think, young man, you should put your gun away. I think . . .

TONY: The problem is that he doesn't think.

MAX: There is an old saying about thieves falling out . . .

PATSY: Who's a thief? What are you saying, you bloody old Jew? No one calls me a thief. I've never stolen a halfpenny in my whole life.

TONY: In a manner of speaking is all he meant, Patsy. In a manner of speaking. That's all. He meant no harm.

STEVO: You and Davey are, after all, supposed to be on the same side.

PATSY: He'd need to watch what he says. What right has he to call people bad names.

MAX: It happens to be my room in which you are brandishing your gun. I have the right to object. This is my friend, my pupil you come to take away. I have a right to object to that too.

PATSY:  You know nothing about all this. Don't you go poking your beaky nose into affairs that don't concern you.

MAX:  Besides . . . (*He rolls up his sleeve*) I think I have the right—the eternal right to protest about violence. (*He holds his arm out to them. Tony and Stevo look at the mark on his arm. He then walks over to Patsy and holds his arm out in front of him*)

PATSY:  What's that anyway?

MAX:  It's my number.

PATSY:  I can see that. What do you have a number on you for?

MAX:  It means that I have lived through a violence more terrible than you could imagine, and I am here, alive, and I demand that you put up your gun.

PATSY:  You stupid old bugger. Who . . .

MAX:  Put it away. (*Slowly Patsy puts away the gun. As he does so, Max rolls down his sleeve again. Tony and Patsy move toward Stevo*) No. You are not to touch him. Not to move. We will now practise. You two gentlemen may, if you wish, sit here until we have done our work . . . in silence. After we have finished to practise, you may discuss with Stevo your trouble. But until then we have no words, no foolishness. You understand?

TONY:  Fair dos. (*He sits down*)

STEVO:  Sit down, Patsy. Do as Max says. We'll sort it all out later on. We'll forget this . . . well, as Max says . . . foolishness. Won't we, Tony? (*Pause*) Won't we, Tony?

TONY:  Yeah. We'll forget it. It was the nerves getting the better of us. Nobody likes this sort of job. After all we've been friend's a long time, Stevo. Right back to school.

STEVO:  Right back to school.

TONY:  We're just doing what we were told to do. You understand?

STEVO:  I understand.

TONY:  Nobody likes . . .

PATSY:  You think I am an "eejit."

TONY:  No. Forget it, Patsy. Forget what I said. You're a great guy. Honest to God. Sit down, there's a good lad.

(*Patsy sits cautiously. There is a moment's relieved silence*)

MAX:  Well. It is well.

STEVO:   "Good," you crazy foreigner.

MAX:   Kate, perhaps you will be kind and make some more tea . . . for our nervous systems. Would you be kind?

STEVO:   Perpetuating the eternal myth that women are angels of mercy and tea makers forever and ever. A-a-amen!

KATE:   I'm making tea because Max asked me . . . politely. He's a gentleman, not like some. (*She goes into the kitchen*)

STEVO:   I must say my nervous system could do with a large Paddy.

MAX:   We will play. (*He sits at the piano and turns the pages*) While we wait for our tea, we will play. You and I, Stevo. The fourth movement, from the beginning. You will be very quiet and listen. Then when we have our tea, we will play from the beginning right through to the end. Maybe you will learn something. Maybe you will not. Probably not. For us, it will be our first audience. A great challenge. We will have to play g . . . well. Are you ready, Stevo?

STEVO:   I'm ready, maestro. Watch out Jimmy Galway. I'm about to start up the ladder.

MAX:   Allegro vivace. One and two . . .

(*They play from the beginning of the* Rondo. *Max sings the cello melody as it comes in. Kate comes in the room and collects the cups, which she brings out to the kitchen. The two men stare at each other in silence. Sometime after bar 55 the kettle whistles. The two men jump and turn towards the kitchen. Max plays on. Stevo runs out through the door with the fiddle and the bow in his hands*)

PATSY:   What the . . . ?

TONY:   Bloody kettle. My mother has one that does that too. It . . . Stevo . . . Stevo . . . Shit . . .

PATSY:   The bastard. (*He is away, through the door after Stevo, pulling the gun out of his pocket as he runs*)

TONY:   Patsy, let him go.

KATE:   (*Coming in*) What's up? What's all the shouting in aid of? Where's Stevo?

MAX:   I think Stevo's done something very foolish.

KATE:   What are you standing there for? Why don't you do something? You stupid, old man, do something.

TONY:   Like what, for Jesus' sake?

KATE:   Go after them. Stop Patsy . . . something . . . not just . . .

TONY:   Why don't you, for instance. Run, scream, cry. Call the cops, why don't you?

(*Kate moves uncertainly towards the door*)

TONY:   You could save his life perhaps. Not the old man. He couldn't. It's not his problem, is it? He's just an old freak playing the piano. Spouting a bit of air. What's bloody art when people are dying in the streets? But you . . . run, girl. You could save his life . . . You. After all . . . you . . .

KATE:   No. I didn't know. I swear to God, I didn't know.

TONY:   We all know, so we do, love . . . so don't give me that one.

KATE:   (*Starting to cry*) I didn't know. Oh, God, oh, God . . .

MAX:   Very foolish.

TONY:   I was at school with him.

MAX:   So you said. It doesn't seem to matter much though . . . to have any relevance . . . does it?

TONY:   Ever seen a corpse?

MAX:   Yes. I've seen a corpse.

TONY:   Just a bundle on the ground. That was what I thought when I . . . a bundle. I wouldn't have hurt Stevo. I'd like you to believe that.

MAX:   Hadn't you better go? Your friends . . .

TONY:   I just wouldn't want you to think . . .

MAX:   It doesn't matter what I think. All that matters is what you think in yourself . . . of yourself. It is most important to respect yourself. Only that way can you respect other people . . . their dignity. We do possess that, you know. Dignity. He was starting to learn about himself. It seems he left it a bit too late. Do go away. Go. You too, Kate.

KATE:   No. Please. Don't send me away. I want to stay there with you.

MAX:   Andante un poco mosso.

(*Max begins to play. Tony watches him for a moment before going out and closing the door quietly behind him*)

KATE:   Where could I go? (*She picks up the cello*) Where? I swear to you I didn't know, Max. Do you believe me?

(*Max continues to play. After a moment Kate picks up the bow and begins to play as the curtain falls*)

*Martin Jones*
# OLD SOLDIERS

# Martin Jones

Born in Elizabeth, New Jersey, in 1946, Martin Jones is the son of an engineer whose work required the family to move every two or three years. Some of the places Mr. Jones has called home include Denver, Memphis, pre-Castro Cuba, Niagara Falls, St. Louis, Philadelphia, Chicago, Ann Arbor, Montreal, Florida, and southern California. In 1968 he received a B.A. in English and Theatre from Hillsdale College (Michigan). This was followed by an M.A. from Eastern Michigan University in 1970 and a Ph.D. in Playwriting and Dramatic Theory from Southern Illinois University at Carbondale in 1977.

Since finishing college, Mr. Jones has worked as Playwright-in-Residence at Northern Illinois University and as drama professor at the University of Virginia and Bowdoin College, where he was theatre director and Playwright-in-Residence. After teaching for several years, Mr. Jones left academic theatre to work professionally as an actor, playwright, and director. He founded the Mother Wit Improvisational Theatre Company and has worked with several Chicago area theatres as a performer or director.

*Old Soldiers*—a tragicomedy focusing on the illusions of a World War I veteran—first came to the editor's attention in 1974 when it was originally produced by Southern Illinois University at Carbondale for the American College Theatre Festival. Directed by Christian H. Moe, the play won the regional new play competition for its performance in Milwaukee at the regional festival in 1975 and was ranked second in the national competition. The play was later produced by the Academy Theatre in Atlanta in 1977, and in January 1980 it had its Mid-West professional premiere at the Performance Community in Chicago where it ran for over six weeks. Mr. Jones started writing *Old Soldiers* after listening to stories of his grandfather's experiences in World War I. The author reflects: "Some of the anecdotes were so hilarious and touching, I had to put them into a play. The character of Tom is not really modeled after my grandfather, but is a composite of several old men I met while working at a retiree's hotel while I was in college." *Old Soldiers* appears in print for the first time in this collection.

Other plays by Martin Jones include: *Daughters*, produced by the Guthrie Theatre Studio in Minneapolis in September

1980, by Chicago's Goodman Theatre new play series in January 1980, and in November 1981 by the Victory Gardens Theatre in Chicago; *Zoology*, produced by the Chicago Dramatists Workshop; *Cabbages and Kings*, produced by the Northern Illinois Fine Arts Festival; and *Night Train*, a television play, videotaped by WSIU-TV. His latest short play, *Flamingos*, was presented in an Actors Equity showcase production in New York City, in January 1983, at the Nameless Theatre.

Currently residing in Brunswick, Maine, Mr. Jones is now associated with the Portland Stage Company, and is at work on a new play and a volume of short stories.

The author dedicates *Old Soldiers*: "To my grandfather, Barney Monroe Martin, 1894–1980."

# Characters:

MR. MCMURTY
TOM
DICK
LUCILLE SAMMONS

# Time:

November 11, 1962, 9:45 P.M.

# Scene:

*The interior of the lobby of the St. James Hotel in Chicago. The St. James is one of those once elegant hotels that has lost business to motels. The clientele is now made up of old men who prefer its security to the horrors of an old folks' home.*

*It has been raining lightly for some time. A wet American flag has been hung near the doorway to dry. A banner reading "Welcome Harry!" hangs over the bannister of the staircase.*

*An old record player sits on an end table near the fireplace. As the play begins, "I'm Just Wild About Harry" concludes on the record player. The needle on the record player fails to reject.*

*Mr. McMurty, a man in his late sixties, is practicing golf at an indoor putting green. The wall clock strikes the quarter hour and McMurty misses his putt.*

MCMURTY:   Damn! Bogey five! (*He retrieves his ball and pulls several more from his pocket and drops them on the floor. He pulls out his watch and checks the time with the wall clock and sets the time on his watch. McMurty lines up for another putt. Tom, a man in his seventies enters from the dining room, wiping his mouth on a napkin. He stops upstage near the end of the register desk. Tom puts the napkin in his pocket and removes a Benzedrine inhaler from another pocket and inhales deeply*) Evening, Tom.

TOM:   Evening. Any calls?

MCMURTY:   (*Returning to his putting*) No.

(*Tom crosses to the record player, drawn by the sound of the needle scratching. He removes the record carefully, inspecting it closely for damage*)

TOM: If you're going to play this record . . . please be careful about the needle . . . we can't afford to damage it anymore . . . this thing's an antique . . . been in the hotel for as long as I can remember . . .

MCMURTY: Sorry . . . I'll be more careful, Tom . . .

(*Tom places the record on a shelf behind the desk where it will be safe. Tom looks at the wall clock*)

TOM: Is that the correct time?

MCMURTY: (*Checks his watch*) Yes. Did you have a good dinner?

TOM: (*Setting his watch*) Fine . . . just fine . . . (*Moves downstage to observe the putting*) Better score tonight?

MCMURTY: Forty-three on the back nine . . . two bogeys and a birdie so far this round. (*He moves the cup to a new position*)

TOM: That should make it about par.

MCMURTY: About. (*He misses a putt*)

TOM: One over.

MCMURTY: Hmph! (*He lines up for another putt*)

TOM: Have dinner?

MCMURTY: No . . . how was it?

TOM: Potatoes were cold.

MCMURTY: No?

TOM: And the fishsticks were hard.

MCMURTY: Hard?

TOM: Overcooked.

MCMURTY: Sorry to hear that.

TOM: (*Sits on ottoman*) Everything they make is overcooked. Must be part of their culture. Overcook everything.

MCMURTY: I wouldn't know . . . Not as good as old Hester used to do, eh?

TOM: Not quite. I've seen many cooks come and go here . . . but Hester, now there was a cook. (*He uses inhaler*)

MCMURTY: Shouldn't do that, bad for the nose.

TOM: Really?

MCMURTY: Destroys the blood vessels, hard on the liver, and can damage the brain cells. Habit forming, too.

TOM: (*Looks at inhaler*) I didn't know that.

MCMURTY: Benzedrine . . . terrible stuff. Fellows in my outfit used to chew on the cotton stuffing to get at the juice. Kept them out of their heads for hours. Give it up—you'll never make eighty if you don't.

TOM:   I've already outlived you.

MCMURTY:   Ten years.

TOM:   (*Puts inhaler in ashtray*) Maybe you're right. Don't need a habit at my age.

MCMURTY:   Of course I'm right. Worse than smoking. (*Pause*)

TOM:   Have you seen Dick tonight?

MCMURTY:   No. (*Pause*) Didn't he have dinner with you?

TOM:   Not tonight . . . He went up to his room after the parade, to change his clothes. I haven't seen him since . . . I thought maybe you had.

MCMURTY:   No, sorry . . . perhaps, he's still in his room. Have you checked to see?

TOM:   No? I'll have to do that. I'll buzz his room.

(*Tom crosses to house phone, lifts receiver*)

MCMURTY:   Heard anything from your missing friend?

TOM:   Harry? . . . No, but he'll be in tonight.

(*Tom replaces phone on hook*)

MCMURTY:   A damn shame he missed the parade. Very impressive. Pity there was such a small turnout.

TOM:   Small! It was a disgrace. I would be ashamed to be called an American after that piddlin' display of patriotism . . . No, I'm almost glad Harry wasn't here to see it, he would have been ashamed.

MCMURTY:   Dick could've used some help with those flags. (*Points to flags*) I think they were heavy for him. He was really draggin' when he came in here.

TOM:   His heart was broken. (*Pause*) The American Legion wasn't even there!

MCMURTY:   It *was* raining.

TOM:   Macy's and Gimbel's never call off a parade for a sprinkle. Half of the drum section of that junior high band didn't show. Three snares, two trumpets, and a miserable piccolo!! A disgrace to the boys who served their country!

MCMURTY:   There have been other wars since yours, Tom.

TOM:   Only a few.

MCMURTY:   Not many people around remember Armistice Day.

TOM:   What do you mean? Everyone I know remembers

Armistice Day. (*Proclamation*) The eleventh hour of the eleventh day of the eleventh month . . ."

MCMURTY: How many people do you know, Tom? . . . Who are still alive?

TOM: *I* remember, Dick remembers, Harry remembers . . .

MCMURTY: (*Laughs*) Harry must have forgotten! Or maybe, he got too old for it, eh, Tom?

TOM: Harry'll be here! You'll see!! The three of us have made every Armistice Day reunion for 43 years! No club, lodge, or organization in the world has an attendance record like ours.

MCMURTY: (*Laughs*) Oh, I believe you, Tom. I'm impressed.

TOM: We'll see, Mr. Bigmouth!

MCMURTY: Relax, Tom, I'm only kidding you.

TOM: Kidding!! The Armistice of the Great War is nothing to laugh about.

MCMURTY: I never said that, Tom. Aren't you being just a bit extreme?

TOM: You're damn right, we're extreme! A true patriot is always extreme.

MCMURTY: Don't take it so serious, Tom. You'll give yourself a coronary.

TOM: (*Trembling*) I've never been healthier. (*Silence*) I'll be a pallbearer at your funeral.

MCMURTY: (*Yawns*) If you say so, Tom.

TOM: (*Sneezes, goes to ashtray and retrieves inhaler, inhales deeply and sniffs*) Harry's never been late before. (*Pause*) He's been held up or he'd be here. Prob'ly the damn trains! You miss one and you might as well pitch a tent. They don't run regular anymore. One thing you can say for Mussolini, he made the trains run on time. (*Tom looks out the window. McMurty picks up a newspaper and ignores him*) With all this rain . . . no tellin' where he's stranded. (*Pause, then suddenly*) You don't think he's had an accident, do you?

MCMURTY: Was he driving?

TOM: No, he hates automobiles, doesn't trust the damn things.

MCMURTY: Maybe he got on the wrong train.

TOM: Harry's not blind. He's made this trip so many times, he could find his way here in the dark.

MCMURTY: (*Looks at his watch*) He's going to have to this time. It's almost ten.

TOM: (*Dials on house phone*) Dick doesn't answer.

MCMURTY: Must be asleep.

TOM: He was very tired.

MCMURTY: Why don't you leave a message in his mailbox?

TOM: No, it's not necessary. I'll let him sleep. I'll wake him when Harry arrives.

MCMURTY: Could I interest you in an after-dinner drink?

TOM: None for me. (*Sneezes. Pause*) Mr. Giacconni said no drinking in the lobby.

MCMURTY: What Mr. Giacconni doesn't know won't hurt him. (*Goes to the mailboxes. Removes a bottle and two glasses from one of the mail slots behind the hotel desk*)

TOM: I don't want any. (*He sneezes*)

MCMURTY: Of course you do. It will take care of that cold you're getting.

TOM: I don't need any liquor.

MCMURTY: Of course you do. We'll have a toast! (*Pours a drink for both of them*)

TOM: Where's Giacconni tonight?

MCMURTY: Took the night off.

TOM: What a nerve . . . leaving a bunch of kids in charge of this hotel. I don't like all this part-time help he brings in here. Foreigners. They steal all the silver.

MCMURTY: They're harmless.

TOM: Arabs!

MCMURTY: (*Correcting*) Iraq.

TOM: He what?

MCMURTY: (*Laughs*) Iraq, it's a country.

TOM: Never heard of it.

MCMURTY: It's near Saudi Arabia.

TOM: I thought so . . . I can always tell an Arab. They smell . . . like olive oil or something. (*Uses inhaler*)

MCMURTY: How can you tell what anyone smells like, you've always got Benzedrine rammed up your nose. (*Tom sneezes*) You've caught a cold marching up and down in the rain, like a fool.

TOM: (*Sneezes*) I didn't see you out there today.

MCMURTY: It wasn't my war. Go ahead, destroy your nose.

TOM: (*Using inhaler again*) It's my nose . . . mind your own business! (*Tom steps on golf ball and almost falls*) Would you mind picking up your damned golf balls. I could've broken my neck.

MCMURTY: (*Rolls back carpet into place and picks up golf balls*) You know something, Tom?

TOM: What?

MCMURTY: You've become a sour old fart, lately. (*Silence*)

TOM: At least I can say that I'm proud of the army I served in.

MCMURTY: What was that supposed to mean?

TOM: Exactly what I said.

MCMURTY: (*Picks up the putter threateningly*) If you make another lousy crack about the Abraham Lincoln Brigade, I swear to God, I'll . . .

TOM: You'll what? You'd strike a defenseless old veteran . . . wouldn't you? Hit him with a club, eh?

MCMURTY: This is a putter, not a club. Don't you know anything?

TOM: Don't you dare threaten me with that *thing* . . . you . . . you . . .

MCMURTY: If you say communist . . . I'll crack your head. I warned you before Tom, the Lincoln Brigade was the finest regiment ever to fight for the cause of freedom. (*Pause*) And I wasn't drafted.

TOM: (*Snorts*) The *American* army wouldn't have had you!

MCMURTY: Always looking for a fight, aren't you?

TOM: I refuse to discuss this matter any further, Mr. McMurty, act your age.

MCMURTY: *You* grow up. (*Long pause*)

TOM: I don't believe in bickering. (*Gestures toward kitchen*) It leads to disrespect. The service industries are in bad enough shape as it is.

MCMURTY: (*Pours a drink*) You make my liver inflame when you start in on that . . .

TOM: Sorry, I won't bring it up again.

MCMURTY: (*Hands a drink to Tom*) Here's to your health.

TOM: (*Reluctantly*) And yours. (*Silence. Tom crosses over and picks up the putter, examines it*) Very nice. I'd like to have one like this someday.

MCMURTY: There's an interesting story behind that putter.

TOM: I know, you've told me before.

MCMURTY: It was given to me by the greatest golfer of them all, Bobby Jones . . .

TOM:   Is that a fact?

MCMURTY:   Yes, Sir! Beat him by two strokes, back in '26. Did I ever tell you about how it happened?

TOM:   Yeah, several times.

MCMURTY:   Hmm? Several times? I'll have to watch that.

(*Silence. Tom crosses to the window and looks to the street*)

TOM:   (*Finally, sighing*) It's rained all day. (*Rubs leg*) Terrible on my arthritis.

(*McMurty pulls out watch, discovers it has stopped, squints at wall clock, but cannot see it*)

MCMURTY:   What time do you have? My watch seems to have stopped.

TOM:   (*Producing his watch*) Nine fifty-five. Harry gave me this watch. Solid silver! Keeps perfect time . . . Even has an inscription on the back. La Belle Epoque . . . that's French . . . means "the good old days." (*McMurty pays no attention to Tom. McMurty sets his watch*) What did you think of dinner tonight?

MCMURTY:   I didn't eat . . . (*Thinks*) Didn't you ask me that before?

TOM:   I . . . I don't think so.

MCMURTY:   Yes . . . I remember . . . you said the potatoes were cold. (*Chuckles*) You're getting senile.

TOM:   (*Irritated by his mistake*) No, it's the weather. When it rains . . . arthritis . . . acts up and . . .

MCMURTY:   (*Under his breath*) In the brain.

TOM:   (*To himself*) I can't seem to keep my thoughts . . . (*Trailing off. Pause. Then, vindictive*) Well, you'll just have to do without . . . they stopped serving at nine.

MCMURTY:   I'm having a late dinner in my room.

TOM:   Are you?

MCMURTY:   Yes.

TOM:   Alone?

MCMURTY:   Of course not. Mrs. Sammons is joining me for dinner.

TOM:   Oh, my God, she's not coming here tonight?

MCMURTY:   Yes, she is, Tom. Tuesdays and Thursdays.

TOM:   You cannot have a woman in your room tonight!

MCMURTY:   Why not?

TOM:   Because . . . because Harry wouldn't like it!

MCMURTY:   Harry isn't here.

TOM: He'll be here. And when he comes and finds out that you've got a . . . a . . . woman, up for the night . . . Harry will be furious . . . I just don't know what he might do.

MCMURTY: Harry will never know. We won't make any noise.

TOM: No, I'm afraid I cannot allow it. Any other time, but not tonight. Not on our reunion.

MCMURTY: It's too late, Tom. Everything's arranged. Be reasonable.

TOM: You be reasonable. This is not going to be suitable, not one bit.

MCMURTY: Tough shit, Tom.

TOM: What?!!?

MCMURTY: You heard what I said.

TOM: You're disgusting.

MCMURTY: No, just enjoying my retirement.

(*Dick appears on the landing at the bottom of the stairs dressed in a WWI uniform with gas mask on his face and wearing a steel helmet. He stomps to attention and salutes Tom and McMurty. Dick mumbles something that is garbled by the mask*)

MCMURTY: (*Laughing*) Is it another gas attack, Mr. Weaver?

(*Dick crosses downstage, speech still unintelligible*)

TOM: Take off that ridiculous gas mask. I can't understand a word you're saying.

DICK: (*Takes off mask and is without his glasses*) Harry?

TOM: No, it's Mr. McMurty.

MCMURTY: Put on your glasses, Dick.

DICK: (*Dick fumbles in tunic, looking for glasses*) I heard voices, I thought maybe Harry was here.

TOM: Not yet.

MCMURTY: Tom and I were having a drink. Care to join us?

DICK: Yes, I would, thank you. You know, I fell asleep right after the parade. I thought I might lie down for a few minutes before dinner . . . I must have dozed off . . . (*Yawns*) I suppose I missed dinner?

MCMURTY: Yes, it's after ten.

TOM: Dinner wasn't very good tonight.

DICK: Is it ever?

MCMURTY: (*Rises*) I'll see if I can find you some leftovers in the kitchen. (*Exits*)

DICK: (*Calls after him*) Bring another glass, will ya? (*Crosses over to examine flag which is drying by door*) Do you think it's dry enough to fold?

TOM:   I suppose. (*Tom crosses to Dick. They begin folding the flag*) Your uniform is wet.

DICK:   I know and I slept in it, too. Hope I don't catch a cold.

TOM:   I'll loan you a Benzedrine.

DICK:   That would be nice.

TOM:   Mrs. Sammons is coming to visit McMurty again.

DICK:   Really, what a pleasant surprise. I haven't seen her for some time now. Let's see . . . how long has it been?

TOM:   Tuesday.

DICK:   (*Folding the flag*) That recent?

TOM:   Don't let it touch the floor.

DICK:   Sorry. . . . You know, I like Mrs. Sammons, she knows so many fine stories.

TOM:   What about Harry?

DICK:   Oh, dear, I forgot. He won't like it, will he?

TOM:   Not at all.

DICK:   What will he do?

TOM:   I don't know. (*Tom notices McMurty coming*) Ahem! (*McMurty enters from dining room with a glass and a box of crackers*)

MCMURTY:   This was all I could find. (*Hands the crackers to Dick*) The cooks said they would make you an egg.

DICK:   No, thanks, crackers will be fine.

MCMURTY:   Well, let me pour you a drink. (*Pours the drink and sniffs the air*) Do you smell something peculiar?

TOM:   (*Points to Dick*) It's his uniform.

DICK:   (*Sniffs his sleeve and extends it to McMurty*) Yes, it smells like horsehair when it's damp.

MCMURTY:   Whew, that's terrible! You ought to change out of those clothes before you catch pneumonia.

DICK:   (*Chewing on a cracker*) I have to be in uniform when Harry gets here.

MCMURTY:   Says who?

TOM:   Harry says.

DICK:   It's a tradition.

MCMURTY:   (*To Tom*) Where's your uniform?

TOM:   At the cleaners.

DICK:   He means they lost it at the cleaners . . . six years ago!

MCMURTY:   Oh, that's too bad. Perhaps, you can get another one at the Army-Navy surplus store.

TOM:   It wouldn't be the same thing.

DICK:   Harry would never approve.

MCMURTY:   (*Pause*) I'd be interested in meeting Harry. What does this Harry look like? Perhaps I've met him before. Another city maybe?

DICK:   Oh, no. You've never met Harry before.

MCMURTY:   How do you know?

DICK:   If you had met Harry, we'd know. Harry would have told us.

MCMURTY:   Oh. (*Pause*) Suppose I ran into him in the past year, before I moved here. It is possible. Maybe we sat together on a train, shared a table in a cafeteria . . . who knows?

TOM:   It's not likely. He lives very far from here.

MCMURTY:   So did I. Last year.

DICK:   But you would remember if you had seen him.

TOM:   Harry is the type of man you don't forget.

MCMURTY:   I knew a Harry about six months ago. I was in a hospital in Kansas City . . . minor gallstone ailment, nothing serious. There was a fellow in the same room, the next bed, actually—undergoing exploratory surgery of . . . the colon, I believe. We hit it off pretty well . . . trading war stories and the like. He said he was in the artillery during the First World War. Served in France, somewhere around Nancy—1918.

TOM:   (*Unimpressed*) Lots of people served in France.

DICK:   What outfit was he in?

MCMURTY:   301st Field Artillery, I believe.

DICK:   (*Sigh of relief*) No . . . that's not our Harry, different regiment.

MCMURTY:   Now, I could be wrong about the number of the regiment, it's been a long time. My memory isn't what it used to be. It could have been the 103rd, I'm not sure anymore.

DICK:   103rd! That's our outfit.

TOM:   Easy, Dick. What did this Harry of yours look like?

MCMURTY:   He was about your height, Tom.

DICK:   Our Harry was much taller.

MCMURTY:   Practically bald, brown eyes . . . medium build.

TOM:   Harry has blue eyes.

DICK:   And a full head of bushy blond hair.

MCMURTY:   Said he was a captain in the gunnery.

DICK: A lieutenant. *(Pause)* Nope, you've got the wrong man.

MCMURTY: I guess so.

TOM: *(After a pause)* Besides, Harry has never been to Kansas City.

*(Pause)*

MCMURTY: Funny coincidence. *(Pause)* No matter, the wrong Harry.

DICK: What else did this Harry have to say?

MCMURTY: Nothing . . . Only knew him for a day or two. He died on the operating table. Never saw him again after they wheeled him into surgery.

*(Long pause. Tom looks out the window, takes a large sip of his drink. Dick picks lint off the flag. Dick finally breaks the silence)*

DICK: How . . . how old was he?

MCMURTY: In his sixties, I imagine. *(Tom rises and crosses to window. McMurty tries to smooth things over)* No need to worry . . . There must have been hundreds of men named Harry in your outfit.

DICK: *(Pouring a drink)* Yes . . . hundreds. *(Pause)* Tom tells me that your lady friend is coming this evening.

MCMURTY: *(Consults his watch)* Yes, she should be here directly.

DICK: Tom's worried about . . . about Harry, and how it would look with a woman here and . . .

MCMURTY: Doesn't like females, eh?

DICK: Who?

MCMURTY: Harry.

DICK: No, Tom. Harry was always a ladies' man.

MCMURTY: Oh.

TOM: *(Looks out the window)* Miserable weather!

MCMURTY: Been raining for hours . . . I remember a night like this in Spain. *(Tom looks upward and shakes his head)* We'd been camped in this little town for days, don't have nothin' to eat but hardtack. There was about two hundred of us and we were all hungrier than hell. There wasn't a thing to eat in all of Spain. Then, I'll be damned if a big white duck didn't fly out of the bell tower of the little church. I threw my submachine gun up and let'er rip. I must have been lucky cause he caught the whole damn clip. Ripped 'em from eyehole to asshole. Feathers all over the square. Before all the feathers could light, I had him plucked, spitted, and over a fire. Before

I knew what was happening, there was about a hundred and fifty guys standing around watching me cook that duck. I'll never forget the hungry look on these guys' faces, you shoulda' heard the begging and pleading. And one guy said, "Listen, McMurty, if I had a duck, I'd give you half" . . .

TOM: (*Has had enough*) What in th ehell are you talking about?

MCMURTY: HMM? Huh? Oh, I'm sorry, I thought it was funny.

(*Long pause*)

DICK: It was raining like this the night I married my first wife . . .

TOM: Oh, Jesus . . .

DICK: Schenectady . . . or was it Columbus? I don't know. I spent my honeymoon in one of them.

MCMURTY: Which one?

DICK: My first wife.

MCMURTY: I know that. Which town?

DICK: I don't know. I can't remember.

TOM: Do you remember her name?

DICK: (*Slight hesitation*) Edith . . . Edith was my first wife. Dorothy was my second.

MCMURTY: Are you sure, Dick?

DICK: Of course. How could I forget something like that?

TOM: I could.

DICK: That's because you never married.

TOM: Possibly.

DICK: Were you ever married, Mr. McMurty? I can't recall you mentioning anything about a wife.

MCMURTY: No . . . sorry to say I never met the right woman.

DICK: Too bad.

TOM: I don't think I'd have the patience to put up with a woman's qualms. Always sick and complaining. No. I don't think I'd enjoy that prospect. Friends are better than wives.

MCMURTY: Well . . . now that might be debatable.

DICK: Friends don't complain as often as wives. Believe me, I know.

TOM: I've heard you bellyache enough.

DICK: Who said I was your friend? (*Pause*) My best friend is Harry.

MCMURTY: And who is Harry's best friend?

TOM: Me, of course.

DICK:   I am. Harry said he liked me the best . . . on several occasions.

TOM:   Don't be absurd. You're a crybaby. Nobody likes crybabies.

DICK:   (*Infantile*) I am not a crybaby!

TOM:   Yes, you are.

DICK:   I am not! I have never cried in my entire life.

(*McMurty finds this very amusing*)

TOM:   Yes, you have. I've seen it.

DICK:   When?

TOM:   St. Remy. November the 11th, 1918, at 11 o'clock in the morning. You cried at your post. Standing next to a howitzer with a shell cradled in your arms . . . tears were streaming down your face. You looked like a pathetic puppy.

DICK:   (*Protesting*) THE WAR WAS OVER!

TOM:   You looked ridiculous. Holding a shell like it was a loaf of bread . . . it was weak.

DICK:   Everybody cries when a war is over!

TOM:   I didn't.

DICK:   Well . . . you have no feelings. You're . . . you're . . . malignant!

TOM:   What's that supposed to mean?

DICK:   (*Laughing*) Ha. Ha. Really caught you with that one.

(*Tom looks to McMurty to see if a joke has passed that all but Dick have missed. McMurty shrugs*)

TOM:   (*To McMurty*) What does he mean?

MCMURTY:   Dunno. It was a rather strange choice of words, I must say. (*He chuckles. To Dick*) Haven't heard that one in a long time.

(*Long pause*)

TOM:   (*Confused*) Well . . . at least I'm not a namby-pamby!

DICK:   Namby-pamby! (*Howls*) Oh, that's good! Baby talk! Ha. Ha.

TOM:   That wasn't funny. (*Turns to McMurty*) Did I say something funny?

MCMURTY:   (*Laughs*) No.

TOM:   (*To Dick*) You're getting drunk. He gets like this everytime he drinks . . . makes an incredible ass of himself. (*Agitated*) Where's Harry? (*Pause. Pours a drink*) It's getting late.

DICK:   Maybe he's not coming this year.

TOM:   (*Gives Dick an icy stare*) We'll see.

(*Long pause*)

DICK: I saw Tom cry once.

TOM: You never! When?

DICK: At Coetquidan. (*To McMurty*) It was during a gas attack. (*To Tom*) You didn't get your mask on in time.

TOM: It was the gas ... I didn't cry.

DICK: Tears were in your eyes.

TOM: My eyes were watering from the gas.

DICK: They were tears ... all the same.

TOM: Doesn't count. Only cowards cry ... people who are afraid of life.

DICK: Something they're ashamed of?

TOM: What are you getting at?

DICK: Oh, nothing, Tom.

TOM: (*To Dick*) Don't say anything you'll regret later.

DICK: (*Nervously changes the subject. To McMurty*) What about you? Do you cry?

MCMURTY: Not often ... on certain occasions ... if something moves me ... a sad movie, a lost love ...

TOM: I never knew you were in love.

MCMURTY: Oh, yes ... many times when I was young. (*Pause*) There was a girl in Pittsburgh during the war ...

DICK: Which war?

MCMURTY: The second.

DICK: (*Disappointed*) Oh.

MCMURTY: Her name was Katherine, a dancer. She worked in a canteen for the USO ... one of those dime-a-dance places. She wanted to be a famous ballerina someday ... (*Pause*) She was very beautiful, long gorgeous legs. (*Sighs*) A wonderful girl ... I never knew anyone who enjoyed life so much. We used to visit museums when she wasn't working ... museums and of course, the ballet. We were very happy and very much in love. Three months later she met a sailor. He promised to take her to New York ... bright lights, Broadway ... they were married within a week. Shortly afterwards her sailor was shipped out. Guadalcanal. He never returned. Katherine left Chicago ... moved to California. We used to write to each other for a while. Then one day there were no more letters. I never saw her again. (*Pause*) C'est la vie!

DICK: (*Visibly moved*) That is such a sad story. You never tried to find her again?

MCMURTY: No.

TOM:   Too bad. What about Mrs. Sammons? Do you love her?

DICK:   What a terrible thing to ask!

TOM:   (*Gleeful malice*) If you got married, you would have to move out of the hotel. Mr. Giacconni doesn't rent to couples.

(*Phone rings. Tom and Dick rise*)

TOM:   Harry!

DICK:   (*Moves quickly toward the phone*) I'll get it.

TOM:   (*Beats Dick to the phone*) I've got it. (*Lifts receiver*) Hello, Harry? (*Pause*) Who?

DICK:   Is it Harry?

TOM:   (*Shoos Dick away*) Yes, he is. Just a moment, please. (*To McMurty*) It's for you.

DICK:   (*Disappointed*) It wasn't Harry.

MCMURTY:   (*Crosses to phone and takes receiver*) Thank you. Hello? Yes. I've been worried. You said an hour ago. I see. Of course, dear.

(*McMurty turns his back so that the rest of the conversation cannot be hard. Tom and Dick move away*)

TOM:   It's that damn woman.

DICK:   Mrs. Sammons?

TOM:   (*Nods. Pours another drink*) When that woman gets here . . . don't mention anything about Harry. (*McMurty hangs up the phone and crosses back to them*) You keep your mouth shut in front of Mrs. Sammons, understand?

DICK:   All right.

MCMURTY:   I'm afraid you gentlemen will have to excuse me. (*Picks up the putter*) I must change into something more suitable for dinner.

DICK:   Mrs. Sammons is coming?

MCMURTY:   Yes, and I must get changed . . . she'll be here shortly. Seems they're having some kind of trouble at the club tonight.

TOM:   Is that so?

DICK:   What kind of trouble?

MCMURTY:   I dunno. She didn't say. Well, gentlemen, talking with you has been a pleasure . . . it's been stimulating as usual. (*Picks up the whisky bottle*) If you don't mind, we'll be needing this. I'm sure you can find another bottle in the kitchen. I hope your friend Harry arrives. Look forward to meeting him.

DICK:   Yes, in the morning, Mr. McMurty. You can count on it.

MCMURTY:   Yes . . . well, until morning . . . good evening!

TOM:   Evening.

DICK:   Have a jolly time.

MCMURTY:   You, too. (*Pause. Confidential*) Oh, say listen, when Mrs. Sammons arrives, you'll send her up to my room, O.K.?

DICK:   We'll do that. Good night.

MCMURTY:   Have a nice reunion. 'Night. (*Exits up the stairs*)

DICK:   Well, that was abrupt.

TOM:   (*Sulking*) Ignoramus!

DICK:   Who? McMurty?

TOM:   Yes, that stupid Irish mick, McMurty!

DICK:   SSSH! He'll hear you.

TOM:   Who cares? (*Pause, then contemptuously*) A ballerina! I bet he's never even been to Pittsburgh. (*Pause*) I'll bet he never met Bobby Jones, either.

DICK:   I wouldn't be surprised. (*Pause*) Who is Bobby Jones?

TOM:   A baseball player.

DICK:   Oh. Never heard of him. I think I'll have another whisky.

TOM:   He took the bottle with him.

DICK:   (*Notices Tom's full glass*) Where did you get that?

TOM:   I refilled before he left. You've got to look out for yourself when an Irishman is near a bottle of whisky.

DICK:   (*Starts for the dining room*) I'll see if there's another bottle in the pantry.

(*Dick exits. Tom takes out inhaler again. He paces around the room and sits in an easy chair. He rises and pulls a golf ball out of the cushion, tosses the ball behind the sofa. He rises and crosses to the desk. He goes behind register and looks through the contents of the various mailboxes. He finds an apple, puts it in his coat pocket. Tom reads a postcard. He hears steps approaching. Tom pockets the postcard. He crosses back to the easy chair sipping his drink. Dick enters carrying a bottle of cooking sherry*)

DICK:   (*Looking at wall clock. Shakes his head*) It's getting late.

TOM:   What have you got in that bottle?

DICK:   Cooking sherry.

TOM:   Ugh! You're not going to drink it?

DICK:   All there was . . . cupboard's bare.

TOM:   There was a bottle of Scotch in there three days ago.

DICK: (*Pours a drink*) Perhaps McMurty drank it.

TOM: Scotch isn't his drink. I wonder what could have happened to it?

DICK: (*Sits on couch, pulls out a golf ball*) Is this yours?

TOM: No. I've been sitting on them all night.

(*Dick pockets the ball*)

TOM: I bet those Arabs know what happened to that fifth of Scotch I placed in the pantry last week.

DICK: I'll go ask them . . .

TOM: Don't bother . . . they'll lie to you . . . There was a full bottle in there three days ago. One of those miserable bastards unlocked the cabinet for me . . . He was standing right next to me when I locked it up. (*Mutters*) Every time trouble comes their way, they put on the dumb show . . . pretend they can't understand English.

DICK: You think one of the kitchen staff drank it?

TOM: Who else?

DICK: Not me.

TOM: Can't trust immigrants for a minute. Everything disappears around here now. (*Pause*) I left my razor on the sink one morning. When I came back twenty minutes later, it was gone. Now who would steal someone else's razor? It's unsanitary. It's like wearing someone else's underwear.

DICK: I don't know. Who would?

TOM: What were they doing when you went into the kitchen?

DICK: Washing dishes.

TOM: Probably loading up their pockets with silverware and salt shakers. Believe me, I've seen it happen. When I was down in Miami a few years ago, when they started to let Cubans in—those greasers took all the jobs away from the coloreds. Cubans the reason we got so many coloreds on welfare.

DICK: Is that so?

TOM: And all the time those Cubans were stealing anything they could get their hands on. You had to nail everything down. I've seen'em take the plumbing out of a men's room.

DICK: It's a dirty shame.

TOM: You damn well better believe it. Foreigners are the death of the service industries. (*Tom runs his hand along the top of the fireplace mantle*) You don't have to look far to see that.

DICK: Used to be a man took pride in his job . . . not anymore, nope.

TOM:   They're having a terrible time with 'em over in England.

DICK:   Who?

TOM:   Those Pakiis, that's who.

DICK:   Pakiis?

TOM:   Pakistanis . . . They got'em all over the place in England.

DICK:   Coming out of the woodwork, eh?

TOM:   By the thousands . . . every day! Most of them can't read or write . . . can't get decent work . . . rapists, killers, all sorts. None of them speak a word of English, they say. Dirtiest people in the world. Never take a bath.

DICK:   I thought that was the Chinese.

TOM:   The what?

DICK:   Chinese! It's the Chinks that never bathe.

TOM:   (*Guffaws*) Shows how much you know.

DICK:   It's true. I read it somewhere . . . I know I did.

TOM:   Where? . . . Where did you read such nonsense? (*Pause*)

DICK:   I can't remember . . . But, I did read it. It said the Chinese were the dirtiest people on earth!

TOM:   Bull!

DICK:   Maybe it was the Japanese . . .

TOM:   You didn't read that. You made it up. Ask Harry when he gets here. He'll know. (*Pause*) Next you'll be telling me that some Chinaman invented gunpowder.

DICK:   I read that, too . . . the same article.

TOM:   (*Swings at Dick*) You idiot! That's a myth. Everyone knows the English invented gunpowder . . . 1066, I believe. (*Long silence*)

TOM:   Look it up if you don't believe me.

DICK:   I believe you.

(*The front door opens. Lucille Sammons enters. She is a heavy-set, middle-aged woman with frosted hair-do. She wears a plastic raincoat, galoshes, and carries a bucket of Kentucky Fried Chicken*)

LUCILLE:   (*Shaking her raincoat*) Ooh! That weather . . . it's miserable. How are you boys, tonight?

DICK:   Just fine, Mrs. Sammons. How are you?

TOM:   Fine.

LUCILLE:   (*Removing galoshes*) What a night! I thought I'd never get out.

DICK:   Exciting night at the club?

LUCILLE:   You'll never believe what happened.

DICK:   Here, let me hang up that raincoat by the radiator. Tell us all about it.

LUCILLE:   It was just unbelievable. There was a brawl right there in the lounge. Two fellows got into it at the bar . . . turned over tables, throwing glasses . . . they smashed the glass on the jukebox.

DICK:   Amazing! What started it?

LUCILLE:   Oh, who knows? Probably fighting over some woman.

TOM:   It figures.

DICK:   I hope you weren't hurt.

LUCILLE:   Not me. I stayed out of it. When two drunks get going at each other . . . I know enough to stay put . . . don't get involved. Brother, what a mess they made. We had to close early. It took until a half-hour ago just to sweep up the glass.

DICK:   Tsk, tsk . . . terrible business.

LUCILLE:   Whew, what a night! Any excitement around here this evening?

TOM:   We were having an after-dinner drink with Mr. McMurty before you arrived.

DICK:   It was after your dinner, not mine.

TOM:   He slept through dinner again . . . second time this week.

DICK:   I can't help it. I get tired easily these days.

LUCILLE:   Poor thing. (*She hands bucket of chicken to Dick*) Have a piece of fried chicken.

DICK:   Oh, no, I couldn't, Mrs. Sammons . . . it's your dinner.

LUCILLE:   Call me Lucille. Go on, I've got plenty. Mac never eats more than a wing or two.

DICK:   (*Taking a piece*) Thank you.

(*Lucille sits on one of the easy chairs, rises and extracts a golf ball from under the cushion*)

LUCILLE:   (*Holding the ball*) What in hell . . .

TOM:   One of McMurty's toys . . . he's got them all over the hotel.

LUCILLE:   (*Putting the ball in an ashtray*) Damn fool. Someone could hurt himself. How is Mac this evening, feeling well?

DICK:   He looked O.K. to me.

LUCILLE:   I worry about him. He drinks too much. Have

two pieces, Dick. Go on. How about you, Tom? (*Offers the bucket*) Chicken?

TOM:   No, thank you. I've already eaten.

(*Lucille takes a piece of chicken*)

DICK:   Umm. This is marvelous.

LUCILLE:   It is quite good.

DICK:   I was starved. I haven't been this hungry since we were in France.

LUCILLE:   In France?

TOM:   During the war.

LUCILLE:   You were in France? "Oh, how lovely."

TOM:   It wasn't so lovely then . . . there was a war going on.

LUCILLE:   No, I guess it wouldn't be so much fun during a war. (*Sighs*) Paris in the spring. I've never been to Europe, but someday I'm going. Morty has been promising to take me to France for years . . . the bum, he never makes enough money . . . at least, that's what he says. "Next year we'll go," he says, "next year." When next year finally rolls around: one weekend fishing in the Ozarks.

TOM:   Morty?

LUCILLE:   My husband. (*Pause*) I should say my former husband . . . We separated . . . temporarily.

DICK:   Oh, that's too bad.

TOM:   Hmm, I thought you were a widow.

LUCILLE:   No such luck. Never happen to this girl. If he ever did kick off . . . I'd end up with a pile of dough . . . Then I could travel. . . . Ha! Fat chance. Instead I end up working six nights a week slopping tables in a crummy bar, dodging the gooses of dirty old men. No offense, boys!

DICK:   We don't mind, do we, Tom?

TOM:   No. (*Pause*) I don't pinch waitresses.

LUCILLE:   (*To Tom*) Whatever gave you the idea that I was a widow? (*Laughs*) I better change my wardrobe. I didn't know that I looked like I was in mourning.

DICK:   Earlier tonight he thought Mr. McMurty had never been in love. Can you imagine that? (*To Tom*) But he set you straight didn't he? (*To Lucille*) Told us all about an old flame, a ballerina in Pittsburgh during the war . . . such a sad story . . . (*Realizes he has said the wrong thing*) Ooops, I shouldn't have said that.

TOM:   You always find a way to put your foot in your mouth, don't you?

DICK:   Please don't tell him I said anything...

TOM:   See the mess you've gotten yourself into this time. Big mouth?

LUCILLE:   Don't worry. I don't care anything about other women Mac has known. Ancient history.

DICK:   Are you sure?

LUCILLE:   (*A lie*) Doesn't bother me a bit.

DICK:   Whew, that's a relief. (*Trying to smooth things over*) Why don't you have a drink with us, Mrs. Sammons.

LUCILLE:   Why, thank you. You boys shouldn't be drinking in the lobby. You know what will happen if you get caught.

DICK:   Giacconni's not here tonight.

TOM:   Anyway, it's a special occasion.

LUCILLE:   Really? What?

TOM:   Don't you know what day this is?

LUCILLE:   (*Thinks*) Uhh ... November the 11th. (*Pause*) So? What's so special about today?

TOM:   The Armistice!

LUCILLE:   Huh?

DICK:   World War I. It was over today. Forty-three years ago.

LUCILLE:   Oh? ... So, that's why you're wearing the costume!

TOM:   COSTUME!

LUCILLE:   I wondered ... I thought it was a masonic lodge outfit or something.

DICK:   (*Hurt*) This was my uniform. (*Pause. Sad*) We had a parade.

LUCILLE:   (*She pats Dick's arm*) I'm sorry, Dick. I didn't know. (*Pause*) Well World War I was a bit before my time ... but, just the same ... let me propose a toast to two of the finest old gentlemen I have ever had the privilege of meeting.

DICK:   That was very kind of you.

LUCILLE:   To your health! (*She drinks and gags*) God, what is that awful concoction?

DICK:   Cooking sherry.

TOM:   We did have some whisky, but Mr. McMurty took the bottle for your dinner party.

LUCILLE:   Why, that conniving old bastard! Leaving you

boys with cooking sherry to celebrate your holiday ...
Wait until I get hold of him ... I'll give him ...

TOM: It's all right, Mrs. Sammons. We'll manage.

LUCILLE: Will you stop being so formal, Tom? Call me
Lucille. (*She begins to rummage in her purse*) I just happen to
have a little something with me. (*She pulls out a pint of vodka*)
One of the fringe benefits of working in a tavern.

DICK: Oh, you really shouldn't go to the trouble.

LUCILLE: (*Taking their glasses*) Nonsense. If you're going to
have a toast, it must be done properly. An important occasion
like ... Armistice Day certainly deserves a more civilized oil
than this. (*She looks around for a place to dump the glasses of sherry*)
Now where can I dump this drink? (*She crosses to the potted
plant*) This will do. (*She pours the sherry into the plant*)

TOM: Oh, no ... not there, please!

LUCILLE: Don't fret, Tom ... it will do that plant a world
of good. (*She pours vodka into their glasses*) Hope you don't mind
vodka.

DICK: Vodka is fine.

LUCILLE: (*She hands them their drinks*) Here you go ... Now,
let's try that again. To the Armistice!

TOM & DICK: To the Armistice!

(*They clink their glasses together in a silent toast. Tom and Dick
sip their drinks. Lucille leans against the fireplace mantel and
drains her glass in one long swallow. She sets the glass down hard
on the mantel*)

LUCILLE: Ahh, much better. (*Sighs*) Well, why don't you
tell me *all* about the war.

DICK: Everything?

LUCILLE: Sure, why not? How many Germans did you kill?
(*Pause*) It was the Germans we fought in that war?

TOM: Yes ... and the Austrians.

LUCILLE: I remember ... "Kick the Kaiser!" Right? Well,
how many did you get?

DICK: I don't actually know. I never counted.

TOM: We were too far away to see what we were shooting.

DICK: The artillery ... you know, big cannons.

TOM: (*He points to Dick's shoulder insignia*) The 103rd Field
Artillery, 26th Division. We fought on the Hindenburg Line.

DICK: Tom and I fired a howitzer. Couldn't see where the
shells landed. When we went through a village and saw the
rubble, only then did we know if we ever hit anything. (*Pause*)

Of course, it could have been German shells. No way of telling. (*Pause*) The only Germans I saw were dead or prisoners.

LUCILLE:  Sounds fascinating.

DICK:  Actually it was pretty boring . . . loading a howitzer gets to be a routine job after awhile.

LUCILLE:  I'll bet both of you were decorated as heroes.

TOM:  I didn't get any medals.

DICK:  Me either. (*Pause*) Harry was the only one that got a medal.

TOM:  (*To Dick, vindictive*) I warned you not to say . . .

DICK:  I forgot.

LUCILLE:  Who's Harry?

TOM:  Harry Palmer. Our buddy during the war. He's coming here tonight for our reunion. Harry comes every Armistice Day . . . it's a tradition.

DICK:  But he's late this year. Very late.

(*Tom gives him a look as if to suggest he be silent*)

LUCILLE:  How nice to have a good friend for such a long time. I hope he arrives in time for your party.

TOM:  Harry missed the parade, but he'll be here before morning.

LUCILLE:  So . . . Harry was a hero?

DICK:  Yes, wounded many times . . . a real soldier.

LUCILLE:  Were you wounded, Tom?

TOM:  No. I made it through without a scratch.

DICK:  I dropped a shell casing on my foot once. Almost got tetanus. (*Pause*) Tom had dysentery.

TOM:  I did not.

DICK:  Yes, you did. After you ate some French bread.

TOM:  (*Correcting*) I was sick . . . but, I did not have dysentery.

DICK:  He's being brave, but believe me, you never saw anyone so sick in your life.

LUCILLE:  How awful! What happened?

TOM:  Oh, those miserable Frenchmen. Some idea of a practical joke on the American liberators. It makes me furious to think about it. We entered this deserted town after a week of shelling.

DICK:  Lamarche-en-Woerve.

TOM:  Yes . . . Lamarche-en-Woerve   . I'll never forget that rotten hole. We were looking for food, so we went into this deserted French bakery . . . I took a loaf of bread and some wine. There was no one around . . . so, we sat on a curb under a streetlamp and began eating.

DICK: And then Tom turns to me after he finished half a loaf and says to me, "This bread tastes funny . . ."

TOM: I should have noticed it earlier . . . but, I was too hungry at the time.

DICK: So, Tom cracks open his loaf of bread, and sure enough, there was a core of horse shit right down the center of the loaf.

TOM: Those bastards baked it right into the bread.

DICK: He thinks they did it on purpose. I'm sure it was an accident. The bakery was next door to a stable.

TOM: Accidents like that don't happen. I know it. (*Lucille starts giggling*) The Frogs were laying for us. (*Pause*) Don't tell me the dung just walked into that bakery and jumped into the oven. Someone put it there, dammit!

(*Dick and Lucille are laughing*)

DICK: There wasn't any in my loaf.

TOM: Go on, laugh. It wasn't funny . . . not one bit. I nearly puked my guts out.

DICK: (*Laughing*) A pretty good way to catch a thief when the baker is away.

TOM: Very funny. If I ever catch the Frenchy that did that, I'll . . .

DICK: And ever since that night . . . Tom refuses to eat another piece of French bread.

(*Dick and Lucille howl*)

TOM: Shut up, both of you! It wasn't funny. (*Dick and Lucille try to stop laughing, but can't. Tom turns to Dick*) I'm going to punch you in the mouth if you don't stop laughing.

LUCILLE: I'm sorry, Tom. I just got tickled.

TOM: (*Snorts*) Hmpf.

LUCILLE: Don't sulk. We're laughing at the story, not you.

TOM: We'll see. (*To Dick*) Just you wait, big mouth!

DICK: You told the story!

TOM: Who brought it up?

(*Silence. Tom uses the inhaler*)

DICK: You shouldn't do that.

TOM: (*Throwing the inhaler*) Why is everybody so damned concerned about my nose?

(*Silence. Tom sits sulking. All are quiet. Lucille dries away tears. Dick drinks quietly. Suddenly Lucille snickers and she and Dick break up again*

TOM: (*Furious*) All right, DAMMIT! ENOUGH!

(*All sit quietly again. Tom closes his eyes. Lucille tries desperately to subdue her chuckles. No sound. Dick and Lucille shake occasionally as they try to hold it in. A smile will break out from time to time. Tom is looking for revenge, finally he opens his watch and speaks*)

TOM: I think you are going to be late for your dinner, Mrs. Sammons. I'm sure Mr. McMurty has heard you *cackling* down here and probably wonders what . . .

DICK: Tom! Don't be rude!

LUCILLE: That's all right, Dick. I can take a hint . . . The chicken is getting cold. (*Rises*) I'd better go.

DICK: Not until Tom apologizes. Well, Tom . . .

LUCILLE: Forget it. It's not important. Tom's right . . . I've overstayed my welcome.

DICK: Sometimes Tom can be so rude. He doesn't mean it . . . He doesn't know what he's saying sometimes . . .

TOM: Oh, yes, I do.

LUCILLE: No explanations necessary. Well . . . see you later, gentlemen.

DICK: (*He hands the vodka bottle to her*) Don't forget your bottle.

LUCILLE: You keep it. (*Pause*) It's a party!

(*Tom stares out the window*)

DICK: Good night.

(*Lucille starts up the stairs*)

DICK: I want to apologize for Tom since he won't do it himself.

LUCILLE: (*Without looking back*) I've forgotten it.

(*Lucille is gone. Silence. Dick turns from the staircase and crosses down to Tom*)

DICK: That was vicious and cruel!

TOM: She deserved it! (*Turns*) And you deserve a swift kick in the ass!

DICK: You have no concern for other people's feelings. You never think of anyone but yourself. You're a selfish bully! (*Pause*) Sometimes I wonder why I stay with you.

TOM: You are a simpering brat! No one else would put

up with you. If you were half as concerned about Harry as you are about that whore's fried chicken . . .

DICK: Mrs. Sammons is not a whore!

TOM: Oh! What do you think they do up there two nights a week?

DICK: They have dinner and talk . . . and she reads to him. I know, I've heard them.

TOM: Naïve.

DICK: Well, so what if they do sleep together. Is it any of your business? They're in love.

TOM: (*Chokes*) Love! Is that what you call it? At McMurty's age, it's . . . disgusting!

DICK: Everything is disgusting to you. Who do you think you are? (*Pause*) Well . . . to me, you're disgusting.

(*A scream is heard from upstairs*)

DICK: What was that?

TOM: (*Sarcastic*) Love.

DICK: Tom, if you don't apologize to Mrs. Sammons, I'll . . . (*Bravely*) I'll move out of this hotel. Tonight! I swear it, I'll leave.

TOM: No, you won't. You've got no place to go.

DICK: I'm serious. (*Pause*) I'll move out tonight.

TOM: (*Laughs*) Ha, Ha! Why don't you move in with Harry . . . that would be a good one.

(*Lucille appears on the landing of the stairs. She is shaking. Tears are on her cheeks. She moves slowly to the bannister, staring vacantly*)

TOM: Something wrong, Lucille?

LUCILLE: (*Hesitant*) Mr. McMurty . . . is . . . dead!

DICK: Oh, my God!

(*Dick slumps on the foot of the stairs*)

TOM: (*Recites*)
"In Flanders Fields the poppies blow.
Between the crosses, row on row.
That mark our place; and in the sky
The larks, still bravely singing, fly
Scarce heard amid the guns below."

(*Dick sits with his head in his hands, muttering to himself. Tom continues to recite "Flanders Field"*)
"We are the dead. Short days ago
We lived, felt dawn, now sunset glow,

Loved and were loved, and now we lie in
Flanders Fields."

LUCILLE: (*Hysterical*) There is a man dead upstairs and all
you can do is recite poetry! WILL SOMEBODY PLEASE DO
SOMETHING!

(*No one moves. Pause*)

TOM: What would you suggest, Lucille?

LUCILLE: Call an ambulance, dammit!

(*Pause.*)

TOM: What for?

DICK: (*Mumbling to himself*) Oh, dear, oh, dear.

LUCILLE: (*To Tom*) What did you say?

TOM: (*Slow and deliberate*) I said . . . what for? He's dead
isn't he? Why would he need an ambulance? A coroner would
be more appropriate.

LUCILLE: You're an animal.

TOM: SLUT!

DICK: Tom . . . don't . . .

TOM: (*To Dick*) You stay out of this!

LUCILLE: If you're looking to tangle with me . . .

TOM: I wouldn't waste my time. (*Tom starts for the stairs*) If
you'll excuse me, now . . . I'm going to see if I can find my
bottle of Scotch.

LUCILLE: (*Grabbing Tom by the arm*) WHERE DO YOU
THINK YOU'RE GOING?

TOM: Upstairs. (*Pause*) Take you hand off my arm, before
I kick your teeth in.

LUCILLE: (*Releasing her grip*) You stay out of his room!

TOM: Believe me, I won't go near him. (*Tom goes upstairs*)

DICK: I'm really sorry, Lucille. (*No response*) I can't understand it. He seemed so healthy a few minutes ago . . . Must
have been a heart attack . . . you never know.

(*Lucille lights a cigarette and stares out the window on the front
door ignoring Dick*)

DICK: What are you going to do now?

LUCILLE: I don't know . . . (*Long pause. She wipes away a
tear*) Dammit!

DICK: Is there anything I can do?

LUCILLE: No . . . thanks. I'll be all right. (*Pause*) Damn him!
I knew this would happen. That old bastard would never listen
to me . . . I told him not to drink . . . but would he listen? Oh,
no . . . even the doctors warned . . . but he never paid any

attention. Mac never listened to anyone. He knew whisky would kill him. How the hell can someone destroy themselves that way? It doesn't make any sense . . . Well, I hope he's happy . . . if he wanted to die that badly . . . I hope he's got what he wanted now! Jesus!

DICK:   Lucille . . . before Tom comes back . . . I want to say one thing. Tom doesn't mean to say the things he does . . . I know, deep inside he cares a great deal about Mac . . .

LUCILLE:   DAMMIT! Will you stop apologizing, Dick! Why do you have to be sorry for everything that happens?

DICK:   But, you've got to understand about him . . .

LUCILLE:   Oh, for Christ's sake! What is there to understand?

DICK:   He doesn't mean everything he says.

LUCILLE:   Oh, yes, he does! That son-of-a-bitch means every word that comes out of his mouth. Stop pretending that Tom is a nice guy, because he's not.

DICK:   He's my friend.

LUCILLE:   And you don't need to apologize for your friends. Tom is old enough to look out for himself.

DICK:   Lucille . . . you don't understand . . . he needs me here . . .

LUCILLE:   What for? His "yes" man?

DICK:   No . . .

LUCILLE:   What does he give you in return?

DICK:   Companionship.

LUCILLE:   That kind of companionship you don't need. What about your other friend? . . . What's his name? . . . Harry. Why don't you live with him? Certainly it would be better for you . . .

DICK:   I can't . . . that's not possible.

LUCILLE:   Why not?

(*Tom comes down the stairs with a bottle of whisky*)

DICK:   (*He notices Tom, whereas Lucille does not*) I . . . I can't tell you. I don't want to talk about it right now . . .

LUCILLE:   (*She notices Tom, to Dick*) Why don't you want to talk about it? What are you afraid of?

TOM:   Leave him alone! He doesn't want to talk about Harry because I told him not to . . . (*Tom crosses to table and pours a drink*)

LUCILLE:   Let Dick make his own decisions. Stop trying to run his life!

TOM: (*To Dick*) What did you tell her?

DICK: Nothing.

TOM: Your big mouth is going to get you into trouble. (*Tom holds Dick by the sleeve*)

DICK: (*Pulling away*) Stop threatening me! I didn't tell her anything . . .

LUCILLE: (*Noticing the bottle for the first time*) Where did you get that bottle?

TOM: On the nightstand in McMurty's room.

LUCILLE: I TOLD YOU NOT TO GO IN THERE!

TOM: Madame, I live in this hotel, not you. I'll go anywhere I damn well please.

LUCILLE: Don't you have any respect for anything?

DICK: Tom. This time you've gone too far.

TOM: (*To the room in general*) When I was in France during the war, and a soldier died next to me in a trench . . . we didn't have time for burials and eulogies over the dead . . . just a quick prayer, then we took his dog tags, cigarettes, food, dry socks and anything else he wouldn't need . . . You'll do anything, and I mean *anything* to stay alive just one more day. (*Tom picks up McMurty's putter*)

DICK: (*A devastating blow*) Even strip the clothing . . .

TOM: (*A warning to Dick*) War is war.

DICK: That's no excuse . . . There isn't any more war, TOM!

TOM: Yes, that's one of the problems in this country today . . . a good war, with trenches and gas would straighten out these jellybellies damn quick!

LUCILLE: (*Quietly, but with intense emotion*) A man that I loved and respected is dead . . . and he is going to be given a decent burial. I will not allow his body to be picked over by vultures. (*To Tom*) Take your filthy hands off that putter.

TOM: (*Holding it away from her*) Mac promised this putter to me when he was gone . . . I'm claiming it now. (*To Dick*) You had better get your claim in now before she tries to pick the hotel clean . . .

DICK: (*Angry*) This is not time to argue about possessions. (*To Lucille*) We had better call someone . . .

(*Pause*)

TOM: (*Nonchalantly examining the putter*) I thought Mac looked very peaceful when I was up there . . . a little pale, but very peaceful. (*To Lucille*) Did you know that this putter was given to him by Bobby Jones? Did you know that?

DICK: Tom . . . How can you behave this way?

TOM: It's easy . . . Just watch me, and learn. You should know, BIG MOUTH. Just had to mention him, didn't you? Couldn't you have waited . . . oh, no . . .

*(Lucille crosses to desk phone, lifts receiver and dials. Tom notices her suddenly)*

TOM: What do you think you're doing?

LUCILLE: Calling the police.

*(Tom slams the head of the putter near the phone, narrowly missing Lucille's hand)*

TOM: No, you're not! Get away from that phone. *(Tom rips the cord out of the wall)*

DICK: TOM!

LUCILLE: *(Frightened)* You could have killed me with that thing!

TOM: This is not a matter for the police.

*(Dick starts to protest, but is silenced by Tom)*

TOM: You stay out of this!

LUCILLE: Put that club down, or so help me . . .

DICK: No. I will not stay out of this.

*(Tom raises the putter like a weapon. Dick and Lucille freeze)*

TOM: SHUT UP! Both of you. *(Pause)* Now . . . very calmly . . . now, we are going to sit down quietly like civilized human beings and talk this out . . . SIT!

*(They reluctantly sit)*

LUCILLE: You're insane!

TOM: QUIET! *(Tom relaxes somewhat)* First, is the matter of claim on the deceased's possessions, notification of the next of kin and the proper authorities . . . Care for a drink? No? Well, when Harry gets here, he'll decide how to settle this affair. Harry is an expert in the matter of property settlements . . . He was once a lawyer before he retired . . .

LUCILLE: You're . . . a lunatic!

*(Dick rises)*

TOM: I told you to sit down.

DICK: Put that golf club down, Tom.

LUCILLE: Be careful, Dick!

DICK: I'm not afraid of you. *(To Lucille)* He won't hurt you. *(Dick starts wearily for the stairs)*

TOM: Dick, don't try to sneak off. *(Panic)* Where are you going?

DICK: I've had enough, Tom . . . I told you I was leaving . . . I'll pack a suitcase . . . and send for the rest of my things in the morning.

TOM: You are not going anywhere . . . Not until Harry arrives!

LUCILLE: (*To Dick*) Is there another phone around here?

TOM: (*Almost pleading*) What is Harry going to think?

DICK: (*To Lucille*) There's a pay phone on the corner at the drugstore. I'll get my coat.

(*Lucille rises carefully, moves around Tom toward the door*)

LUCILLE: I'm leaving, now, Tom. Understand? Don't you dare try to stop me . . . Are you coming with me, Dick?

DICK: Yes.

TOM: (*Blocking Dick's way*) No, he's not going anywhere.

DICK: Get out of my way, Tom.

TOM: You can't leave . . . You're not going with her.

DICK: Yes . . . yes, I am. You are not going to tell me what to do . . . or what to think, no more . . . It's over.

TOM: (*Defensively*) Harry will be furious if you're not here.

DICK: (*Crying*) Dammit, Tom, will you stop. There isn't going to be any Harry . . .

TOM: Harry will be here.

LUCILLE: I'm leaving. Dick, if you're going with me . . .

DICK: (*A realization that he must destroy Tom in order to save him*) Lucille . . . stay for a few minutes . . . there's something I want you to hear.

TOM: (*Afraid of what is to follow*) NO!

DICK: Tom, it's over. Harry is not coming this year. Harry is not going to be here, like he wasn't here last year . . . or the year before . . . Harry is dead!

TOM: NO! HE'S ALIVE!

(*Pause*)

DICK: You took the gloves off his body at Coetquidan. You broke his frozen fingers to get the gloves off his hands . . . Remember?

TOM: No . . . it's not true. The face and chest were blown away . . . There were no dog tags . . . some unidentified doughboy . . . He escaped! Remember . . . I saw him in Paris riding in an automobile after the Armistice . . . and that time on the train outside London . . . It was Harry!

DICK: Someone who looked like Harry.

TOM: You can't say that.

DICK: (*Mainly to Lucille*) Harry died at Coetquidan in 1918 before the Armistice . . .

TOM: No, he did not.

DICK: And . . . we're responsible for the way he died.

TOM: This is not the truth!

DICK: Yes, it is! Shut up, Tom! I'm going to say it . . . the way it really happened . . . (*Tom is crushed. Pause*) It was a winter night, during heavy artillery barrage . . . Tom and I were pinned down in a trench . . . and near the barbed wire, about fifty feet away in another trench, was a wounded soldier . . . Harry! He was calling to us . . . he cried for help for almost an hour.

TOM: Pah! The oldest trick in the book. All the Germans used it . . . they all spoke English. They were trying to trick us . . . they call for help and when you stick your head out you get shot!

DICK: This was no German. It was Harry . . . I was going to crawl to him, but Tom wouldn't let me go. Tom said it was a German . . . and then . . . he threw a grenade into the other trench . . . and everything was silent. No more cries for help . . . It was Harry . . . calling to us . . .

TOM: We don't know that!

DICK: After the barrage . . . we crawled to the other trench and then we saw the uniform . . . it was one of our boys . . . The face was gone . . . we were freezing . . . we took the gloves and boots . . . so we could stay alive a bit longer . . . (*Dick sniffles*) We never reported the killing . . .

TOM: It was an accident! Happens all the time in battle! It was someone else . . . Harry is alive! He will be here tonight! I'll show you . . .

LUCILLE: Oh, my God, I think I'm going to be sick . . . (*She goes out the front door*) I've got to get some air . . .

TOM: (*Refusing to give in*) They never identified the body . . .

DICK: Dammit! Will you stop? (*Dick grabs the watch from Tom's vest*) You took the watch off his body! This one!

TOM: Harry gave that watch to me!

DICK: No! I saw you take it . . .

TOM: That's a lie!

DICK: You didn't think I could see you take the watch . . . while I was removing his boots . . . Tom, you can't hide it from me . . . I knew it was Harry . . . and so did you!

I know why you stole the watch . . . so I wouldn't know . . . I understand it was an accident, Tom . . . we don't need to pretend anymore.

TOM: I didn't steal it . . . Harry said . . . it was O.K.

DICK: Admit it, please . . . Will you say . . . Harry is dead!

TOM: (*A last attempt*) But, there were no dog tags . . .

DICK: (*Quietly*) Tom. He's not coming. Let it go!

TOM: (*Breaking down*) I am *not responsible!* . . . Is it my fault some idiot doesn't know when to take cover . . . and gets himself wounded . . . ? Huh? Serves him right, goddamit! Stupid idiot . . . I can't take the blame.

DICK: No one is blaming you . . . Let go, Tom.

TOM: I . . . I can't . . .

DICK: You have to . . .

TOM: Always that one hope . . .

DICK: (*Pause*) Where was he last year?

TOM: I was not a coward! Never . . . you hear? I never got any medals . . . but I am no coward!

DICK: I know . . . I never said you were.

(*Pause*)

TOM: (*Vindictive*) And I thought you believed . . . all this time . . . and I thought you believed. Why? Why did you stay with me . . . deceiving me? If you never believed Harry was alive . . . then why did you stay with me after your wife died?

DICK: I don't know. (*Pause*) I was lonely . . . I thought you needed me.

TOM: Pah! I have never needed anyone. I managed without you during your marriages . . . I can get along without you now . . . Go, on . . . get out of here, you ungrateful . . . (*Tom breaks down crying*)

DICK: And I needed you . . . (*Pause*) I wanted to believe . . . for you . . . I just couldn't . . . I'm sorry . . . I . . . (*He trails off*)

(*Dick goes up the stairs. After a pause, Tom rises and crosses to get a drink and looks around the room. He notices the "Welcome Harry!" banner. He sets his drink on the register desk. He slowly takes down the banner and stuffs it into the fireplace. Dick comes down the stairs wearing an overcoat*)

DICK: I put a blanket over his face. The eyes were open.

TOM: (*Drying his eyes with handkerchief*) Where's your suitcase?

DICK: In my room. I'll pack it later. I don't know where to begin. What to take . . . I've collected so many things.

TOM: Where will you go?

DICK: I don't know. (*Pause*) We have to bury McMurty first. Lucille is going to need help . . . she . . . (*He trails off*)

TOM: (*Handing the putter to Dick*) Give this to her . . . I never liked golf, anyway. (*Long pause. Then with great difficulty*) Will you stay . . . after tonight?

DICK: I don't know. (*Pause*) There would have to be a lot of changes.

TOM: I need someone to talk to . . . without McMurty around to argue with . . . well . . .

DICK: We'll see . . . I've got to help Lucille make a phone call first. We'll talk about it later . . .

(*Dick goes out the front door*)

TOM: I'll leave a light on for you.

(*Tom stands in the middle of the room staring at the banner in the fireplace*)

Curtain

*Tom Huey*

# IT AIN'T THE HEAT, IT'S THE HUMILITY

## Tom Huey

Tom Huey makes his debut as a published playwright with the appearance of *It Ain't the Heat, It's the Humility* in this anthology. This play together with two other short plays, *Reservations* and *Why Are the Clouds Shaped Like Pennsylvania and Top Hats?* constitute a trilogy under the collective title *The Magic City.*

A native of Birmingham, Alabama, now residing in Greensboro, North Carolina, Mr. Huey has developed a keen ear for individual and social differences in Southern speech patterns. These nuances are powerfully evident in the parallels and differences Mr. Huey draws between a retired Southern judge and his Black gardener as comparisons between their two families emerge.

His other plays include *Against the Middle* and *The Whitening of the Godwins and the Starrs*, both performed by Greensboro ACT Company with subsequent productions by members of Lee Strasberg's Actors Studio at the Circle Theatre in Los Angeles in 1977; *Wild Air*, premiered by Los Angeles Actors Theatre in 1978 with subsequent workshop productions by the Seattle Repertory Theatre in 1980 and the McCarter Theatre of Princeton, New Jersey in 1981.

Mr. Huey also is author of four books of poetry and a published novel, *Sixteen People Who Live Downtown.* A young writer, now thirty-three years old, Mr. Huey has demonstrated a creative gift that promises interesting development.

The author dedicates this play: "For Diane White and William Bushnell, Jr."

## Characters:

CHARLES BROWNLOWE *74, white*
WILLIAM SHAKERS *74, black*

*The patio of the Brownlowe home in Mountain Brook, a pleasant, if exclusive suburb of Birmingham. Center left is a wrought-iron table and four wrought-iron chairs. Right is the garden. Down is the golf course the Brownlowe home borders, Birmingham Country Club, specifically the fourth hole on the East Course. Up is the house.*
*Judge Charles Brownlowe is supervising the weeding of his garden. He stands over William, who hunkers in the loam, steadily though slowly pulling weeds from between rows of crocuses, irises, dwarf azaleas, aucubas, etc. The Judge wears almost outlandishly baggy clothes: pants, shirt and suspenders from at least the Fifties if not the Forties; pants that would billow in the breeze and a shirt so loose the five or six pens and pencils and a glasses case clipped to his pocket make the pocket drop almost to his waist. The Judge also wears a wide-brimmed, floppy straw hat that is frayed at the edges but is banded by an elongated Confederate flag design.*
*William, who is also seventy-four, wears the Judge's clothes too. These hand-me-downs appear equally outlandish on William, though it should be pointed out that both outfits, the Judge's and William's shouldn't draw attention away from the drama but should be easily noticed once attention is drawn to them by the action of the scene. At any rate, William has souped-up his working clothes somewhat by wearing a broad swath of cloth—once a dress or robe—around his waist, in a manner resembling the Zouave of French Algeria. Every now and then, when William moves through the garden to a spot which is rocky and hurts his knees, he will take off the cloth and lay it under his knees, pausing but to adjust his own suspenders a little tighter.*
*It is a suffocatingly hot August twilight. The Judge and William move through it as if in slow motion. On the wrought-iron table is a pitcher of iced tea and two glasses.*

JUDGE: Don't dig up that one.
WILLIAM: Naw sah.
JUDGE: I said don't dig up that one.
WILLIAM: Which one?
JUDGE: That one you're diggin' up.

WILLIAM:   This here's a weed, Judge.

JUDGE:   Not that one.

WILLIAM:   This here's what I diggin' up.

JUDGE:   No, that one.

WILLIAM:   I ain't gon' dig up this one.

JUDGE:   Well, what's your hand around that one for?

WILLIAM:   I gots to suppo't my sef.

JUDGE:   Well, don't dig that one up.

WILLIAM:   Naw, sah.

JUDGE:   That's something supposed to bloom, I think.

WILLIAM:   Yas, sah.

JUDGE:   What is it, anyway?

WILLIAM:   Dwa'f iris.

JUDGE:   A what?

WILLIAM:   Dwa'f iris.

JUDGE:   (*Crossing to the iced tea*) Well, don't you dig it up.

WILLIAM:   Naw, sah.

JUDGE:   I'm pourin you some ice tea. Well, I don't know: all the ice is gone. (*Feels the pitcher*) But it's still cool. The pitcher's sweatin' more than we are.

(*William gets up slowly, moves his weed box somewhere else, pulls off his band of cloth and kneels on it, weeding*)

JUDGE:   Where did you get that rag, William?

WILLIAM:   Mrs. Brownlowe give me it.

(*Judge hands William his tea and resumes his position over William's shoulder. While William continues to work, Judge studies William's cloth. Finally*)

JUDGE:   What was it before it was what it is now?

WILLIAM:   Garland's dress.

JUDGE:   What do you mean Garland's dress?

WILLIAM:   It was up in he room, up there with his things.

JUDGE:   My son was certainly no angel, William, but one thing he never was, was a . . . wearer of dresses.

WILLIAM:   Weren't his dress, Judge.

JUDGE:   Well, dammit, you just said . . .

WILLIAM:   When you an' Mrs. Brownlowe went off some judge meetin'.

JUDGE:   What?

WILLIAM:   When Garland brought home that guhl an' you come home early an' Garland send her out the winnow in your robe.

JUDGE:   I don't keep my robes at home, William.

WILLIAM:   Weren't your bench-sittin' robe, was your bed-time robe.

JUDGE:   The hell, you say!

WILLIAM:   I just tellin' you what . . .

JUDGE:   Stand up, William!

WILLIAM:   (*Standing up*) Yas, sah.

JUDGE:   Hold that thing out an' let me make sure . . .

WILLIAM:   (*Holds out the dress*) You . . .

JUDGE:   Well, William, this looks like my robe to me.

WILLIAM:   Naw, sah.

JUDGE:   I can't be sure in this light, but it looks like my robe.

WILLIAM:   If it you' robe, then you doin' some strange things in the bedroom.

JUDGE:   (*Inspecting it a little more closely, sort of picking at it with his hands, holding his glasses ready to inspect even more closely . . . but not putting his glasses on*) Well, I don't know, William, you've grimed the thing up so much that it's impossible to make a clear identification, but, an' you can be completely candid with me, why in the world would you wear my robe around your waist, an' sit on it in the loam, when you could ask for a pillow, or a cushion, or even an inner tube, an' I would give it to you?

WILLIAM:   'Cause it ain't no robe. Garland left home, Mrs. Brownlowe give off his old things, and one thing hung up there was this here dress. (*Resuming his weeding*) Said to me, "William, I don't want to touch this here dress. Git it outta my sight." Sifonia couldn't git inna it. You know how big Sifonia is. Couldn't even git one laig on through it. Sifonia gon' *use* it cover pillow with, in fact, but my knees started actin' up roun' then, so *I* used it *like* a pillow. (*Pause*) Only diff'ence is, *ain't* no pillow. (*Pause*) Ain't no robe either.

JUDGE:   What are you diggin up there!

WILLIAM:   Weed.

JUDGE:   Don't dig up that one.

WILLIAM:   Which one?

JUDGE:   The one you're diggin up.

WILLIAM:   I ain't diggin that one.

JUDGE:   Then what hell you doin'?

WILLIAM:   Suppo'tin' myself.

JUDGE:   Well, let's see if we can have a little less support an' a little more diggin'. (*Pause. The Judge pulls out a large clean handkerchief and wipes his head with it. William does the same thing, but with a dirtier handkerchief)* An' I suppose that is Garland's slip you're wipin' your face with?

WILLIAM:   Naw, sah.

JUDGE:   Well, that's a true true relief.

WILLIAM:   It's your kerchief.

JUDGE:   No, William, it's yours.

WILLIAM:   Well, you done give me it.

JUDGE:   I was pleased to give it to you.

WILLIAM:   I's pleased to git it.

JUDGE:   I'm sure you were.

WILLIAM:   You done gimme more than I can wear at a time.

JUDGE:   Well, you know, ninety-nine percent of these clothes are pure cotton.

WILLIAM:   Yas, sah.

JUDGE:   What's that?

WILLIAM:   Wild flower.

JUDGE:   A weed?

WILLIAM:   I ain't put it in the ground here. It done come up on its own.

JUDGE:   You mean it was carried here by the wind.

WILLIAM:   Yas, sah.

JUDGE:   Then it's a weed.

WILLIAM:   That ain't its name.

JUDGE:   What?

WILLIAM:   I say that ain't its name.

JUDGE:   What the hell difference does it make?

WILLIAM:   *(Pulling it up)* Sah.

JUDGE:   A weed is a weed is a weed, William.

WILLIAM:   Yas, sah.

JUDGE:   An' I'll tell you another thing. A weed is also your friend.

WILLIAM:   Yas, sah.

JUDGE:   Because the day there are no more weeds in this garden, then that is also the day when there is no more green stuff for your pockets.

WILLIAM:   Yas, sah.

JUDGE:   *(Picking up the pulled flower)* Pretty thing, though, this weed, eh?

WILLIAM:   That a white-fringed aw-kid.

JUDGE:   *(Throwing it down)* A white-fringed what?

WILLIAM:   Aw-kid.

JUDGE:  An *orchid*, is that what you're saying?

WILLIAM:  Yas, sah.

JUDGE:  An' you're tellin me you pulled up an orchid?

WILLIAM:  Yas, sah.

JUDGE:  Just to spite me.

WILLIAM:  Naw, sah.

JUDGE:  But now, you just let it sit there.

WILLIAM:  Can't plant it back, done tored off the ruts.

JUDGE:  Well, hide it in the box. Mrs. Brownlowe sees it pulled up, she'll have another stroke. She comes to the window every day. She knows the garden by heart. You ought to be shot.

WILLIAM:  Yas, sah.

JUDGE:  I give you my clothes, I pay you good money, I bring you ice tea, and what do you do? Use my robe for a pillow and pull up my wife's favorite flowers. You ain't a spring chicken no more.

WILLIAM:  You ain't neither.

JUDGE:  What was that?

WILLIAM:  Say, Sifonia laid up in the bed like Mrs. Brownlowe.

JUDGE:  Symphonia, Symphonia, where do you think up these names?

WILLIAM:  She ain't had no stroke.

JUDGE:  Won't work?

WILLIAM:  I tole her, tonight I come home, she ain't cooked my supper, I'm gon' tie my chain to that bedsted an' tote her fat ass to the junk yard.

JUDGE:  How many does Symphonia make?

WILLIAM:  Five . . .

JUDGE:  My God.

WILLIAM:   . . . that I married.

JUDGE:  No wonder you and Garland got along so well together. Whorin' was the bond that made you friends.

WILLIAM:  Where Garland at?

JUDGE:  Who knows. Probably with some whore. Who cares.

WILLIAM:  Garland took off an' never come back?

JUDGE:  That's right.

WILLIAM:  Nelson come home.

JUDGE:  How's that?

WILLIAM:  My son, Nelson.

JUDGE:  What about him?

WILLIAM:   I say he come home. He run off like Garland, but he come home.

JUDGE:   Didn't I give him one of my suits?

WILLIAM:   Yas, sah.

JUDGE:   The double-breasted zoot-suited affair?

WILLIAM:   Yas, sah.

JUDGE:   The one with the padded shoulders?

WILLIAM:   Yas, sah.

JUDGE:   What the hell did I give it away for?

WILLIAM:   You done got a hundred suits, you said.

JUDGE:   Well, now I got ninety-nine.

WILLIAM:   That suit done come back into style.

JUDGE:   That suit was a Palm Beach. A Palm Beach never goes out of style. A Palm Beach creates its own style. What does Nelson do in it? Whore?

WILLIAM:   I 'spect he does some of that.

JUDGE:   I knew it. An what's worse, whorin' in Birmingham. You know I have my position to maintain. For all I know he's out there now, whorin' down Twenty-First Street, lettin' everybody know he's in Judge Brownlowe's Palm Beach Suit.

WILLIAM:   You wants it back . . .

JUDGE:   Want it back? After Nelson has whored about in it? I'd rather send it to the furnace on the end of a fishin' pole!

WILLIAM:   Well, Nelson, he 'preciate that suit to such an extent, he done kept it clean all along.

JUDGE:   I'm sure he has.

WILLIAM:   Member when I had that operation on my phosphate?

JUDGE:   Your what?

WILLIAM:   When they worked on my phosphate.

JUDGE:   The prostate operation? How could I forget the prostate operation? I paid for the prostate operation.

WILLIAM:   Well, Nelson, he was in Baltimore then, an' he send me down a pitcher of him in that suit an' said hi to you in the bottom of the corner.

JUDGE:   William.

WILLIAM:   Sah.

JUDGE:   What's that shinin' object you're diggin' up?

WILLIAM:   (*Holds up a mirror*) This here's a mirror.

JUDGE:   What's a mirror doin' in the garden?

WILLIAM:   Settin' there.

JUDGE:   What the hell's it sittin' there for?

WILLIAM:   'Cause I set it there.

JUDGE:   What did you set a mirror in the garden for?

WILLIAM:   Keep the haints off Sooty's grave.

JUDGE:   This is where you buried Sooty?

WILLIAM:   Yas, sah.

JUDGE:   You buried our dog in the garden?

WILLIAM:   Yas, sah.

JUDGE:   Does Mrs. Brownlowe know about it?

WILLIAM:   I done told her, I did.

JUDGE:   An' what did she say.

WILLIAM:   She done told me to bury Sooty there in the first place.

JUDGE:   How long's that been?

WILLIAM:   I can't recollect.

JUDGE:   Nine years.

WILLIAM:   That right.

JUDGE:   When Garland left.

WILLIAM:   That right. When Armstead run naked through Homewood.

JUDGE:   What?

WILLIAM:   Armstead, my brother.

JUDGE:   Ran naked through Homewood?

WILLIAM:   Yas, sah.

JUDGE:   What the hell for?

WILLIAM:   You got him outta jail.

JUDGE:   I did?

WILLIAM:   Then you got him in Bryce Mental.

JUDGE:   Oh, yes. He was crazy.

WILLIAM:   Yas, sah.

JUDGE:   Armstead. I'm sorry about old Armstead. Remember when you and he and Garland and I laid that flagstone up at the lake?

WILLIAM:   Yas, sah.

JUDGE:   Made a patio in the side of a veritable mountain. God. It was like a rain forest. Do you remember the mosquitoes?

WILLIAM:   I 'member Armstead an' Garland got stung on the head by them hornets.

JUDGE:   Oh, my goodness. That's right! Reduced the boy to tears and sent your lunatic brother into the lake, head first.

WILLIAM:   When he run naked through Homewood, he claimed it was them hornets stingin' his head all over again.

JUDGE:   He did?

WILLIAM:   Yas, sah. An' what he claimed he was lookin' for was a large lake to jump into head first to cool the sting.

JUDGE:   Old Armstead. Where's Armstead?

WILLIAM:   Drownt.

JUDGE:   Say, what?

WILLIAM:   I says he drownt, Judge.

JUDGE:   In a lake?

WILLIAM:   Yas, sah. He found him a lake down at Bryce. Over by an open field. They couldn't git to him in time.

JUDGE:   I'm sorry to hear that, William.

WILLIAM:   Yas, sah.

JUDGE:   Old Armstead could work like a mule. He must of laid half that flagstone himself.

WILLIAM:   Garland, he loved that lake.

JUDGE:   Loved to whore up there is what he loved.

WILLIAM:   Well, when you good at somethin' you likes to share it.

JUDGE:   Why didn't we get stung, William?

WILLIAM:   Had on these here hats.

JUDGE:   That's right! Always wear a hat when you work. You can't work in the sun without a hat on your head. An' look what it did. Saved us from the hornets.

WILLIAM:   I got one stung me.

JUDGE:   On your head?

WILLIAM:   Naw, sah.

JUDGE:   Where then?

WILLIAM:   On my dick.

JUDGE:   Do you have to use such language.

WILLIAM:   That where he stung me.

JUDGE:   Well, it must of put you out of commission, at least.

WILLIAM:   Yas, sah. But I's with LaWanda then an' she liked the new size of it so much, I hads to get drunk to do it.

JUDGE:   I don't want to hear any more of that talk. And from you, of all people. A seventy-four-year-old man. First you steal my robe. Then you pull up my wife's favorite orchid. Then you remind me of Garland. Then you talk trash with a child's mirror in your hand. Give me that thing. (*Holding the mirror to his face, turning it over*)

WILLIAM:   What you think bout what I wrote on the back of that mirror, Judge?
JUDGE:   What the hell is it?
WILLIAM:   A dawg prayer.
JUDGE:   A dog what?
WILLIAM:   It says what it is there.
JUDGE:   (*Reading with difficulty*) Oh . . .
WILLIAM:   Lawd.
JUDGE:   Lod, is what you have here.
WILLIAM:   Lawd, that right.
JUDGE:   L-O-D.
WILLIAM:   .Lawd.
JUDGE:   "Oh, Lod, Sooty was good,
Keep the "aints"?
WILLIAM:   Haints.
JUDGE:   What you've got here is "aints" . . . that's what a country man calls an ant.
WILLIAM:   Haints.
JUDGE:   "Keep the aints in the woods."
WILLIAM:   Yow.
JUDGE:   "Oh, Lod, Sooty was good,
Keep the aints in the wood."
(*Pause. Judge taps the mirror on his glasses reflectively, then hands the mirror back to William*)
JUDGE:   If you're such the poet, why didn't you put it on a stone?
WILLIAM:   Stone don't work like no mirror. Plus you's 'gainst Sooty buried here in the first place.
JUDGE:   It's a trashy thing to do, that's for sure. But once you do something, you don't half-ass around, you don't scrawl on mirrors. You chisel it in granite. You even buy a little granite sculpture if you like. A little vase, perhaps, with some geraniums in it . . .
WILLIAM:   Stone ain't no mirror.
JUDGE:   I see. Now you're not only the gardener, you the authority on God around here?
WILLIAM:   Yas, sah.
JUDGE:   You are?
WILLIAM:   Naw, sah.
JUDGE:   And my ideas you simply ignore. (*Looks up at the bedroom window. Mrs. Brownlowe has wheeled herself over and is now looking down at them. Pause*) Hello, Eunice. (*To William*)

Turn around and wave to Mrs. Brownlowe. (*With forced loud-
ness, and slowly, as to a deaf person*) HELLO, EUNICE. (*Waves
exaggeratedly, slowly*) DOESN'T IT ALL LOOK GOOD? (*Pause*)
OLD WILLIAM DOESN'T KNOW WHEN TO STOP! (*Pause*)
DO YOU, WILLIAM?
    WILLIAM:  Naw, sah.
    JUDGE:  WILLIAM SAID HE WASN'T GOING TO STOP
UNTIL IT'S SHIPSHAPE OUT HERE IN THE GARDEN.
(*Pause*) I'M GOING TO SUPERVISE A LITTLE MORE NOW,
EUNICE. YOU GO ON AND WATCH THE NEWS. (*Turns
around*) She won't watch the news. (*Pause*) She'll sit right there
with her eyes on my back 'till she scoots off to the other side
of the room. (*Pause*) It's a terrible, terrible, shame, William.
There you have a woman. (*Pause*) A wife. (*Pause*) Not the fifth.
Not the fourth. Just the first. (*Pause*) There you have the
woman you have lived with forty-five years. (*Pause*) That's
what you have up there. (*Pause*) And that's all that you have.
(*William moves once more, this time rising to pour some more iced
tea. Judge watches William absent-mindedly, finally paying attention
to the way William is drinking his iced tea*) Is she still in the
window?
    WILLIAM:  Naw, sah.
    JUDGE:  Is the window open or closed?
    WILLIAM:  Closed.
    JUDGE:  Good.
    WILLIAM:  Guess she done scooted off.
    JUDGE:  I just can't bear her eyes on my back. I just can't
stand someone looking down on me. I don't care who she
is . . . (*William flicks at his tea*) What the hell are you doin' to
the tea?
    WILLIAM:  There's a gnat on my lemon.
    JUDGE:  Well, throw away the lemon, for God's sake.
    WILLIAM:  Lemon, the best part.
    JUDGE:  What?
    WILLIAM:  I say when you ain't got no ice, lemon the best
part of the tea.
    JUDGE:  So you're an authority on ice tea now?
    WILLIAM:  Plus you gets stung, lemon draws out the po'sin.
    JUDGE:  You know all about God, and now you know all
about iced tea. The next you're going to tell me is if I take a
lemon upstairs and stick it in her mouth, she'll throw away
her electric wheelchair and run down here and weed with us?

WILLIAM:  Naw, sah.

JUDGE:  Well, she would be doin' more than you're doin', wouldn't she?

WILLIAM:  Yo.

JUDGE:  (*Shrugging, hurrying a little to get the spade and weed box himself*) I suppose it's just my burden. (*Digging*) If I thought it was my curse, I suppose I would just blow my brains out. But I suppose it's my cross. I suppose the good Lord knew what he was doin' when he stuck me with a whorin' son, a dyin' woman and a lemon-suckin' nigger.

WILLIAM:  Yas, sah.

JUDGE:  Say what?

WILLIAM:  Say, Lawd knew what he's doin' awright.

JUDGE:  Well, since you're on such good terms with Him, why don't you ask Him why it is that I must pay you to watch me work?

WILLIAM:  Don't haves to ask Him.

JUDGE:  Oh, so you know why?

WILLIAM:  Yas, sah.

JUDGE:  And why is that?

WILLIAM:  'Cause you likes to mess an' meddle.

JUDGE:  What?

WILLIAM:  Said 'cause you likes to . . . (*Judge rises to his full height, turns to scold William, catches himself, weaves a little, lowers himself to his knees like a dog and tries to catch his breath*) The blood done rushed to your haid.

JUDGE:  I'm all right. It's this heat.

WILLIAM:  (*Assisting him to sit down*) You all right, the blood done rushed to your haid. But it ain't the heat.

JUDGE:  So now you're a doctor? It's the *heat*!

WILLIAM:  Naw, sah. It ain't the heat, it's the humility.

JUDGE:  Lost my breath . . . in the humil . . .

WILLIAM:  You all right?

JUDGE:  Got a little fat-headed.

WILLIAM:  Yas, sah.

JUDGE:  A little thick-eyed. (*Pause*) Thought I was . . . (*Pause*)

WILLIAM:  Just set.

JUDGE:  A little winded. (*Pause*) Well. All over the . . . (*To the flowers*) What are these . . .

WILLIAM:  Ain't nothin no mo'.

JUDGE:  What were these?

WILLIAM:   Can't tell, you on 'em like that.

JUDGE:   Well, help me up, for God's sake!

WILLIAM:   (*Pulls off his swath of cloth*) Set your knees on this dress of Garland's like I does.

JUDGE:   I wouldn't touch that thing with a ten foot pole! Get me in the chair, William, the chair!. (*William and Judge make it to the chair, William supporting him all the way*) That's better.

WILLIAM:   That was poke, knotweed, pinkweed an' heart-leaf you done squashed.

JUDGE:   What's that?

WILLIAM:   I say you done squashed all the weeds, Judge. You done good.

JUDGE:   I did.

WILLIAM:   You done kilt the weeds an' spared the aw-kids. You done fell down in a educated manner.

JUDGE:   Get over there and work, and leave me alone!

WILLIAM:   Yow.

JUDGE:   Whew.

WILLIAM:   We done gone past first dark.

JUDGE:   I know.

WILLIAM:   We done worked straight into night.

(*Suddenly the automatic flood lights come on*)

JUDGE:   The flood lights!

WILLIAM:   Ain't it funny what darkness do.

JUDGE:   Now we can really see.

WILLIAM:   In darkness light, all the flowers lose their color. Everythin' look the same.

JUDGE:   William:

WILLIAM:   Yas, sah.

JUDGE:   William.

WILLIAM:   Yow.

JUDGE:   Do you remember that birthday party for Garland, the one he wanted at night?

WILLIAM:   On the barbeque pit.

JUDGE:   And you got that pony cart.

WILLIAM:   Armstead got that.

JUDGE:   But you drove it over here.

WILLIAM:   Armstead led that pony, an' I clucked it along.

JUDGE:   Where on earth did you get that pony cart?

WILLIAM:   Armstead got it.

JUDGE:   It was *the* party. It made Garland so happy. All his friends got to ride around the block. Under the street lights. What child gets such a treat these days? A ride around the block at night in a pony cart with a real Shetland pony.

WILLIAM:   Armstead stolt it.

JUDGE:   Garland, Garland, Garland.

WILLIAM:   Then after that party, we give Nelson a party with it. Then Armstead took that pony to Blount County an' set it loose.

JUDGE:   Our boys.

WILLIAM:   You 'member Nelson.

JUDGE:   Of course I remember Nelson. I gave him the Palm Beach Suit.

WILLIAM:   You 'member Garland?

JUDGE:   You know I do, but I can't stand to.

WILLIAM:   What you care to 'member, Judge?

JUDGE:   Perhaps what never happened.

WILLIAM:   There ain't no medicine for that.

(*Judge looks at William as if he is going to tell him something very important—straight in the eye and William returns the stare—then Judge diverts his attention to William's hands*)

JUDGE:   What's that?

WILLIAM:   Heartleaf.

JUDGE:   Heartleaf?

WILLIAM:   Yas, sah.

JUDGE:   Heartleaf. What does it do?

WILLIAM:   Set there.

JUDGE:   Is it *supposed* to be there!

WILLIAM:   It come up wild.

JUDGE:   Then it's a weed.

WILLIAM:   Wild flower.

JUDGE:   But it blew in here by chance.

WILLIAM:   Yas, sah.

JUDGE:   Then it's a weed.

(*Pause*)

A heart weed.

(*Pause*)

So what are you lookin' at me for? PULL IT UP!


Blackout

*John Bishop*
# CONFLUENCE

# John Bishop

When John Bishop's *The Trip Back Down* made its Broadway debut in 1977, the author was hailed as "a talented new playwright with a voice that rings true." This promise was further demonstrated in his *Cabin 12* (published in *Best Short Plays 1979*), the sensitive study of a father and son in a strange town, arranging for the burial of their son and brother.

Mr. Bishop continues to develop the talent evident in his earlier work with his contribution for this anthology—*Confluence*. It was first produced in January 1982, in an evening of one-act plays along with Beth Henley's *Am I Blue* (elsewhere in this volume) and Lanford Wilson's *Thymus Vulgaris* (in *Best Short Plays 1982*) at New York's Circle Repertory Theatre, where Mr. Bishop serves as dramaturge and resident playwright. *Confluence* was cited by Douglas Watt of the *New York Daily News* as "the centerpiece of last night's triple bill . . . a small, pure gem, its every facet shining. Lean in the writing, and beautifully acted and staged, it is stunning."

Fame has a different meaning to each of the three characters—a former Pittsburgh Steeler; his actress girlfriend; and a Hall-of-Fame third baseman now confined to a wheelchair. As the former football star and the former baseball player share nostalgic athletic glories, an understanding develops between them that makes their present limitations and future expectations more bearable.

*Confluence* was followed in March 1982, by Circle Rep's production of Mr. Bishop's full-length play, *The Great Grandson of Jedediah Kohler,* a satire on the impact of Hollywood's image of the old West. John Beaufort of the *Christian Science Monitor* called the play "a wildly funny broadside of comic iconoclasm."

Mr. Bishop is a graduate of Carnegie-Mellon University. He acted for three years, then turned his talents to directing, staging musicals in Dallas for five summers and later for the Pittsburgh Civic Light Opera Company. In 1979–80 Mr. Bishop received a Literary Fellowship from the National Endowment for the Arts. His most recent one-act, *How Women Break Bad News*, premiered at the Philadelphia Festival of New Plays in the spring of 1982.

# Characters:

CHUCK (CHICK) JANOLA, *forty-five*
KATHY MILLAN, *twenty-five*
EARL DOUCHETTE, *seventy-one*

# Scene:

*It is summer in a park in the small town of Confluence, Pennsylvania.*

*Chuck (Chick) Janola enters. He is strongly built and looks young for his age. He wears well-cut jeans, a light-weight summer blazer and a Lacoste shirt. He sits on a bench center stage.*

*Kathy Millan enters. She is exceptionally pretty, blonde, slim. She carries two small paper sacks.*

KATHY:   I got you some yogurt.
JANOLA:   Thanks.
(*Kathy takes out two cups of yogurt from the sacks. Also a small box of raisins and a tin of cinnamon, the ingredients of which she mixes into the yogurt*)
JANOLA:   You're a regular walking Baskin Robbins. (*He looks ahead at the river*) You know how many bridges there are in this place? Seven. Seven bridges. Christ, we don't have seven bridges in Pittsburgh, and this town, with maybe 500 people has got seven bridges.
KATHY:   There's easily seven bridges in Pittsburgh.
JANOLA:   Name 'em.
KATHY:   Name seven bridges in Pittsburgh? (*Laughs*) Eat your yogurt and shut up. (*They eat quietly a moment*) Pretty here.
JANOLA:   I thought you'd like it.
KATHY:   How'd you ever find it?
JANOLA:   Drivin' around yesterday. Saw the name on a map. Confluence.   I   thought   the   name   was ... I   don't know ... interesting. So I drove over. Hung around here all day. (*Pointing ahead*) That's the Youghiheny. The other two rivers come in from . . . well . . . over there, one of them. And we drove across another on the way in. The Laurel Hill, I think.

KATHY: "Rafts for rent."

JANOLA: What?

KATHY: On that sign over there . . . there, across the river . . . and down.

JANOLA: Oh. Yeah.

KATHY: Be fun.

JANOLA: Yeah.

KATHY: Maybe we'll come here and rent one on our day off.

JANOLA: That river's movin' pretty fast. Not careful, you'll end up somewhere in West Virginia.

KATHY: Doesn't it go to Pittsburgh?

JANOLA: They. When it gets around that bend . . . behind those houses . . . it's three rivers become one. "They."

KATHY: "It." Three rivers become on is "it."

JANOLA: Well, anyhow I don't think "it" goes to Pittsburgh. I don't know where it goes.

KATHY: Goes to the sea.

JANOLA: Maybe.

KATHY: Be fun to rent a raft.

JANOLA: Need someone who knows how to handle one.

KATHY: I'll bet Bob does. Or Griff.

JANOLA: Who's Griff?

KATHY: Oh, you met him last night. The tall guy who's the T.D.

JANOLA: Tall guy?

KATHY: With a beard. Blonde. Smoking a joint.

JANOLA: Oh, yeah. I didn't talk to him much.

KATHY: He doesn't talk much.

JANOLA: He's the what? The T.D.?

KATHY: Technical director. He's in charge of building the sets . . . the lights . . . that stuff.

JANOLA: Tough job.

KATHY: For him . . . it's just a job. He's an artist.

JANOLA: You mean like a painter?

KATHY: Yeah. (*Beat*) He's very good.

JANOLA: So what's he doing in a summer stock company?

KATHY: A job. (*Beat*) You should see his work.

JANOLA: Why?

KATHY: Maybe you could use him.

JANOLA: Painting displays?

KATHY: Why not?

JANOLA:    They don't work out . . . artists. Painting art deco skylines for the Little League show tends to depress them.

KATHY:    It would depress me.

JANOLA:    It depresses everyone. Especially the husbands of the women dancing in front of the skyline. But it *really* depresses artists. (*They laugh*)

KATHY:    Griff's not like that. He needs a job in the fall. (*Beat*) I said maybe you'd talk to him.

JANOLA:    Okay. (*Beat*) You've seen his work.

KATHY:    Ummm. It's good.

JANOLA:    Where'd you see it?

KATHY:    He's got some of it with him.

JANOLA:    In his room?

KATHY:    Yeah. (*Looks at him*) There was a whole bunch of us went there, Chuck. I didn't go to see his etchings. God!

JANOLA:    Okay.

KATHY:    Christ, you haven't been here 24 hours and you've had me making it with practically every guy in the company.

JANOLA:    Practically? Who'd I miss?

KATHY:    I'm serious, Chuck. I'm getting tired of it. Real tired.

JANOLA:    Yeah. I noticed. I noticed how tired you were last night.

KATHY:    What's that mean? (*No answer*) What's it mean? (*Beat*)

JANOLA:    Forget it.

KATHY:    I told you I was exhausted. I didn't want to stop for a beer. I didn't want to eat . . .

JANOLA:    I was hungry.

KATHY:    'Cause I was very tired and I was afraid . . . oh, damn! (*Turning to him*) Listen Chuck, I said maybe you should wait, come out next week . . .

JANOLA:    It's your opening.

KATHY:    I told you it was a bad time. It's the first show. Everyone is very tense and a lot of energy . . . all the energies are going toward just one thing.

JANOLA:    (*Dryly*) Yeah.

KATHY:    (*Slamming down her yogurt cup*) Damn! (*There's a moment of silence*) Chuck, can you try and understand how important this is to me? I haven't been on stage that much and . . .

CHUCK: What are you talking about? All the stuff you did last year?

KATHY: I'm talking about professionals, Chuck. These are professionals. And I've got a lot to learn. A lot. And I want to be good, Chuck. I mean regardless of the show . . . me . . . I want to feel I've succeeded, you know? And it just takes total concentration, and I don't have the time to be . . . well, to be the way I'd like to be with you. And dammit Chuck, I *do* get tired. I get real tired.

JANOLA: At 25 years old?

KATHY: What's that got to do with it?

JANOLA: (*After a moment*) I shouldn't have come, I guess.

KATHY: I just wish you could understand the pressure.

JANOLA: I do. I know what pressure's like. I know what you're going through. I just get . . . I don't know . . . selfish, I guess.

KATHY: It's not like you.

JANOLA: What's that mean? It *is* me.

KATHY: Being jealous is definitely *not* you. For four years you don't care where I go or when I come home . . . now, all of a sudden we're back in the middle ages.

JANOLA: Yeah. Okay, I'm being' dumb. I don't even understand it myself. I just hear myself saying words and . . . (*Shakes his head*) I don't know. Maybe it's 'cause it's the first time you've been away or something.

KATHY: Why does that matter?

JANOLA: A lot of younger guys, for one thing.

KATHY: I was around young guys in Pittsburgh. Besides, that's just numbers. You're the youngest guy I know. (*Janola only nods*) Chuck, honey, there's no one. No one to be jealous of. I'd tell you. I wouldn't do that to you. I'd ask you not to come.

JANOLA: (*Smiles*) You *did* ask me not to come.

KATHY: I did not. I said maybe it'd be better if you waited.

JANOLA: Hell, I wasn't going to miss your opening night.

KATHY: (*After a moment*) Remember that big tent thing you built for Westinghouse? That thing with all the equipment in displays inside. What was it called?

JANOLA: Geodesic dome.

KATHY: Yeah. And the opening was a real big deal. With the chairmen of God-knows how many boards and their wirehaired wives. And everyone in black tie. And you said I couldn't come with you because you were too nervous? (*Janola nods*) Same thing.

JANOLA:   I dropped a deviled egg on the guy from Mellon Bank.

(*They laugh*)

KATHY:   Yeah, I forgot about that.

JANOLA:   And, as long as we're on the subject, remember what went on in the car before we went in?

KATHY:   I was only tryin' to get your attention.

JANOLA:   And last night I was only . . .

KATHY:   (*Laughing*) I know . . . same thing.

(*They kiss. They hold the embrace for a moment. Then she looks at his watch*)

KATHY:   We gotta' get back.

JANOLA:   Okay.

KATHY:   Line rehearsal.

JANOLA:   You looked real pretty on that stage last night.

KATHY:   Thank you.

JANOLA:   You like it up there, don't you?

KATHY:   (*Beaming*) I love it.

JANOLA:   (*Nods . . . then, quietly*) I could tell. (*Beat*) Most of those others from New York?

KATHY:   Most.

JANOLA:   And what do they tell you?

KATHY:   What do you mean?

JANOLA:   About New York. About going to New York. They tell you to go, right?

KATHY:   (*Shrugs . . . evading*) They say I'd probably get some commercials.

JANOLA:   Probably would. You certainly got Pittsburgh sewed up.

KATHY:   I want to act.

JANOLA:   That's acting, isn't it?

KATHY:   I mean really act. And study. I've got so much to learn and . . . (*Her voice drifts off. She stares ahead at the river. Janola studies her. After a moment she speaks*) I've got to get back to the theater.

JANOLA:   Take the car.

KATHY:   What?

JANOLA:   Take the car. I'll get a cab.

KATHY:   (*Laughs*) Where are you going to get a cab in Confluence, Pennsylvania, for Christ's sake?

JANOLA:   Well, they must have at least one.

KATHY:   Chuck, take a look around. I've never been here before . . . but trust me . . . they don't have at least one.

JANOLA:   Okay, I'll hire an ambulance.

KATHY:   Chuck . . .

JANOLA:   I'll pay someone to drive me back. It's no big deal. What time's the opening?

KATHY:   8:30. Chuck . . .

JANOLA:   Take the car.

KATHY:   Why?

JANOLA:   I want to stay here.

KATHY:   Here?

JANOLA:   I like it here. I feel good here. I . . . want to stay. Don't worry, I'll be there for your show.

KATHY:   (*Studies him a moment*) I'll be back to get you. About 4 . . . 4:30. Okay?

JANOLA:   I said I'll get to the theater.

KATHY:   How? It's over twenty miles. I'll be back to get you.

JANOLA:   (*Rising*) Okay. Let's go.

KATHY:   (*Determined*) I said . . . I'll be back to get you. (*Smiles*) You stay here. Take a nap in the sun. What the hell you want to hang around that theater for anyhow, right? It's lovely here. Stay. I don't mind coming back. Fact, it'll be kinda' pleasant. Okay?

JANOLA:   Okay.

(*She kisses him. Then kneels next to where he sits on the bench*)

KATHY:   Hey, I'm sorry about last night.

JANOLA:   Good thing you didn't shower first, you'd probably fallen asleep in there.

KATHY:   Tonight, to be safe, we'll shower together.

JANOLA:   Okay. But if you doze off, I'm gonna' throw the bath mat over you and leave you in the tub.

(*She laughs. At this point they are standing close together. They kiss*)

KATHY:   I've missed you, Chuck. I really have. And I'm glad you're here. (*She reaches up to lightly touch his face*) I love you, Chuck.

JANOLA:   I love you, Kath.

(*They kiss*)

KATHY: You'll be all right here?

JANOLA: Sure.

KATHY: Suppose you get bored?

JANOLA: I'll rent a raft.

KATHY: I'll bet you're good with one.

JANOLA: I never been on one.

KATHY: But I'll bet you're good anyhow. (*Kisses him*) Back at 5:30.

(*She goes. Janola watches her. After a moment he takes off his jacket and lays it over the back of the bench. He sits down and leans back . . . face to the sun . . . and closes his eyes. Lights shift to indicate a passage of time. Janola is asleep. . . . From offstage we hear the whirr of an electric motor. Presently a man appears riding in a battery operated wheelchair. He is Earl Douchette, an amputee. He is neatly dressed and has a robe over his lap and one remaining leg. He drives his chair up next to the bench where Janola sits. He looks Janola over. Then takes an apple and knife from his pocket . . . cuts a small section from the apple and begins to eat it. Janola wakes and turns to look at Earl.*)

EARL: (*Noticing the look*) Nice day.

JANOLA: Yes. (*Stretches*) Fell asleep.

EARL: Easy to do on a day like this. (*Cuts off a piece of the apple and offers it to Janola*) Apple?

JANOLA: No, thanks.

EARL: (*Looking out*) River's real frisky today. (*Beat*) You with that little black and silver sports car?

JANOLA: With it? Uh . . . it's mine.

EARL: Young lady drove it off 'bout an hour ago.

JANOLA: My girl friend.

EARL: Don't misunderstand me. I didn't think she stole it. I just bring it up 'cause I was wondering if you were the fella was asking about me yesterday.

JANOLA: Oh! You're . . . Earl Douchette? (*Earl nods. Janola stands and walks to Earl to shake hands*) Yes, I was asking. My name is Janola . . . Chuck Janola.

EARL: (*As they shake*) Pleased to meet you. You from a newspaper?

JANOLA: No, no . . . nothing like that. I just saw the window and . . . well . . . asked about you.

EARL: Oh.

JANOLA:   I saw you play. Knew who you were . . . so when I saw the window . . .

EARL:   Well, I'm glad you're not a reporter. That'd mean somebody died.

JANOLA:   Oh?

EARL:   Onliest time they come around. When somebody I played with died.

JANOLA:   No. I just . . . was asking.

EARL:   Oh, I see.

JANOLA:   I . . . uh . . . I saw you play your last game.

EARL:   My last one?

JANOLA:   Yes.

EARL:   My last one. (*Beat*) You from around here?

JANOLA:   No.

EARL:   Oh, of course not. You wouldn't have had to ask.

JANOLA:   I was driving around here yesterday.

EARL:   How come?

JANOLA:   Just driving.

EARL:   Passing time?

JANOLA:   In a way.

EARL:   On vacation?

JANOLA:   Well, sort of.

EARL:   Where are you from?

JANOLA:   Pittsburgh. (*He waits but Earl just nods*) So anyhow . . . I was driving around and I got . . . well . . . kinda drawn here.

EARL:   Drawn here?

JANOLA:   By the name.

EARL:   Confluence.

JANOLA:   Yes.

EARL:   Three rivers come together here. And a creek.

JANOLA:   Yes.

EARL:   Yep.

(*A pause*)

JANOLA:   And so I stopped to look around the town. It was so pretty.

EARL:   Which'd take all of three minutes, I guess.

JANOLA:   Just about. And when I walked by the hardware store I saw the window with all your stuff . . . trophies and all. So . . . (*He lets the sentence die*)

EARL:   My son's idea. He come over to the house one day

and took all that junk out of the basement. Would have taken the scrapbook my wife had kept but I wouldn't let him. The mice weren't finished eating it. Goes and puts it all in the store window where it can gather dust and spider webs, not to mention dead fruitflies. All pretty embarrassing, if you ask me. (*Beat*) But then, people seem to need it. Ever notice that? Sure, you're old enough to have noticed that.

JANOLA:   Noticed what?

EARL:   People need to touch accomplishment. Pick a thread off it's coat. Have it around to look at. You ever an athlete?

JANOLA:   I played football.

EARL:   Well, then, you know. Where'd you play?

JANOLA:   College at Tulane. Then with the Steelers.

EARL:   Pittsburgh Steelers? How long?

JANOLA:   Eight years.

EARL:   (*Stares at him and beams*) Well, damn me, that's wonderful! (*Drives his chair closer to Janola*) Do you know how long it's been since I talked to anyone who played ball for a living? This is great! (*Leans over and taps Janola's arm*) There's a lot we know that the other's don't, you know.

JANOLA:   There is?

EARL:   You mean you haven't found that out?

JANOLA:   I'm . . . not sure I have.

EARL:   (*Laughs*) Of course you have. (*Laughs again. Then a beat before he speaks again*) So . . . what do you think of this place?

JANOLA:   I like it here.

EARL:   I've been up where they all begin.

JANOLA:   What?

EARL:   The rivers. Fact, I was born next to one of 'em. Back up in those mountains. Up there where the Youghiheny begins. That's the Youghiheny coming in from over there. (*Points*) The rowdy one. Churning and splashing. Banging against the rocks till they're as smooth as a baby's ass. A hard charger, the Youghiheny. A maverick. She'll overflow occasionally and move everybody out of their houses along Laurel Street. 'Bout once every five years. She just moves everybody out for the hell of it. Fills up their cellars and tries to drown their cats. Yeah, she's a hell raiser. And I was born right alongside her. (*Beat*) You play in Forbes Field?

JANOLA:   Yes.

EARL:   I don't think I ever played but two games in Forbes Field. Exhibitions.

JANOLA:   It's torn down now.

EARL:   Well, what isn't? (*Beat*) Wrigley Field is still there. Least it was last summer. I saw it on TV.

JANOLA:   You watch much baseball?

EARL:   Some. Not all the time. But I watch it. Makes my son angry 'cause I turn the sound off. But I know what's going on, I guess. And all the players got names on their shirts nowadays. I just don't like all the talk.

JANOLA:   I hardly ever watch football.

EARL:   No?

JANOLA:   Hardly ever.

EARL:   You're how old?

JANOLA:   Forty-five.

EARL:   (*After a beat*) Yeah, there was a time I didn't watch much baseball either. (*Pause*) I come out here every day. Sure. Rain or whatever. My son's wife fusses over me if it's cold. But I come out. Check the rivers. Make sure they're still runnin'. (*Beat*) What you should do is come here in the winter sometime. After a snow. Late afternoon sky is a light purple. Them trees up there, green and white. The snow along the banks a kind of dark blue. And what's left of the sun bounces around on the river ice in a sort of pale yellow. It's like a goddamn Christmas card around here, I'll tell you.

JANOLA:   (*After a beat . . . quietly*) I like it here. (*Beat*) I feel . . . I don't know why . . . I didn't come from any place like this . . . mountains, rivers . . . but it feels like home somehow.

EARL:   There's mountains in Pittsburgh.

JANOLA:   I was raised in Ohio.

EARL:   No mountains in Ohio.

JANOLA:   No.

EARL:   Some hills.

JANOLA:   Some.

EARL:   Around Cincinnati. Where abouts in Ohio you from?

JANOLA:   Mansfield. About 70 miles south of Cleveland.

EARL:   That's not so far from here.

JANOLA:   No.

EARL:   So drop back sometime and take a look at winter. (*Beat*) Cleveland. I spent some real dull nights in Cleveland.

JANOLA:   I believe it.

EARL:   Yessir, in Cleveland, even when you're havin' fun you're still half bored.

JANOLA:   You played your last game there.

EARL:   (*Thinking*) Yes, I did. (*Beat*) And you saw it.

JANOLA:   Yes.

EARL:   I'm surprised you remember.

JANOLA:   Well . . . you looked right at me, Earl.

EARL:   I did?

JANOLA:   Right at me.

EARL:   (*Smiling*) You're sure of that now?

JANOLA:   (*Smiles*) Yep.

EARL:   That would'a been '46. I think we finished 437 games out that year. I recollect it was surely a twilight season. (*Laughs*) I don't even recall who won.

JANOLA:   Yankees?

EARL:   I don't know. May have. Or Detroit or Boston. Lotta tough teams that year. Everyone back from the war. Williams, Greenberg, Doerr, that big right hander the Tigers had . . . what was his name? Later became a manager. (*They sit quietly a bit*) What's your line now?

JANOLA:   What?

EARL:   What kinda work you do?

JANOLA:   Displays. (*Beat*) I have a company. We build displays, point of sale, billboards . . . stuff like that.

EARL:   You a carpenter?

JANOLA:   No. It began as a summer job. In college . . . New Orleans. Mostly muscle work. Driving the truck . . . setting the stuff up . . . and, well, when I joined the Steelers, I hooked up with a company in Pittsburgh.

EARL:   Now it's your company.

JANOLA:   Yeah. Janola Displays. Yeah, it's mine.

EARL:   Me, I came back to the hardware store. Bought it with my first Series split. (*Beat*) You know, I ran that damn store for eleven years longer than I played ball. Twenty-nine years. Amazing, when you think about it.

JANOLA:   What is?

EARL:   In the terms of the years of my life . . . I'm a hardware store owner.

JANOLA:   C'mon, you're in the Hall of Fame, for Christ's sake.

EARL:   And . . . and, if I can live another twelve years . . . baseball will rank third. My second profession will then be river watcher. In fact, I sometimes think that's what it was all about. So's I'd be able to watch these rivers. (*Beat*) I would say it's best now. This time of year. Because it stays light longer. And you can watch the sun set by following the patterns of light and dark across the river. At the very last light, just as the kids come out to bottle fireflies, there is . . . right there in front of that elm . . . a final golden, bright triangle on the water. And if you look up to that mountain there . . . you'll see a circle of orange around the very top of it. A circle that gets smaller as it slides slowly up that stand of pine . . . till one last glimmer touches the top of the trees and then blinks out. It's night . . . and the moon is already sitting over there . . . waiting.

(*Pause*)

JANOLA:   Yeah . . . well, I could sit here . . . watching the light change . . . for a long time.

EARL:   Could you?

JANOLA:   Yes, I could.

EARL:   I think you're too young yet.

JANOLA:   (*Laughs*) I'm not young.

EARL:   Sure you are. (*Beat*) You must have been very young when you saw me play.

JANOLA:   Twelve.

EARL:   And I was younger then, than you are now. (*Smiles*) Time is a shifty thing, isn't it?

JANOLA:   I used to pretend to be you.

EARL:   How's that?

JANOLA:   With a rubber ball. Throwing it against our back porch steps. I'd be you . . . "The Emperor of the Infield" . . . scooping up that ball and firing it back at the steps. Trouble was, I had a very wild arm. I kept punching holes in the screen door or knocking the rain spout off the edge of the house. Even broke a couple windows.

EARL:   With a rubber ball?

JANOLA:   Oh, I could throw.

EARL:   I guess you could.

JANOLA:   I just couldn't throw *straight*. (*Laughs*) It got so bad my *mother* encouraged me to take up football.

EARL:   And shortly after . . . some kid somewhere was pretending to be . . . (*Leans in for name*)

JANOLA:   (*Quietly*) Yeah . . . Chick Janola.

EARL:   Chick Janola. Time is a shifty thing. (*Yawns*)

Oh . . . 'scuse me. Doctor says I'm low on potassium. I tend to fall asleep at the drop of a hat. I think it's more likely I'm just plain low on everything.

JANOLA: Well listen, if you want to take a nap.

EARL: No. Let's talk. (*Beat*) You been over to the dam?

JANOLA: Drove past it.

EARL: They built that in '52. (*Beat, as if he is going on, then . . .* ) I'm not sure why. (*Pause*) You played football.

JANOLA: Yep.

EARL: Rough game. 'Course baseball could be rough too, you know.

JANOLA: Of course.

EARL: We had some rough boys played that game.

JANOLA: I'll bet.

EARL: Medwick comes to mind. Slaughter . . . hell, practically that whole damn team.

JANOLA: Ty Cobb was a hard nose, wasn't he? Did you play against him?

EARL: Well, Cobb . . . he was the real goods when it came to that. He didn't play to beat you. He played to destroy you.

JANOLA: How come?

EARL: (*Shrugs*) Who knows? His old man shot his mother and told the police he thought she was a burglar. That mighta had something to do with it.

(*They laugh*)

JANOLA: I thought it was the other way around. Mother shot the father.

EARL: Whatever.

JANOLA: Did you play against him?

EARL: When I was comin' in, he was goin' out. First time I saw him was in the 8th inning of a game in Detroit, when they stuck me in for my glove. The Georgia cracker himself led off the inning with a single.

JANOLA: I thought he was called the Georgia Peach?

EARL: I don't know what they called him . . . but he was a cracker.

JANOLA: And did he steal second on you?

EARL: (*Mock serious, pointing to amputated leg*) How do you think I lost this?

JANOLA: (*Getting into the spirit*) Took your leg, did he?

EARL: He played angry.

JANOLA: Well, that's pretty damn angry.

(*They smile at each other. A pause. Then Earl points out toward the rivers*)

EARL: Look! There he comes!

JANOLA: What?

EARL: There! Comin' around that turn. The kid in the canoe. He's been at it for two days and ain't made it yet . . . Oh! There he goes! (*Laughs*) Is he up? I can't see him. He wears a life jacket so . . .

JANOLA: Yes. There . . . on the other side of the canoe. See!

EARL: Oh, yeah. (*Laughs*) He'll go back and try her again. Comes from way up river, I think. But damn that river's a hellion at that bend. Hey! Here comes another! Look at him fight her! C'mon!

(*Janola begins to root with him*)

EARL: C'mon! Stay with it! Look at him handle that paddle! Ride 'em cowboy!

JANOLA: Atta' way kid! Stick with it! You got it! You got it!

(*They both give a whoop of joy*)

EARL: Made it! He made it! Nice goin'!

JANOLA: Aaaal . . . right!

EARL: God, I love to watch 'em. (*Beat*) We used to take that same damnfool ride. On inner tubes . . . cellar doors . . . anything we could find. It's a helluva' river. But you know something? Up there at the source . . . that roughneck is nothin' but a little stream. A ribbon of water a three-year-old kid could step across. A sliver of melted ice and snow . . . slippin' its way around pebbles. Uncertain, skittish, breakin' in two at a rock . . . windin' down the mountain . . . pickin' it's way carefully. Then . . . beginning to gather strength. Movin' faster . . . gettin' stronger. Not splittin' at rocks . . . knocking them out of the way. Pourin' down the mountain . . . barreling into town . . . hell-bent for somewhere. Not knowin', not carin' . . . just hell-bent for somewhere. And then comin' together with the other two. And somehow calmed by that. Slowin' down. Flowing on south . . . fuller, quieter. A real river now . . . deep and steady and a half mile wide . . . moving easily toward the sea. (*Beat*) Another canoe comin'! Hey, looks like a girl this time! It is! Whoop! Over she goes! (*Chuckles*) Ever ride a river?

JANOLA: Nope.

EARL: Oh that's right, you're from Ohio. (*Beat*) What made you go to that particular game?

JANOLA: Your last one? Because it was. My grandfather took me. He said we should see Earl Douchette's last game.

EARL: Did I play? I wasn't playin' steady then.

JANOLA: You pinch hit in the ninth. Singled. Got to second somehow.

EARL: Oh, yeah.

JANOLA: (*After a pause*) And then the game was over. There weren't too many people in the stands and those that were, left quickly. It was fall and that stadium can get chilly in the late afternoon. I remember looking out over center field and seeing white caps on Lake Erie. The shadow of the stadium cut across the infield . . . halfway to center. Sun shone on the outfield grass. You stood on second a moment . . . then kinda kicked the bag . . . and walked across the infield toward the foul line. An umpire came up and shook your hand . . .

EARL: (*In a low voice*) Eddie Rommel.

JANOLA: . . . and then, when you reached the dugout steps, you stopped, turned and looked around. Your eyes swept the entire stadium and then . . . you looked right at me.

EARL: I did?

JANOLA: Right at me. I said, "Grandpa, he's lookin' at me." "No," said Grandpa, "He's just takin' a last look around is all." "No," I said, "He's lookin' right at me. He's tryin' to tell me something. What's he tryin' to tell me, Grandpa?" (*He laughs. Earl joins in*) You stood there on the dugout steps with the sun dying in front of you and that cold breeze coming in from the lake . . . you stood there looking right into my eyes. And then you turned and went into the dugout. "He went with class," my Grandpa said.

EARL: (*After a beat*) I don't know. Is there a classy way of going out? Or does it just look that way? (*Beat*) That was a nice story, son. I wish I could reply that it meant something. That I was, indeed, trying to speak to you across that field. But the only thing I recall is looking around that park . . . and wondering . . . would it ever be that good again?

JANOLA: And . . . ?

EARL: (*With some anger*) Don't you know the answer?

JANOLA: Were you angry?

EARL: Were you?

JANOLA: Yes.

EARL: Of course! I hate to lose! (*Still with some anger*) I couldn't even watch a bunch of jug-eared kids play ball back of the school. I became a hardware man. As if I had never been the fastest, quickest, son of a bitch who ever stood on the dirt between second and third. I drank Seagrams and sold pin hinges! Of course I was angry. And I'm going to be just as angry the next time. (*Beat*) I'll tell you something, Chick. I watch the ball games now. But I never think . . . I make *sure* I never think about how it felt. 'Cause the terrible thing is that the body remembers. The muscles remember. And that's the memory you gotta' avoid . . . the way it felt. You can recall the high times and you might smile and feel good. But if you allow in the memory of how it *felt* . . . you're gonna' have to do one hell of a lot of drinkin' later. (*Beat . . . calming*) Hell, you know all of that.

JANOLA: Yeah. I know that.

EARL: Sure you do.

JANOLA: I just thought you only had to do it once.

EARL: Oh, hell no. You keep doin' it. You just keep doin' it.

JANOLA: (*Lightening mood*) Well . . . Grandpa said you did it well.

EARL: (*Lightening also*) I just went whilst I could still walk.

JANOLA: A lot don't. A lot hold on.

EARL: That's 'cause they aren't payin' attention. (*They both laugh*) The trick, I suppose is to do it quick and simple . . . and leave your laundry behind. (*Beat*) Not bad huh? I just made it up.

JANOLA: Yeah? Well, maybe you oughta put it in a fortune cookie.

EARL: Put it on a bumper sticker.

JANOLA: Stick it in *Reader's Digest*.

EARL: Stick it in your ear.

JANOLA: Shove it up your ass. (*They smile at each other. A pause . . . then*) Yeah, you ain't the only one hates to lose, Earl. (*Beat*) The year after I quit I went to the Steelers' opening game. But I left at the half. Left Forbes Field and got in my car and drove back to the town . . . the field where we played in high school. Stood there in the moonlight waiting for ghosts. Waiting to see seventy-five boys pour out of the gym door in dirty white practice jerseys and yellow, grass-stained, canvas pants. Waited to see those small, tight jogging steps and hear the clatter of cleats on concrete. Waited for one . . . to say goodbye to him. For it was to be a kind of exorcism. We had reached the point where the two of us could go no further together. And I knew, as I stood next to my car, looking at a dark, empty field . . . I knew that I had finally been beat. (*Beat*) I carried the ball nine times in a row once in high school. Nine times in the last minutes of a game that everyone thought was lost. Nine times I took it to 'em. And came into the huddle after the fourth time screaming at my teammates that if they had given up, they could at least get the fuck out of my way. See, I believed that someone could beat Mansfield High, could beat Tulane, could beat the Steelers . . . but they could never beat Chick Janola. (*Beat*) But that night, I stood by my car knowing I could be beat. Time had beat me. Time had beat me real good. And I hoped I'd never have to come up against that son of a bitch again.

(*Janola looks at Earl, but Earl is asleep. Janola smiles. Sits staring ahead for a long moment. Then he looks off left in the direction that Kathy exited. He seems to come to some kind of an inner decision. He takes an envelope from his pocket, removes a card from the envelope and opening the card writes something on it. When he finishes, he holds the card in his hand as he sits thinking. From offstage we hear a car horn. Then Kathy's voice*)

KATHY: (*Off*) Chuck! Chuck, you ready to go?

(*Janola waves a hand and stands*)

KATHY: (*Off*) I'm going into that store a second. Need some Kleenex.

(*The horn has awakened Earl*)

EARL: Oh . . . sorry. Guess I ran out of potassium (*Seeing Janola putting on coat*) Leavin' Chuck?

JANOLA: Yeah, have to go, Earl.

EARL: (*Noticing envelope*) You want to mail that letter, there's a box right over next to the grocery store.

JANOLA: No. No, this is . . . just a card. Friend of mine . . . my girl, is opening in a play tonight. Up in Jennerstown.

EARL: Actress?

JANOLA: Yep. This is just a card . . . to wish her luck. (*Beat*) And a long career.

EARL: (*Yawns*) Oh, excuse me. It's that river breeze. Makes me as sleepy as a cat in the sun.

JANOLA: Well, you go back to sleep, Earl.

EARL: Been real nice talkin' to you, Chick.

JANOLA: Good talkin' to you, Earl.

EARL: If you decide to see this place in the winter. Look me up. Who knows . . . I may still be around. (*He settles back to his nap*)

JANOLA: I'll do that. I'll be back when the snow falls.

EARL: Good.

(*Kathy runs on. Holds stage left*)

KATHY: Chuck, honey . . . we have to hurry. I've got a lot to do.

JANOLA: (*Crosses to her*) I know you do, Kath. (*Puts an arm around her. Looks at her*) I know you do.

(*He gives her a short kiss. They walk off. Earl sleeps. Lights fade to black*)

End

*Beth Henley*

# AM I BLUE

# Beth Henley

Beth Henley's Southern gothic comedy *Crimes of the Heart* received the 1981 Pulitzer and Critics' Circle Prizes. Simultaneously, productions of two other full-length plays were announced: *The Miss Firecracker Contest* at Buffalo's Studio Arena Theatre and *The Wake of Jamey Foster* at the Hartford Stage Company, with director Ulu Grosbard slating a Broadway opening for the fall of 1982. Miss Henley's good fortune appeared to be an overnight success—yet actually her overnight success had been several years in the making.

After finishing *Crimes of the Heart* in 1978, Miss Henley sent it to a number of regional theatres, which returned it without production. Then a playwright friend sent the script to the Actors Theatre of Louisville where Jon Jory's staff had the sensitivity and wisdom to select it as a co-winner of the 1978 Great American Play Contest. An ATL production attracted local Louisville praise and regional productions. But despite the efforts of an enthusiastic agent, no Broadway producer could be interested in taking the play to the Great White Way. Eventually director Melvyn Bernhardt urged Lynne Meadow to produce the script at her Manhattan Theatre Club, which had rejected the script earlier. This time Ms. Meadow looked favorably on the material, and her exciting production there attracted producers for a move to Broadway in November 1981.

After receiving a Bachelor of Fine Arts degree in Theatre from Southern Methodist University in Dallas and studying acting for a year at the University of Illinois, Miss Henley moved to Los Angeles to attempt a career as an actress. Not finding the doors open to her performing abilities—luckily for theatre lovers—she turned her hand to screenwriting and playwriting.

*Am I Blue*, here published in an anthology for the first time, was written when Miss Henley was a sophomore in college, but it was not professionally produced until Manhattan's Circle Rep chose it for an evening of one-acts in January 1982, along with *Confluence* by John Bishop (elsewhere in this volume) and *Thymus Vulgaris* by Lanford Wilson (in *Best Short Plays 1982*). *Am I Blue* is a tender and riotous tale of a naive college freshman expected on his eighteenth birthday to prove his manhood to fraternity brothers by a successful visit to a New Orleans bordello. Instead of fulfilling his mission, the freshman is intercepted by one of Miss Henley's daffy Southern belles for a far more engaging evening. Frank Rich, reviewer for the *New York Times*, observes, "Along the way we sample Miss Henley's wondrous gift for creating sweet comedy out of Southern eccentricities—as well as her ability to reveal the sad loneliness beneath the spunk."

With Miss Henley just skipping past her thirty-first birthday, we trust her zany imagination will create many more entertaining characters, which *Time* magazine reviewer Richard Corliss describes as "the most engaging bunch of eccentrics since the days of the young William Saroyan."

## Characters:

JOHN POLK, *seventeen*
ASHBE, *sixteen*
HILDA, *a waitress, thirty-five*
*Street People*: BARKER, WHORE, BUM, CLAREECE

## Scene:

*A bar, the street, the living room of a run-down apartment.*

## Time:

*Fall 1968*

*The scene opens on a street in the New Orleans French Quarter on a rainy, blue bourbon night. Various people—a whore, bum, street barker, Clareece—appear and disappear along the street. The scene then focuses on a bar where a piano is heard from the back room playing softly and insistinctly "Am I Blue?" The lights go up on John Polk, who sits alone at a table. He is seventeen, a bit overweight and awkward. He wears nice clothes, perhaps a navy sweater with large white monograms. His navy raincoat is slung over an empty chair. While drinking John Polk concentrates on the red and black card that he holds in his hand. As soon as the scene is established, Ashbe enters from the street. She is sixteen, wears a flowered plastic raincoat, a white plastic rain cap, red galoshes, a butterfly barrette, and jeweled cat-eye glasses. She is carrying a bag full of stolen goods. Her hair is very curly. Ashbe makes her way cautiously to John Polk's table. As he sees her coming, he puts the card into his pocket. She sits in the empty chair and pulls his raincoat over her head*

ASHBE:   Excuse me . . . do you mind if I sit here please?
JOHN POLK:   (*Looks up at her—then down into his glass*) What are you doing hiding under my raincoat? You're getting it all wet.

ASHBE:　Well, I'm very sorry, but after all it is a raincoat. (*He tries to pull off coat*) It was rude of me I know, but look I just don't want them to recognize me.

JOHN POLK:　(*Looking about*) Who to recognize you?

ASHBE:　Well, I stole these two ash trays from the Screw Inn, ya know right down the street. (*She pulls out two glass commercial ash trays from her white plastic bag*) Anyway, I'm scared the manager saw me. They'll be after me I'm afraid.

JOHN POLK:　Well, they should be. Look, do you mind giving me back my raincoat? I don't want to be found protecting any thief.

ASHBE:　(*Coming out from under coat*) Thief—would you call Robin Hood a thief?

JOHN POLK:　Christ.

ASHBE:　(*Back under coat*) No, you wouldn't. He was valiant—all the time stealing from the rich and giving to the poor.

JOHN POLK:　But your case isn't exactly the same, is it? You're stealing from some crummy little bar and keeping the ash trays for yourself. Now give me back my coat.

ASHBE:　(*Throws coat at him*) Sure, take your old coat. I suppose I should have explained—about Miss Marcey. (*Silence*) Miss Marcey, this cute old lady with a little hump in her back. I always see her in her sun hat and blue print dress. Miss Marcey lives in the apartment building next to ours. I leave all the stolen goods, as gifts on her front steps.

JOHN POLK:　Are you one of those kleptomaniacs? (*He starts checking his wallet*)

ASHBE:　You mean when people all the time steal and they can't help it?

JOHN POLK:　Yeah.

ASHBE:　Oh, no. I'm not a bit careless. Take my job tonight, my very first night job, if you want to know. Anyway, I've been planning it for two months, trying to decifer which bar most deserved to be stolen from. I finally decided on the Screw Inn. Mainly because of the way they're so mean to Mr. Groves. He works at the magazine rack at Diver's Drugstore and is really very sweet, but he has a drinking problem. I don't think that's fair to be mean to people simply because they have a drinking problem—and, well, anyway, you see I'm not just stealing for personal gain. I mean, I don't even smoke.

JOHN POLK:   Yeah, well, most infants don't, but then again, most infants don't hang around bars.

ASHBE:   I don't see why not, Toulouse Lautrec did.

JOHN POLK:   They'd throw me out.

ASHBE:   Oh, they throw me out too, but I don't accept defeat. (*Slowly moves into him*) Why it's the very same with my pickpocketing.

(*John Polk sneers, turns away*)

ASHBE:   It's a very hard art to master. Why every time I've done it, I've been caught.

JOHN POLK:   That's all I need, is to have some slum kid tell me how good it is to steal. Everyone knows it's not.

ASHBE:   (*About his drink*) That looks good. What is it?

JOHN POLK:   Hey, would you mind leaving me alone—I just wanted to be alone.

ASHBE:   Okay. I'm sorry. How about if I'm quiet?

(*John Polk shrugs. He sips drink, looks around, catches her eye, she smiles and sighs*)

ASHBE:   I was just looking at your pin. What fraternity are you in?

JOHN POLK:   S.A.E.

ASHBE:   Is it a good fraternity?

JOHN POLK:   Sure, it's the greatest.

ASHBE:   I bet you have lots of friends.

JOHN POLK:   Tons.

ASHBE:   Are you being serious?

JOHN POLK:   Yes.

ASHBE:   Hmm. Do they have parties and all that?

JOHN POLK:   Yeah, lots of parties, booze, honking horns, it's exactly what you would expect.

ASHBE:   I wouldn't expect anything. Why did you join?

JOHN POLK:   I don't know. Well, my brother . . . I guess it was my brother . . . he told me how great it was, how the fraternity was supposed to get you dates, make you study, solve all your problems.

ASHBE:   Gee, does it?

JOHN POLK:   Doesn't help you study.

ASHBE:   How about dates? Do they get you a lot of dates?

JOHN POLK:   Some.

ASHBE:   What were the girls like?

JOHN POLK:   I don't know—they were like girls.

ASHBE: Did you have a good time?

JOHN POLK: I had a pretty good time.

ASHBE: Did you make love to any of them?

JOHN POLK: (*To self*) Oh, Christ . . .

ASHBE: I'm sorry . . . I just figured that's why you had the appointment with the whore . . . cause you didn't have anyone else . . . to make love to.

JOHN POLK: How did you know I had the, ah, the appointment?

ASHBE: I saw you put the red card in your pocket when I came up. Those red cards are pretty familiar around here. The house is only about a block or so away. It's one of the best though, really very plush. Only two murders and a knifing in its whole history. Do you go there often?

JOHN POLK: Yeah, I like to give myself a treat.

ASHBE: Who do you have?

JOHN POLK: What do you mean?

ASHBE: I mean which girl. (*John Polk gazes into his drink*) Look, I just thought I might know her is all.

JOHN POLK: Know her, ah, how would you know her?

ASHBE: Well, some of the girls from my high school go there to work when they get out.

JOHN POLK: G.G., her name is G.G.

ASHBE: G.G . . . Hmm, well, how does she look?

JOHN POLK: I don't know.

ASHBE: Oh, you've never been with her before?

JOHN POLK: No.

ASHBE: (*Confidentially*) Are you one of those kinds that likes a lot of variety?

JOHN POLK: Variety? Sure, I guess I like variety.

ASHBE: Oh, yes, now I remember.

JOHN POLK: What?

ASHBE: G.G., that's just her working name. Her real name is Myrtle Reims, she's Kay Reims older sister. Kay is in my grade at school.

JOHN POLK: Myrtle? Her name is Myrtle?

ASHBE: I never liked the name either.

JOHN POLK: Myrtle, oh, Christ. Is she pretty?

ASHBE: (*Matter of fact*) Pretty, no she's not real pretty.

JOHN POLK: What does she look like?

ASHBE: Let's see . . . she's, ah, well, Myrtle had acne and there are a few scars left. It's not bad. I think they sort of give her character. Her hair's red, only I don't think it's really red. It sort of fizzles out all over her head. She's got a pretty good figure . . . big top . . . but the rest of her is kind of skinny.

JOHN POLK:   I wonder if she has a good personality.

ASHBE:   Well, she was a senior when I was a freshman; so I never really knew her. I remember she used to paint her finger nails lots of different colors . . . pink, orange, purple. I don't know, but she kind of scares me. About the only time I ever saw her true personality was around a year ago. I was over at Kay's making a health poster for school. Anyway, My.rtle comes busting in, screaming about how she can't find her spangled bra anywhere. Kay and I just sat on the floor cutting pictures of food out of magazines while she was storming about slamming drawers and swearing. Finally, she found it. It was pretty garish—red with black and gold sequined G's on each cup. That's how I remember the name—G.G.

(*As Ashbe illustrates the placement of the G's she spots Hilda, the waitress, approaching. Ashbe pulls the raincoat over her head and hides on the floor. Hilda enters through the beaded curtains spilling her tray. Hilda is a woman of few words*)

HILDA:   Shit, damn curtain. Nuther drink?

JOHN POLK:   Mam?

HILDA:   (*Points to drink*) Vodka coke?

JOHN POLK:   No, thank you. I'm not quite finished yet.

HILDA:   Napkins clean.

(*Ashbe pulls her bag off the table. Hilda looks at Ashbe then to John Polk. She walks around the table, as Ashbe is crawling along the floor to escape. Ashbe runs into Hilda's toes*)

ASHBE:   Are those real gold?

HILDA:   You again. Out.

ASHBE:   She wants me to leave. Why should a paying customer leave? (*Back to Hilda*) Now I'll have a mint julip and easy on the mint.

HILDA:   This pre-teen with you?

JOHN POLK:   Well, I . . . No . . . I . . .

HILDA:   I.D.'s.

ASHBE:   Certainly, I always try to cooperate with the management.

HILDA:   (*Looking at John Polk's I.D.*) I.D., 11–12–50. Date: 11–11–68.

JOHN POLK:   Yes, but . . . well, 11–12 is less than two hours away.

HILDA: Back in two hours.

ASHBE: I seem to have left my identification in my gold lamé bag.

HILDA: Well, boo-hoo. (*Motions for Ashbe to leave with a minimum of effort. She goes back to table*) No tip.

ASHBE: You didn't tip her?

JOHN POLK: I figured the drinks were so expensive . . . I just didn't . . .

HILDA: No tip!

JOHN POLK: Look, Miss, I'm sorry. (*Going through his pockets*) Here would you like a . . . a nickel . . . wait, wait, here's a quarter.

HILDA: Just move ass, sonny. You too, Barbie.

ASHBE: Ugh, I hate public rudeness. I'm sure I'll refrain from ever coming here again.

HILDA: Think I'll go in the back room and cry.

(*Ashbe and John Polk exit. Hilda picks up tray and exits through the curtain, tripping again*)

HILDA: Shit. Damn curtain.

(*Ashbe and John Polk are now standing outside under the awning of the bar*)

ASHBE: Gee, I didn't know it was your birthday tomorrow. Happy birthday! Don't be mad. I thought you were at least twenty or twenty-one, really.

JOHN POLK: It's o.k. Forget it.

(*As they begin walking, various blues are heard coming from the near-by bars*)

ASHBE: It's raining.

JOHN POLK: I know.

ASHBE: Are you going over to the house now?

JOHN POLK: No, not till twelve.

ASHBE: Yeah, the red and black cards—they mean all night. Midnight till morning.

(*At this point a street barker beckons the couple into his establishment. Perhaps he is accompanied by a whore*)

BARKER: Hey mister, bring your baby on in, buy her a few drinks, maybe tonight ya get lucky.

ASHBE: Keep walking.

JOHN POLK: What's wrong with the place?

ASHBE: The drinks are watery rot gut, and the show girls are boys. . .

BARKER: Up yours, punk!

JOHN POLK: (*Who has now sat down on a street bench*) Look,

just tell me where a cheap bar is. I've got to stay drunk, but I don't have much money left.

ASHBE: Yikes, there aren't too many cheap bars around here, and a lot of them check I.D.'s.

JOHN POLK: Well, do you know of any that don't?

ASHBE: No, not for sure.

JOHN POLK: Oh, God, I need to get drunk.

ASHBE: Aren't you?

JOHN POLK: Some, but I'm losing ground fast.

(*By this time a bum who has been traveling drunkenly down the street falls near the couple and begins throwing up*)

ASHBE: Oh, I know! You can come to my apartment. It's just down the block. We keep one bottle of rum around. I'll serve you a grand drink, three or four if you like.

JOHN POLK: (*Fretfully*) No, thanks.

ASHBE: But look, we're getting all wet.

JOHN POLK: Sober too, wet and sober.

ASHBE: Oh, come on! Rain's blurring my glasses.

JOHN POLK: Well, how about your parents? What would they say?

ASHBE: Daddy's out of town and Mama lives in Atlanta; so I'm sure they won't mind. I think we have some cute, little marshmallows. (*Pulling on him*) Won't you really come?

JOHN POLK: You've probably got some gang of muggers waiting to kill me. Oh, all right . . . what the hell, let's go.

ASHBE: Hurrah! Come on. It's this way. (*She starts across the stage, stops, and picks up an old hat*) Hey, look at this hat. Isn't it something! Here, wear it to keep off the rain.

JOHN POLK: (*Throwing hat back onto street*) No, thanks, you don't know who's worn it before.

ASHBE: (*Picking hat back up*) That makes it all the more exciting. Maybe it was a butcher's who slaughtered his wife or a silver pirate with a black bird on his throat. Who do you guess?

JOHN POLK: I don't know. Anyway what's the good of guessing? I mean you'll never really know.

ASHBE: (*Trying the hat on*) Yeah, probably not.

(*At this point Ashbe and John Polk reach the front door*)

ASHBE: Here we are.

(*Ashbe begins fumbling for her key. Clareece, a teeny-bopper, walks up to John Polk*)

CLAREECE: Hey, man, got any spare change?

JOHN POLK: (*Looking through his pockets*) Let me see ... I ...

ASHBE: (*Coming up between them, giving Clareece a shove*) Beat it, Clareece. He's my company.

CLAREECE: (*Walks away and sneers*) Oh, shove it, Frizzels.

ASHBE: A lot of jerks live around here. Come on in.

(*She opens the door. Lights go up on the living room of a run-down apartment in a run-down apartment house. Besides being merely run-down the room is a malicious pig sty with colors, paper hats, paper dolls, masks, torn up stuffed animals, dead flowers and leaves, dress-up clothes, etc., thrown all about*)

My bones are cold. Do you want a towel to dry off?

JOHN POLK: Yes, thank you.

ASHBE: (*She picks up a towel off the floor and tosses it to him*) Here. (*He begins drying off, as she takes off her rain things; then she begins raking things off the sofa*) Please do sit down. (*He sits*) I'm sorry the place is disheveled, but my father's been out of town. I always try to pick up and all before he gets in. Of course, he's pretty used to messes. My mother never was too good at keeping things clean.

JOHN POLK: When's he coming back?

ASHBE: Sunday, I believe. Oh, I've been meaning to say ...

JOHN POLK: What?

ASHBE: My name's Ashbe Williams.

JOHN POLK: Ashbe?

ASHBE: Yeah, Ashbe.

JOHN POLK: My name's John Polk Richards.

ASHBE: John Polk? They call you John Polk?

JOHN POLK: It's family.

ASHBE: (*Putting on socks*) These are my favorite socks, the red furry ones. Well, here's some books and magazines to look at while I fix you something to drink. What do you want in your rum?

JOHN POLK: Coke's fine.

ASHBE: I'll see if we have any. I think I'll take some hot Kool-Aid myself.

(*She exits to the kitchen*)

JOHN POLK: Hot Kool-Aid?

ASHBE: It's just Kool-Aid that's been heated, like hot chocolate or hot tea.

JOHN POLK: Sounds great.

ASHBE: Well, I'm used to it. You get so much for your

dime, it makes it worth your while. I don't buy pre-sweetened, of course, it's better to sugar your own.

JOHN POLK:   I remember once I threw up a lot of grape Kool-Aid when I was a kid. I've hated it ever since. Hey, would you check on the time?

ASHBE:   (*She enters carrying a tray with several bottles of food coloring, a bottle of rum, and a huge glass*) I'm sorry we don't have Coke. I wonder if rum and Kool-Aid is good? Oh, we don't have a clock either.

(*She pours a large amount of rum into the large glass*)

JOHN POLK:   I'll just have it with water then.

ASHBE:   (*She finds an almost empty glass of water somewhere in the room and dumps it in with the rum*) Would you like food coloring in the water? It makes a drink all the more aesthetic. Of course, some people don't care for aesthetics.

JOHN POLK:   No, thank you, just plain water.

ASHBE:   Are you sure? The taste is entirely the same. I put it in all my water.

JOHN POLK:   Well . . .

ASHBE:   What color do you want?

JOHN POLK:   I don't know.

ASHBE:   What's your favorite color?

JOHN POLK:   Blue, I guess.

(*She puts a few blue drops into the glass. As she has nothing to stir with, she blows into the glass turning the water blue*)

JOHN POLK:   Thanks.

ASHBE:   (*Exits. She screams from kitchen*) Come on, say come on, cat, eat your fresh, good milk.

JOHN POLK:   You have a cat?

ASHBE:   (*off*) No.

JOHN POLK:   Oh.

ASHBE:   (*She enters carrying a tray with a cup of hot Kool-Aid and Cheerios and colored marshmallows*) Here are some Cheerios and some cute, little, colored marshmallows to eat with your drink.

JOHN POLK:   Thanks.

ASHBE:   I one time smashed all the big white marshmallows in the plastic bag at the grocery store.

JOHN POLK:   Why did you do that?

ASHBE:   I was angry. Do you like ceramics?

JOHN POLK:   Yes.

ASHBE:  My mother makes them. It's sort of her hobby. She is very talented.

JOHN POLK:  My mother never does anything. Well, I guess she can shuffle the bridge deck okay.

ASHBE:  Actually, my mother is a dancer. She teaches at a school in Atlanta. She's really very talented.

JOHN POLK:  (*Indicates ceramics*) She must be to do all these.

ASHBE:  Well, Madeline, my older sister, did the blue one. Madeline gets to live with Mama.

JOHN POLK:  And you live with your father.

ASHBE:  Yeah, but I get to go visit them sometimes.

JOHN POLK:  You do ceramics too?

ASHBE:  No, I never learned . . . but I have this great pot-holder set. (*Gets up to show him*) See, I make lots of multicolored potholders and send them to Mama and Madeline. I also make paper hats. (*Gets material to show him*) I guess they're more creative, but making potholders is more relaxing. Here would you like to make a hat?

JOHN POLK:  I don't know, I'm a little drunk.

ASHBE:  It's not hard a bit. (*Hands him material*) Just draw a real pretty design on the paper. It really doesn't have to be pretty, just whatever you want.

JOHN POLK:  It's kind of you to give my creative drives such freedom.

ASHBE:  Ha, ha, ha, I'll work on my potholder set a bit.

JOHN POLK:  What time is it? I've really got to check on the time.

ASHBE:  I know. I'll call the time operator.

(*She goes to the phone*)

JOHN POLK:  How do you get along without a clock?

ASHBE:  Well, I've been late for school a lot. Daddy has a watch. It's 11:03.

JOHN POLK:  I've got a while yet. (*Ashbe twirls back to her chair, drops, and sighs*) Are you a dancer, too?

ASHBE:  (*Delighted*) I can't dance a bit, really. I practice a lot is all, at home in the afternoon. I imagine you go to a lot of dances.

JOHN POLK:  Not really, I'm a terrible dancer. I usually get bored or drunk.

ASHBE:  You probably drink too much.

JOHN POLK:  No, it's just since I've come to college. All you do there is drink more beer and write more papers.

ASHBE:   What are you studying for to be?

JOHN POLK:   I don't know.

ASHBE:   Why don't you become a rancher?

JOHN POLK:   Dad wants me to help run his soybean farm.

ASHBE:   Soybean farm. Yikes, that's really something. Where is it?

JOHN POLK:   Well, I live in the Delta, Hollybluff, Mississippi. Anyway, Dad feels I should go to business school first; you know, so I'll become, well, management-minded. Pass the blue.

ASHBE:   Is that what you really want to do?

JOHN POLK:   I don't know. It would probably be as good as anything else I could do. Dad makes good money. He can take vacations whenever he wants. Sure it'll be a ball.

ASHBE:   I'd hate to have to be management-minded. (*John Polk shrugs*) I don't mean to hurt your feelings, but I would really hate to be a management mind. (*She starts walking on her knees, twisting her fists in front of her eyes, and making clicking sounds as a management mind would make*)

JOHN POLK:   Cut it out. Just forget it. The farm could burn down, and I wouldn't even have to think about it.

ASHBE:   (*After a pause*) Well, what do you want to talk about?

JOHN POLK:   I don't know.

ASHBE:   When was the last dance you went to?

JOHN POLK:   Dances. That's a great subject. Let's see, oh, I don't really remember—it was probably some blind date. God, I hate dates.

ASHBE:   Why?

JOHN POLK:   Well, they always say that they don't want popcorn, and they wind up eating all of yours.

ASHBE:   You mean, you hate dates just because they eat your popcorn? Don't you think that's kind of stingy?

JOHN POLK:   It's the principle of the thing. Why can't they just say, yes, I'd like some popcorn when you ask them. But, no, they're always so damn coy.

ASHBE:   I'd tell my date if I wanted popcorn. I'm not that immature.

JOHN POLK:   Anyway, it's not only the popcorn. It's a lot of little things. I've finished coloring. What do I do now?

ASHBE:   Now you have to fold it. Here . . . like this. (*She explains the process with relish*) Say, that's really something.

JOHN POLK: It's kind of funny looking. (*Putting the hat on*) Yeah, I like it, but you could never wear it anywhere.

ASHBE: Well, like what anyway?

JOHN POLK: Huh?

ASHBE: The things dates do to you that you don't like, the little things.

JOHN POLK: Oh, well, just the way they wear those false eyelashes and put their hand on your knee when you're trying to parallel park, and keep on giggling and going off to the bathroom with their girl friends. It's obvious they don't want to go out with me. They just want to go out so that they can wear their new clothes and won't have to sit on their ass in the dormitory. They never want to go out with me. I can never even talk to them.

ASHBE: Well, you can talk to me, and I'm a girl.

JOHN POLK: Well, I'm really kind of drunk, and you're a stranger . . . well, I probably wouldn't be able to talk to you tomorrow. That makes a difference.

ASHBE: Maybe it does. (*A bit of a pause and then extremely pleased by the idea she says*) You know we're alike because I don't like dances either.

JOHN POLK: I thought you said you practiced . . . in the afternoons.

ASHBE: Well, I like dancing. I just don't like dances. At least not like . . . well, not like the one our school was having tonight . . . they're so corny.

JOHN POLK: Yeah, most dances are.

ASHBE: All they serve is potato chips and fruit punch, and then this stupid baby band plays and everybody dances around thinking they're so hot. I frankly wouldn't dance there. I would prefer to wait till I am invited to an exclusive ball. It doesn't really matter which ball, just one where they have huge, golden chandeliers and silver fountains, and serve delicacies of all sorts and bubble blue champagne. I'll arrive in a pink silk cape. (*Laughing*) I want to dance in pink!

JOHN POLK: You're mixed up. You're probably one of those people that live in a fantasy world.

ASHBE: I do not. I accept reality as well as anyone. Anyway, you can talk to me, remember. I know what you mean by the kind of girls it's hard to talk to. There are girls a lot that way in the small clique at my school. Really tacky and mean. They expect everyone to be as stylish as they are, and they won't even speak to you in the hall. I don't mind if they don't speak to me, but I really love the orphans, and it hurts my feelings when they are so mean to them.

JOHN POLK: What do you mean—they're mean to the "orpheens?" (*Giggles to himself at the wordplay*)

ASHBE: Oh, well, they sometimes snicker at the orphans' dresses. The orphans' usually have hand-me-down, drab, ugly dresses. Once Shelly Maxwell wouldn't let Glinda borrow her pencil, even though she had two. It hurt her feelings.

JOHN POLK: Are you best friends with these orphans?

ASHBE: I hardly know them at all. They're really shy. I just like them a lot. They're the reason I put spells on the girls in the clique.

JOHN POLK: Spells, what do you mean, witch spells?

ASHBE: Witch spells? Not really, mostly just voodoo.

JOHN POLK: Are you kidding? Do you really do voodoo?

ASHBE: Sure, here I'll show you my doll. (*Goes to get doll, comes back with straw voodoo doll. Her air as she returns is one of frightening mystery*) I know a lot about the subject. Cora, she used to wash dishes in the Moonlight Cafe, told me all about voodoo. She's a real expert on the subject, went to all the meetings and everything. Once she caused a man's throat to rot away and turn almost totally black. She's moved to Chicago now.

JOHN POLK: It doesn't really work. Does it?

ASHBE: Well, not always. The thing about voodoo is that both parties have to believe in it for it to work.

JOHN POLK: Do the girls in school believe in it?

ASHBE: Not really, I don't think. That's where my main problem comes in. I have to make the clique believe in it, yet I have to be very subtle. Mainly, I give reports in English class or Speech.

JOHN POLK: Reports?

ASHBE: On voodoo.

JOHN POLK: That's really kind of sick, you know.

ASHBE: Not really. I don't cast spells that'll do any real harm. Mainly, just the kind of thing to make them think . . . to keep them on their toes. (*Blue-drink intoxication begins to take over and John Polk begins laughing*) What's so funny?

JOHN POLK: Nothing. I was just thinking what a mean little person you are.

ASHBE: Mean! I'm not mean a bit.

JOHN POLK:   Yes, you are mean . . . (*Picking up color*) . . and green too.

ASHBE:   Green?

JOHN POLK:   Yes, green with envy of those other girls; so you play all those mean little tricks.

ASHBE:   Envious of those other girls, that stupid, close-minded little clique!

JOHN POLK:   Green as this marshmallow. (*Eats marshmallow*)

ASHBE:   You think I want to be in some group . . . a sheep like you? A little sheep like you that does everything when he's supposed to do it!

JOHN POLK:   Me a sheep . . . I do what I want!

ASHBE:   Ha! I've known you for an hour and already I see you for the sheep you are!

JOHN POLK:   Don't take your green meanness out on me.

ASHBE:   Not only are you a sheep, you are a NORMAL sheep. Give me back my colors! (*Begins snatching colors away*)

JOHN POLK:   (*Pushing colors at her*) Green and mean! Green and mean! Green and mean!

ASHBE:   (*Throwing marshmallows at him*) That's the reason you're in a fraternity and the reason you're going to manage your mind. And dates . . . you go out on dates merely because it's expected of you even though you have a terrible time. That's the reason you go to the whorehouse to prove you're a normal man. Well, you're much too normal for me.

JOHN POLK:   Infant bitch. You think you're really cute.

ASHBE:   That really wasn't food coloring in your drink, it was poison! (*She laughs, he picks up his coat to go, and she stops throwing marshmallows at him*) Are you going? I was only kidding. For Christ sake, it wasn't really poison. Come on, don't go. Can't you take a little friendly criticism?

JOHN POLK:   Look, did you have to bother me tonight? I had enough problems without . . .

(*Phone rings. Both look at phone, it rings for the third time. He stands undecided*)

ASHBE:   Look, wait, we'll make it up. (*She goes to answer phone*) Hello . . . Daddy. How are you? . . . I'm fine . . . Dad, you sound funny . . . What? . . . Come on, Daddy, you know she's not here. (*Pause*) Look, I told you I wouldn't call anymore. You've got her number in Atlanta. (*Pause, as she sinks to the floor*) Why have you started again? . . . Don't say that. I can tell it. I can. Hey, I have to go to bed now, I don't want to talk anymore, okay? (*Hangs up phone, then softly to self*) God-damnit.

JOHN POLK: (*He has heard the conversation and is taking off his coat*) Hey, Ashbe . . . (*She looks at him blankly, her mind far away*) You want to talk?

ASHBE: No. (*Slight pause*) Why don't you look at my shell collection? I have this special shell collection. (*She shows him collection*)

JOHN POLK: They're beautiful, I've never seen colors like this. (*Ashbe is silent, he continues to himself*) I used to go to Biloxi a lot when I was a kid . . . One time my brother and I, we camped out on the beach. The sky was purple. I remember it was really purple. We ate pork and beans out of a can. I'd always kinda wanted to do that. Every night for about a week after I got home, I dreamt about these waves foaming over my head and face. It was funny. Did you find these shells or buy them?

ASHBE: Some I found, some I bought. I've been trying to decipher their meaning. Here, listen, do you hear that?

JOHN POLK: Yes.

ASHBE: That's the soul of the sea. (*She listens*) I'm pretty sure it's the soul of the sea. Just imagine when I decipher the language. I'll know all the secrets of the world.

JOHN POLK: Yeah, probably you will. (*Looking into the shell*) You know, you were right.

ASHBE: What do you mean?

JOHN POLK: About me, you were right. I am a sheep, a normal one. I've been trying to get out of it, but now I'm as big a sheep as ever.

ASHBE: Oh, it doesn't matter. You're company. It was rude of me to say.

JOHN POLK: No, because it was true. I really didn't want to go into a fraternity, I didn't even want to go to college, and I sure as hell don't want to go back to Hollybluff and work the soybean farm till I'm eighty.

ASHBE: I still say you could work on a ranch.

JOHN POLK: I don't know. I wanted to be a minister or something good, but I don't even know if I believe in God.

ASHBE: Yeah.

JOHN POLK: I never used to worry about being a failure. Now I think about it all the time. It's just I need to do something that's . . . fulfilling.

ASHBE: Fulfilling, yes, I see what you mean. Well, how about college? Isn't it fulfilling? I mean, you take all those wonderful classes, and you have all your very good friends.

JOHN POLK: Friends, yeah, I have some friends.

ASHBE: What do you mean?

JOHN POLK: Nothing . . . well, I do mean something. What the hell, let me try to explain. You see it was my "friends," the fraternity guys that set me up with G.G., excuse me, Myrtle, as a gift for my eighteenth birthday.

ASHBE: You mean, you didn't want the appointment?

JOHN POLK: No, I didn't want it. Hey, ah, where did my blue drink go?

ASHBE: (*As she hands him the drink*) They probably thought you really wanted to go.

JOHN POLK: Yeah, I'm sure they gave a damn what I wanted. They never even asked me. Hell, I would have told them a handkerchief, a pair of argyle socks, but, no, they have to get me a whore just because it's a cool-ass thing to do. They make me sick. I couldn't even stay at the party they gave. All the sweaty T-shirts, and moron sex stories . . . I just couldn't take it.

ASHBE: Is that why you were at the Blue Angel so early?

JOHN POLK: Yeah, I needed to get drunk, but not with them. They're such creeps.

ASHBE: Gosh, so you really don't want to go to Myrtle's?

JOHN POLK: No, I guess not.

ASHBE: Then are you going?

JOHN POLK: (*Pause*) Yes.

ASHBE: That's wrong. You shouldn't go just to please them.

JOHN POLK: Oh, that's not the point anymore, maybe at first it was, but it's not anymore. Now I have to go for myself . . . to prove to myself that I'm not afraid.

ASHBE: Afraid? (*Slowly, as she begins to grasp his meaning*) You mean, you've never slept with a girl before?

JOHN POLK: Well, I've never been in love.

ASHBE: (*In amazement*) You're a virgin?

JOHN POLK: Oh, God.

ASHBE: No, don't feel bad, I am too.

JOHN POLK: I thought I should be in love . . .

ASHBE: Well, you're certainly not in love with Myrtle. I mean, you haven't even met her.

JOHN POLK:    I know, but, God, I thought maybe I'd never fall in love. What then? You should experience everything . . . shouldn't you? Oh, what's it matter, everything's so screwed.

ASHBE:    Screwed? Yeah, I guess it is. I mean, I always thought it would be fun to have a lot of friends who gave parties and go to dances all dressed up. Like the dance tonight . . . it might have been fun.

JOHN POLK:    Well, why didn't you go?

ASHBE:    I don't know. I'm not sure it would have been fun. Anyway, you can't go . . . alone.

JOHN POLK:    Oh, you need a date?

ASHBE:    Yeah, or something.

JOHN POLK:    Say, Ashbe, ya wanna dance here?

ASHBE:    No, I think we'd better discuss your dilemma.

JOHN POLK:    What dilemma?

ASHBE:    Myrtle. It doesn't seem right you should . . .

JOHN POLK:    Let's forget Myrtle for now. I've got a while yet. Here have some more of this blue-moon drink.

ASHBE:    You're only trying to escape through artificial means.

JOHN POLK:    Yeah, you got it. Now come on. Would you like to dance? Hey, you said you liked to dance.

ASHBE:    You're being ridiculous.

JOHN POLK:    (*Winking at her*) Dance?

ASHBE:    John Polk, I just thought . . .

JOHN POLK:    Hmm?

ASHBE:    How to solve your problem . . .

JOHN POLK:    Well . . .

ASHBE:    Make love to me!

JOHN POLK:    What?!

ASHBE:    It all seems logical to me. It would prove you weren't scared, and you wouldn't be doing it just to impress others.

JOHN POLK:    Look, I . . . I mean, I hardly know you . . .

ASHBE:    But we've talked. It's better this way, really. I won't be so apt to point out your mistakes.

JOHN POLK:    I'd feel great, stripping a twelve-year-old of her virginity.

ASHBE:    I'm sixteen! Anyway, I'd be stripping you of yours just as well. I'll go put on some Tiger Claw perfume. (*She runs out*)

JOHN POLK:   Hey, come back! Tiger Claw perfume, Christ.

ASHBE:   (*Entering*) I think one should have different scents for different moods.

JOHN POLK:   Hey, stop spraying that! You know I'm not going to . . . well, you'd get neurotic, or pregnant, or some damn thing. Stop spraying, will you!

ASHBE:   Pregnant? You really think I could get pregnant?

JOHN POLK:   Sure, it'd be a delightful possibility.

ASHBE:   It really wouldn't be bad. Maybe I would get to go to Tokyo for an abortion. I've never been to the Orient.

JOHN POLK:   Sure getting cut on is always a real treat.

ASHBE:   Anyway, I might just want to have my dear baby. I could move to Atlanta with Mama and Madeline. It'd be wonderful fun. Why I could take him to the supermarket, put him in one of those little baby seats to stroll him about. I'd buy peach baby food and feed it to him with a tiny golden spoon. Why I could take colored pictures of him and send them to you through the mail. Come on . . . (*Starts putting pillows onto the couch*) Well, I guess you should kiss me for a start. It's only etiquette, everyone begins with it.

JOHN POLK:   I don't think I could even kiss you with a clear conscience. I mean, you're so small with those little cat-eye glasses and curly hair . . . I couldn't even kiss you.

ASHBE:   You couldn't even kiss me? I can't help it if I have to wear glasses. I got the prettiest ones I could find.

JOHN POLK:   Your glasses are fine. Let's forget it, okay?

ASHBE:   I know, my lips are too purple, but if I eat carrots, the dye'll come off and they'll be orange.

JOHN POLK:   I didn't say anything about your lips being too purple.

ASHBE:   Well, what is it? You're just plain chicken, I suppose . . .

JOHN POLK:   Sure, right, I'm chicken, totally chicken. Let's forget it. I don't know how, but, somehow, this is probably all my fault.

ASHBE:   You're darn right it's all your fault! I want to have my dear baby or at least get to Japan. I'm so sick of school I could smash every marshmallow in sight! (*She starts smashing*) Go on to your skinny pimple whore. I hope the skinny whore laughs in your face, which she probably will because you have an easy face to laugh in.

JOHN POLK:   You're absolutely right, she'll probably hoot

and howl her damn fizzle red head off. Maybe you can wait outside the door and hear her, give you lots of pleasure, you sadistic, little thief.

ASHBE: Thief! Was Robin Hood . . . Oh, what's wrong with this world? I just wasn't made for it, is all. I've probably been put in the wrong world, I can see that now.

JOHN POLK: You're fine in this world.

ASHBE: Sure, everyone just views me as an undesirable lump.

JOHN POLK: Who?

ASHBE: You, for one.

JOHN POLK: (*Pause*) You mean because I wouldn't make love to you?

ASHBE: It seems clear to me.

JOHN POLK: But you're wrong, you know.

ASHBE: (*To self, softly*) Don't pity me.

JOHN POLK: The reason I wouldn't wasn't that . . . it's just that . . . well, I like you too much to.

ASHBE: You like me?

JOHN POLK: Undesirable lump, Jesus. You're cheeks they're . . . they're . . .

ASHBE: My cheeks? They're what?

JOHN POLK: They're rosy.

ASHBE: My cheeks are rosy?˙

JOHN POLK: Yeah, your cheeks, they're really rosy.

ASHBE: Well, they're natural, you know. Say, would you like to dance?

JOHN POLK: Yes.

ASHBE: I'll turn on the radio. (*She turns on radio. Ethel Waters is heard singing "Honey in the Honeycomb." Ashbe begins snapping her fingers*) Yikes, let's jazz it out.

(*They dance*)

JOHN POLK: Hey, I'm not good or anything . . .

ASHBE: John Polk.

JOHN POLK: Yeah?

ASHBE: Baby, I think you dance fine!

(*They dance on, laughing, saying what they want till end of song. Then a radio announcer comes on and says the 12:00 news will be in five minutes. Billie Holiday or Terry Pierce, begins singing, "Am I Blue?"*)

JOHN POLK: Dance?

ASHBE: News in five minutes.

JOHN POLK:   Yeah.

ASHBE:   That means five minutes till midnight.

JOHN POLK:   Yeah, I know.

ASHBE:   Then you're not . . .

JOHN POLK:   Ashbe, I've never danced all night. Wouldn't it be something to . . . to dance all night and watch the rats come out of the gutter?

ASHBE:   Rats?

JOHN POLK:   Don't they come out at night? I hear New Orleans has lots of rats.

ASHBE:   Yeah, yeah, it's got lots of rats.

JOHN POLK:   Then let's dance all night and wait for them to come out.

ASHBE:   All right . . . but, but how about our feet?

JOHN POLK:   Feet?

ASHBE:   They'll hurt.

JOHN POLK:   Yeah.

ASHBE:   (*Smiling*) Okay, then let's dance.

(*He takes her hand, and they dance as lights black out and the music soars and continues to play*)

End

*Norman Holland*

# MORE LIVES THAN ONE

# Norman Holland

The premiere publication of *More Lives Than One* in this collection marks a forty-five year span of play publications for British dramatist Norman Holland. Since his first published play, *The High-Backed Chair*, in the British *Best One-Act Plays of 1938*, Mr. Holland has published seventy-two plays, a book on playwriting, and four play collections . . . one with a foreword by Sir Ralph Richardson. Ten of his plays have been made into films or televised, and twenty-seven, broadcast on radio. His plays have received twenty-six awards and have been performed worldwide with translations into a dozen languages. In 1968 his play *The Small Private World of Michael Marston* appeared in this series, and he adapted Leo Knowles' *The Last Victim* for the 1974 edition.

One of Mr. Holland's seven published full-length plays, *The Militants*—about the English suffragettes—has been performed widely in the British Isles, and additionally in Canada, Australia, New Zealand, Hong Kong, and Sweden. During Queen Elizabeth's Silver Jubilee, Mr. Holland wrote a play about Queen Elizabeth I—*Princess Ascending*—and after presenting published copies to the Queen, was assured by Buckingham Palace that Her Majesty "read your play with interest."

A gentleman of wide experience, Mr. Holland has served as a press officer, an advertising copywriter, and a scriptwriter; and was employed in the British Government Service, engaged in the promotion of British participation in overseas trade fairs. He served in World War II for six years, two months, and ten days, ending his service by lecturing on drama at an Army school. He lectured on playwriting for seven years at London's City Literary Institute, has acted with amateur and professional repertory companies, and occasionally directed productions. He also exercised an early ambition to be a heavy-weight boxing champion by winning thirty-eight fights as an amateur—twenty-six of these "inside the distance."

His interest in Oscar Wilde produced two full-length plays: *To Meet Oscar Wilde*, premiered in Bad Homburg, West Germany, by the International Theatre Workshop in 1981; and *Years of the Locust*, premiered to glowing reviews by the Trinity Square Repertory Company in Providence, Rhode Island in 1968. *More Lives Than One*—focusing on Wilde's last days in prison—was first staged on March 18, 1980, as one of three winners in a competition organized by the Bromley Little

Theatre and was voted best play by the audiences during its two-week run. Additional awards came from the Southampton Theatre Guild and the London Abbey Community Centre.

The author and his wife live in Wimbledon, a suburb of London, where moments away from writing are devoted to gardening.

Mr. Holland dedicates this play: "For Paul Solcumb-Rolley."

*For he who lives more lives than one*
*More deaths than one must die.*
Oscar Wilde
*The Ballad of Reading Gaol*

## Characters:

MAJOR NELSON
"FINGERS" BENNETT
MARTIN, *a warder*
OSCAR WILDE
THE CHIEF WARDER
DAVEY CROSS
CONSTANCE WILDE
THE VOICE OF AUTHORITY
OURSELVES, *the prison visitors*

## Time:

*From the latter half of 1896 to May 17, 1897.*

## Scene:

*The setting provides three locales in Reading Gaol: the cell of Oscar Wilde, the Governor's Office, and a neutral central area. The cell contains a prison bed and a stool. In the Governor's Office are a desk, desk chair, and a visitor's chair. The neutral area accommodates scenes from other areas of the prison. The surrounding walls—with entrances left and right behind the cell and office—provide an uncertain, disturbing dimension to what lies beyond the prison.*

*Footsteps echo, cell doors clang. Abruptly, the noises cease and the voice of Major Nelson, Governor of the prison, is heard:*

NELSON: This is Reading Gaol in the year 1896. Major Nelson, the Governor, speaking. You are here to witness the closing stages of the two-year sentence served here by Oscar

Wilde for acts of gross indecency contrary to the Criminal Law Amendment Act of 1885.

*(Light comes up on the neutral area to reveal Fingers Bennett, a prisoner. His situation and the prison uniform cannot disguise the fact that he is quick-witted, sly, and a born survivor. He looks out front and registers shocked surprise when he sees us. The Voice of Authority announces)*

VOICE: So this is Fingers, Fingers Bennett!

FINGERS: What are you doing out there?
It's no good trying to hide.
What are you doing out there
When you ought to be inside?

I see you! Oh, I see you!
Not one of you worth a pin.
I see you! Oh, I see you!
Everyone steeped in sin.

Hypocrites beyond compare,
Innocent until you're tried—
What are you doing out there
When you ought to be inside?

Lust, envy and adultery,
False witness you have spoken;
All of God's commandments
From one to ten you've broken.

You're each and all as bad as me
Of that there is no doubt—
The only difference I can see
Is that I was found out.

*(Martin, a warder, has entered and stands regarding him)*

MARTIN: So you're back again, Fingers?

FINGERS: *(Turning)* Oh, hullo, Tom. Yes, came in yesterday when you were off duty. You hear how I got done on Lewes Racecourse?

MARTIN: Not a word.

FINGERS: Just listen to this. There I was in the paddock just after the fourth race with enough loot to keep me for a year.

MARTIN: That's when you should have beat it, Fingers.

FINGERS: *(Irritably)* I know that now. Well, I spotted this bloke. Biggish feller. Heavy moustache. I was just going to ease over to him when he drifts across to me. I stumbles against him (*He illustrates, using Martin as a model*), gives him the treatment, apologises, pats him, brushes him off, and helps myself to his watch, wallet, and tiepin. Then, just as I was turning away . . .

MARTIN: You felt a hand on your shoulder.

FINGERS: You're dead to rights, mate. "Come with me, Fingers," he says, "Let's step into the Steward's Tent." He had me by the arm so I hadn't a great deal of choice. Know who it was? (*Martin shakes his head*) It was Superintendent Roberts.

MARTIN: But he did you four years ago at Epsom.

FINGERS: I know. And I thought I had a memory for faces. Anyway, it was five years since. He wasn't even on duty. That's the worst of coppers—they won't live and let live.

MARTIN: What did they give you?

FINGERS: Three years—thank you very much. And that's not the worst. They've barred me for life from Lewes Racecourse and, after Epsom, it's my favourite.

MARTIN: Time you gave it up, Fingers.

FINGERS: What else is there?

MARTIN: Come on—you've got to have a bath.

FINGERS: All right. All right. You trying to teach me prison routine?

MARTIN: This way then.

FINGERS: Just a minute, Tom. (*Surprised, Martin looks back*) Present for you. Catch. (*He throws a small object to Martin who catches it and stares at it incredulously*)

MARTIN: Why, it's my whistle!

FINGERS: Just keeping in practice, Tom. Remember when I was patting you. (*He shakes an admonitory finger*) You look out for yourself. It wouldn't do for it to get about that *anybody* could frisk you. (*As Martin is restoring the whistle to his pocket, Fingers moves toward exit*) I thought you was in a hurry. Come on.

(*He goes with Martin following. Light Out on the neutral area. Light up on cell where Oscar Wilde is seated on the bed. The Voice of Authority calls out loudly*)

VOICE: Get a move on there! Empty those chamber pots!

OSCAR: (*Confused, Oscar rises*) Oh, yes! Oh, yes! At once!

(*He rummages under the bed, produces a chamber pot and has just regained the perpendicular when the Voice is heard again*)

VOICE:   C—Three—Three! Stand by for the Governor's visit!

(*Oscar stands irresolute, holding the chamber pot and comes slowly, sloppily, to attention as Major Nelson enters. Nelson is a man of thirty-six, youthful looking and slight but with an air of quiet authority appropriate to his position. He is carrying a clipboard with some papers held by it*)

NELSON:   Good morning, Wilde.

OSCAR:   You're not . . . not . . .

NELSON:   Oh yes, I am. I am the new Governor. My name is Nelson—Major Nelson. I took over yesterday afternoon and I have availed myself of the first opportunity to come and see you. (*He eyes the chamber pot with marked distaste*) Do you think you could get rid of that . . . thing for a few minutes?

OSCAR:   Oh, yes . . . yes. Right away, sir. (*Hurriedly, he restores the chamber pot to its former resting place under the bed. Then he resumes his former posture*)

NELSON:   Please stand at ease. That is, if you *are* supposed to be standing at attention.

OSCAR:   (*Relaxing*) It is difficult to tell, sir. Part of the trouble is these clothes. They are quite unable to come to attention. Also, it is not a position I find natural to me.

NELSON:   I see. I have been curious to see the most distinguished of my charges. Do you know that the correspondence about you has assumed such proportions that you have a large file to yourself?

OSCAR:   I am not in the least surprised, sir.

NELSON:   In addition, I have heard a great deal about you from Major Isaacson.

OSCAR:   I'm sure you did, sir.

NELSON:   Nothing he said will influence me. One of my first duties has been to study the somewhat extended letter you have been writing to Lord Alfred Douglas over these past weeks. (*Oscar reacts*) Oh, don't be alarmed. Your work is in safekeeping. I have to read it as part of my official duty.

OSCAR:   Will it be returned to me, sir?

NELSON:   Most certainly—when you are released. But I . . . well . . . Never mind. May I say how pleased I am you are writing again.

OSCAR:   Thank you, sir.

NELSON:   My visit this morning, however, is primarily concerned with your work for Her Majesty's Government.

OSCAR:   Oh, dear!

NELSON:   Your work has been something less than satisfactory. For instance, you rarely seem to have fulfilled your quota of oakum picking.

OSCAR:   It was not a task to which I could give my mind, sir.

NELSON:   Oakum picking is not intended to be mentally stimulating.

OSCAR:   I wish you could tell me its purpose, sir.

NELSON:   It has no purpose—it merely provides an occupation. (*He studies the clipboard in his hand*) Then I see you were put to bookbinding.

OSCAR:   That was one of Major Isaacson's less happy inspirations. He was so naive that he thought a writer would know how to bind books. As well expect a musician to construct a piano. No. Bookbinding calls for a degree of manual dexterity which I do not possess. Indeed, in such matters I have a natural clumsiness so remarkable that it amounts almost to a gift.

NELSON:   Have you indeed? You pose a problem. I look at this (*He indicates the clipboard*) and I look at you and I ask myself, "What am I to do with him?"

OSCAR:   I sympathize with you in your dilemma, sir.

NELSON:   There is a job I have in mind for you. Would you care to be the schoolmaster's orderly?

OSCAR:   What would be my duties, sir?

NELSON:   Well, they would not involve any degree of manual dexterity.

OSCAR:   I am relieved to hear it.

NELSON:   In fact, they would be purely nominal. But you would have charge of the library.

OSCAR:   (*Kindling*) The library?

NELSON:   Do you find the proposal attractive?

OSCAR:   I cannot tell you how attractive, sir.

NELSON:   Then perhaps we can discuss the matter in my office this afternoon.

OSCAR:   Your office?

NELSON:   Have you any objection?

OSCAR:   No . . . no. It is only that all my previous visits to the Governor's office have been for the purpose of receiving punishment.

NELSON:   This time it will be different. (*He goes to the limit of the light, pauses and looks back*) I have something to ask you but perhaps the question is indiscreet so early in our acquaintance.

OSCAR:   Questions are never indiscreet. Answers sometimes are.

NELSON:   Very well, Although I have said that I am pleased you are writing this marathon letter to Lord Alfred Douglas, I feel bound to ask: why do you find it necessary to revive so much unhappiness and anguish? It is unworthy of the best in you.

OSCAR:   I am touched that you should think so. It is as the result of an action forced upon me by Lord Alfred that I find myself here. It is something I must do for his sake as well as my own.

NELSON:   You deceive yourself. The letter is full of venom and self-pity. Write it, then tear it up. That would be best for all concerned. (*As Oscar is about to speak, he raises his hand*) No, don't say anything. Think about it.

OSCAR:   Yes, sir. But don't expect me to change my mind. I would be going against my nature.

NELSON:   But, surely, that is what you have been doing for this long time past. (*He nods to Oscar in dismissal and goes out. Oscar stands deep in contemplation but is shaken from his musing as the Voice shouts*)

VOICE:   Get moving there, C—Three—Three! You're late! Get that pot emptied!

(*Oscar stoops, collects the chamber pot from under the bed and rushes from the cell. He exits. Light out on cell. Light up on neutral area as Fingers enters. He regards his audience, appears to assess them and announces*)

FINGERS:   It's true I am a criminal
It's true that I robbed and stole.
The good in me is minimal—
I am a perverted soul.

My mother was a bleeding whore.
My father was a screwman.
I never knew my grandmama—

They say she wasn't human.

Every form of felony
My uncle did commit;
They've got him in the jug, but he
Doesn't mind a bit.

My auntie is a procuress
Of credit and renown;
She's got three lovely daughters
And she's put them on the town.

My sister, Sue, is on the game.
Her pimp's my brother, Joe.
They lead a life of utter shame—
But they make a lot of dough.

Neighbours and friends, do not despise
A poor bastard like me—
For how could I be otherwise
With my heredity?

(*Oscar returns carrying the chamber pot. He plunges into the cell and replaces the chamber pot under the bed. Fingers turns as Oscar enters and calls to attract his attention*)

FINGERS:   Whist! Oscar!

OSCAR:   (*Coming into the light*) Yes?

FINGERS:   I was there—at the first night of *The Importance of Being Earnest.*

OSCAR:   (*Delighted*) Were you really? (*Smiling, he regards Fingers*) Wasn't it an altogether glittering occasion? And you were there at the St. James's Theatre that night . . .

FINGERS:   I was there. In the Dress Circle.

OSCAR:   In the Dress Circle . . . Oh, wasn't it one of the most splendid evenings ever? The witty speeches, the amusing situations with the audience hanging on every word . . . the music of the laughter and then the tremendous applause at the final curtain.

FINGERS:   Oh, I didn't wait until then.

OSCAR:   Didn't wait? You left?

FINGERS:   In the interval between Acts One and Two.

OSCAR:   (*Puzzled*) But why? Were you bored?

FINGERS:   No, no. But I couldn't hang about. I was loaded.

OSCAR:   Loaded?

FINGERS:   I was that. I'd been busy. In my pockets I had (*Counting on his fingers*) five fob watches, seven wallets, three sovereign purses, four tiepins, two brooches, and a necklace. (*He nods*) You're right, Oscar. It *was* what you might call a glittering occasion!

(*He nods and exits. Oscar looks after him and proceeds to count on his fingers*)

OSCAR:   Four—no, five fob watches, three sovereign purses, four tiepins, seven wallets, two brooches, and a necklace. (*He shakes his head in admiration*) What a performance! What an artist!

(*He moves into his cell with the light going out on the neutral area and coming up on the cell. The Voice thunders*)

VOICE:   Stand by C—Three—Three! Stand by for a visit from the Chief Warder!

(*Oscar assumes his approximation of attention as the Chief Warder enters and pauses at the entrance to the cell*)

CHIEF:   Everything all right here, C—Three—Three?

OSCAR:   All right, Chief.

CHIEF:   (*Coming into the cell*) Don't stand like that, Mr. Wilde. You know how it upsets me. I thought we'd come to an arrangement.

OSCAR:   I'm sorry. (*He relaxes*) But, when I hear that terrifying announcement . . .

CHIEF:   Don't say that you've come to attention. I've decided you're the one man I've ever met who is physically incapable of coming to attention. Perhaps if I'd had you as a recruit . . .

OSCAR:   Don't make my blood run cold.

CHIEF:   (*Sitting on Oscar's bed*) How are things, Mr. Wilde? Is time hanging heavy with you?

OSCAR:   Not too badly just now—now that I can read and write. Then there's my library work.

CHIEF:   Ah yes, it all helps to relieve the tedium. That's what gets you down.

OSCAR:   I'm sorry about that, Chief.

CHIEF:   You see, I'll be here for years and I haven't committed any crime that I know of—unless serving one's country is a crime. There isn't much that a soldier can turn to when he leaves the Army. We aren't educated men. We haven't got a trade.

OSCAR: Somebody has to do this work and you do it very well.

CHIEF: You think so? You really think so, Mr. Wilde?

OSCAR: I most certainly do. The worst feature is the penal system itself. But even the penal system can be administered humanely as we have seen.

CHIEF: Nobody could call me soft but, when Major Isaacson was here, I used to go home feeling sick and dirty after a spell of duty. Now that can't be right. It's different now.

OSCAR: It is indeed.

CHIEF: (*Rising*) You could do something when you get out. You could write books and articles. You could speak at meetings. You could do a lot to help those still inside.

OSCAR: I'll do my best. I promise.

CHIEF: Half the people don't know what it's like in here and the rest don't care. I'll get along. (*Recollecting*) Oh, yes. (*He puts his hand in his pocket and brings out a paper bag*) My old lady gave me this for my supper and I've more than enough without it. (*He gives the bag to Oscar*) You have it, Mr. Wilde.

OSCAR: Thank you, Chief.

CHIEF: Eating helps to pass the time—if you give your mind to it. It's a pork pie, Mr. Wilde. Very sustaining. I'll leave the door.

(*He nods to Oscar and leaves. Oscar sits on the bed and peers into the bag. He seems baffled by its contents. Rising, Oscar goes to the neutral area which lights up as the light goes out on the cell. He looks up from his continued examination of the paper bag when he is joined by Davey Cross, a feeble-minded, smiling convict*)

OSCAR: Hello, Davey.

DAVEY: Hello, Oscar. I've been working in the garden.

OSCAR: Good for you.

DAVEY: I like working in gardens. (*Then, his face clouding*) It was in a garden where it happened. I was weeding and she ast' me. This girl did.

OSCAR: Asked you?

DAVEY: Yes, ast' me and ast' me to do it. She kept on asting me. But I wouldn't—not at first. When I did do it, she started shouting. People came and she told them I made her do it. Then they took me away and brought me here.

OSCAR: You can't trust women, Davey.

DAVEY: That's a fact. What you got there, Oscar?

OSCAR: I have it on good authority that it is a pork pie, but I'm not sure what I ought to do with it.

DAVEY: Not sure? (*He laughs*) You eat it, Oscar. That's what.

OSCAR: I don't think I'd care to. Would you . . . would you like it?

DAVEY: I would that. Give it here. (*Oscar proffers the bag. Davey fairly snatches it from him, takes out the pie and drops the bag on the floor. He proceeds to devour the pie, watched by Oscar with absorbed interest*)

OSCAR: Is it all right?

DAVEY: (*Nodding and speaking with a full mouth*) Beautiful.

OSCAR: Hardly how I would have described it . . . but each according to his taste. Enjoy it, Davey.

(*He exits. Davey continues to eat the pie. Fingers comes into the neutral area and stands watching Davey. Suddenly, he roars*)

FINGERS: What are you doing there?

(*Davey ceases to chew and stands frozen in terror, holding the remains of the pie away from him. Slowly, he turns his head and relaxes*)

DAVEY: Gawd! I thought they had me!

FINGERS: (*Moving toward him*) Serve you right if they had. What's that you're eating?

DAVEY: Pork pie. Oscar gave it to me.

FINGERS: Then you'd have got him in trouble, too. (*He points to the bag*) Pick that up. (*Davey picks up the bag and, still eating, holds it in his hand*) Put it away, man! Put it away! They mustn't see it. (*Davey thrusts the bag inside his tunic*) Here's you with most of your sentence served and you go and stick your neck out.

DAVEY: Sorry, Fingers.

FINGERS: Don't be sorry for me. Save your sympathy for yourself. Going out soon, aren't you?

DAVEY: (*Smiling*) You know I am.

FINGERS: Shall I tell you how it will be?

DAVEY: Yes, please, Fingers.

FINGERS: Well, first off, you'll get pissed as a newt.

DAVEY: (*Beaming*) That I will. You know me.

FINGERS: Better than you know yourself. Next, you'll run into a bit of stuff. She'll lead you on and, before you know where you are, you'll be back in here.

DAVEY: No, I won't. Not this time.

FINGERS: You said that last time and the time before and the time before that, didn't you?

DAVEY: (*Reluctantly*) Yes.

FINGERS: I'll tell you something, Davey ... (*He leans forward confidentially*) Women will be the death of you. (*Davey can only nod miserably and is turning to walk away when Fingers calls*) Hey! (*Davey turns to find Fingers smiling at him*) But what wonderful way to go, Davey! (*Davey smiles broadly in response and exits, watched by Fingers. When he has gone, Fingers turns to us*)

FINGERS: Poor little sod! You've got to try to cheer him up!

(*Then he follows Davey out. Light out on the neutral area and up on the office where Nelson is seated at the desk. Martin comes in with a tray upon which are a coffee pot, cream, sugar, and two cups*)

MARTIN: The coffee, sir, as you ordered it, and the prisoners are outside.

NELSON: I'll see the first of them. Send him in.

(*Martin exits, and, a moment later, Oscar enters from the same direction. Oscar comes to his travesty of attention and announces*)

OSCAR: C—Three—Three, sir.

NELSON: Oh, good evening, Wilde. Do sit down. (*Oscar sits on the visitor's chair.*) Is all well with the library?

OSCAR: Very well. I'll be submitting a further booklist shortly.

NELSON: I shall look forward to seeing it. (*He inspects the coffee tray*) It seems they have left two cups. Oh, well ... Do help yourself to coffee.

OSCAR: (*Incredulous*) Coffee!

NELSON: In preparation for your release. Come now. (*Thus urged, Oscar pours a cup of coffee and glances at Nelson*) I won't just now. (*Oscar adds sugar and cream. He sits down to sip the coffee with an expression of bliss. As convenient during the rest of the scene, he replenishes his cup*) It is my function at these talks to give such personal news as may be considered fitting. If I add some news of a more general character, that is my responsibility.

OSCAR: I understand, sir. There's no bad news of my wife ... or the children?

NELSON: No, no. I have to tell you that your Aunt Mary is dead but she was, I understand, an old lady and had been in poor health. Also, you may be interested to learn that Sir Edward Poynter has been appointed President of the Royal Academy. (*Oscar sets down his coffee cup, rises, and turns from Nelson with a distressed expression. Concerned, Nelson also rises*) My dear fellow, I didn't realize . . .

OSCAR:   (*Turning to him*) It was very kind of you, sir, to tell me of my Aunt Mary's death but you might have broken the news of Poynter's appointment a little more delicately.

NELSON:   (*Laughing*) You are a scoundrel! I was quite taken in.

OSCAR:   Sir Edward is so supremely unfitted for the office that one can only assume that those who appointed him were activated by malicious humour and cynical disregard for the consequences of their utterly mistaken action. (*He sits again and takes up his coffee cup*)

NELSON:   He is, in fact, a very able man.

OSCAR:   Not in my book. He suffers from a lack of imagination and that is unforgivable to one in his position.

NELSON:   How do you feel as the date of your release draws nearer?

OSCAR:   Alternatively excited and depressed. . . Continually apprehensive . . .

NELSON:   Quite understandable. Everybody feels much the same as the day looms nearer.

OSCAR:   They do? (*He sighs*) But other prisoners do not have my problem. I am required to wear a mask, to pretend to be other than I am, to deny my every instinct. I find the prospect daunting and shameful. Is this what is demanded of me? To live a lie? If so, I know myself to be unequal to my part in this spectacle.

NELSON:   You are not to distress yourself. It does seem daunting from here but, once you are outside these walls, it will look vastly different. Are you still reading a chapter of the New Testament each day?

OSCAR:   I am indeed and I find it rewarding: such beauty of language . . . such depth of philosophy. One has heard so much of people who have sought help, advice, and reassurance by opening the Bible at random and reading the first passage upon which their eyes come to rest. I made the experiment myself yesterday.

NELSON:   And?

OSCAR:   The Book opened at the second chapter of Joel and the words that met my eyes were these: "And I shall restore to you the years that the locust has eaten . . ." Does it mean that God is going to restore to me these years of deprivation and suffering?

NELSON:   I do not think so. These years could not be restored to you. In a sense, they are wasted years but you can give them value by working to make up for the time you have lost.

OSCAR:   You speak, sir, as if opportunity was the only measure of achievement. How do you know if my talent survives?

NELSON:   It is evident from certain passages in the monumental letter you are writing. (*As Oscar reacts*) You know that I have to read it—it is in the book of rules. Write it and tear it up. That would be best for you and everybody else. (*As Oscar is about to protest*) No, don't say anything. Think about it. (*He consults his watch*) We have, as usual, overrun our time. My fault, I enjoy talking to you.

OSCAR:   And I am deeply ashamed to discover that I have drunk all the coffee. You have had none.

NELSON:   You were meant to drink it. I had already had my coffee. (*Smiling, he raises a hand as Oscar seems about to thank him. Then he picks up a small handbell and rings it. Martin enters*) We have finished, Martin. Goodnight, Wilde.

OSCAR:   Goodnight, sir. Thank you.

(*Martin takes the coffee tray and follows Oscar from the Office. Nelson consults a list and again rings the handbell*)

NELSON:   Next prisoner, please.

(*He is awaiting the entrance of the next prisoner as the light fades. The light comes up on the neutral area. The Chief enters the lighted area. He is looking behind him with some concern. Constance Wilde, a pretty and well-dressed woman in her late thirties, joins him. She is carrying a briefcase*)

CHIEF:   Would you care to rest a moment, ma'am?

CONSTANCE:   (*Intimidated by her surroundings, she looks fearfully about her*) If you please . . . Does it always smell like this?

CHIEF:   Afraid so, Ma'am. It's the arrangements—they leave a good deal to be desired.

CONSTANCE:   Do you know my husband?

CHIEF:   Know Mr. Wilde? Indeed, I do—a very fine gentleman who shouldn't be in this place. But he's bearing up very well and has a good deal of his sentence behind him. All right now, ma'am?

CONSTANCE:   Yes. Yes, let us get on. (*Light up on the office with Nelson seated at his desk. The Chief leads the way and announces*)

CHIEF:   Mrs. Wilde, sir. (*He withdraws immediately. Nelson rises*)

NELSON:   Ah, Mrs. Wilde. I am so glad to meet you.

CONSTANCE:   (*Surprised*) But I had expected . . .

NELSON:   Major Isaacson, no doubt. I have replaced him. I am Major Nelson. (*He takes her hand*) There have been changes here—for the better, I like to think. Please sit down. (*She does so. He follows her example*)

CONSTANCE:   My husband . . . is he well?

NELSON:   I would think in better health and spirits than when you saw him last.

CONSTANCE:   That is good news.

NELSON:   And it will do him a power of good to see you— even in the unhappy circumstances.

CONSTANCE:   I thought it better that I should—

NELSON:   No doubt about it. Also, it seems that your visit is timely when one considers that the date of his release draws nearer. Today you have an opportunity to discuss your . . . your future arrangements.

CONSTANCE:   That is what I had in mind.

NELSON:   If I could just offer you a word of advice . . .

CONSTANCE:   Yes?

NELSON:   Men in his situation are especially sensitive. He will need all the understanding you can give him at this time. (*He smiles*) But I'm preaching to the converted. You'll know just what to say . . . just how to reassure him.

CONSTANCE:   But we've only just met. How can you be so sure?

NELSON:   In time, one becomes a judge of character merely by sitting behind this desk. I consider Mr. Wilde most fortunate to have you waiting for him. Mr. Wilde will be here shortly—I thought it best for you to meet, in the sad circumstances, here in the office. (*He rises, comes round the desk and indicates his own chair*) If you were to sit there . . . (*Constance has risen. She takes his profered hand*) It has been a great pleasure to meet you, Mrs. Wilde.

CONSTANCE:   I am so glad to have met you, Major Nelson.

(*He goes and pauses in the neutral area which becomes lit with his entry. He looks back in her direction*)

NELSON:  So pretty... so charming... Poor woman! (*He exits. Oscar enters, escorted by Martin. They enter the office and the light goes out on the neutral area. Oscar halts when he sees Constance*)

OSCAR:  Constance! (*She rises*) They only told me it was a special visit.

MARTIN:  (*To Oscar*) Would you sit, please? (*Oscar sits in the visitor's chair*) You are to remain seated throughout the interview. (*He then turns to Constance*) I have to be present, ma'am, but I will not interfere unless it becomes necessary.

CONSTANCE:  Thank you.

OSCAR:  It's not the children?

CONSTANCE:  No, they're all right. It's your mother.

OSCAR:  She's not...

CONSTANCE:  She died, Oscar.

OSCAR:  Oh, no! I didn't know she was ill. How did she die?

CONSTANCE:  She caught a chill. It turned to bronchitis and there were complications. She asked for you. They wrote asking if you would be allowed to visit her but the reply, when it came, said it would not be possible.

OSCAR:  (*Stonily*) Not possible.

CONSTANCE:  When they told your mother that the request had been refused, she said, "May the prison help him." She did not speak again.

OSCAR:  Poor Mother! (*His expression changes*) Now I remember. I dreamed of her last night. It seemed she came to me in my cell. She was wearing her hat and coat. I asked her to take them off. She shook her head sadly—and vanished. I woke, slept again, and did not remember until now. It was kind of you, Constance, to come all this way...

CONSTANCE:  I didn't want you to hear officially. I thought it would be better if I told you.

OSCAR:  It is better. Incomparably better. You knew her— knew what she was to me. I shall find time to mourn her. You said the boys were well?

CONSTANCE:  Very well. They're growing, of course—especially Cyril.

OSCAR:  They're getting on at their new school?

CONSTANCE:  Yes.

OSCAR:  And getting used to their new name?

CONSTANCE:   That, too.

OSCAR:   I think of you often, Constance. Sometimes I think of your great responsibility in bringing up the boys.

CONSTANCE:   Then what am I to do, Oscar?

OSCAR:   You must appoint a guardian for them—someone you can trust implicitly. Happily, you can find such a man in your own circle of relatives. Mothers are too indulgent, Constance. One has only to see what his mother has made of Bosie Douglas.

CONSTANCE:   Bosie! Do we have to speak of him? Whenever I hear his ridiculous name, I feel sick to death. I remember what he has done to you . . . to both of us. I should have thought he would have been the last, the very last . . .

OSCAR:   I'm sorry, my dear. I was merely citing him as perhaps the worst example of a spoiled child. Perhaps he'll begin to realize it when he reads the letter I am writing.

CONSTANCE:   (*Rising*) Letter? You're writing a letter to Bosie? What on earth for?

OSCAR:   To show him how horribly he has betrayed our relationship. I want him to know the depth of my suffering, the completeness of my destruction.

CONSTANCE:   If you have the time and the inclination to write, should you not write to me? Or to your sons so that they might arrive at an understanding of your actions? Bosie! When you speak of him, I feel angry (*She sits again*) . . . then sick and wretched.

OSCAR:   So do I . . . and I have more time for dwelling on past misdeeds. But I know I must write to him.

CONSTANCE:   You must do as you please. You say you often think of us. But not, I'm sure, as often as I think of you. I try to reconcile what you told me when I was here before with our lives together . . . with your genius as a writer. And I can't! I just can't!

OSCAR:   I cannot excuse—I can only seek to explain it. What the paradox was to me in literature, I expressed as perversity in my life. It seems to me now . . . inescapable. As an artist, I was impelled to fulfill my nature—every part of it.

CONSTANCE:   Then I hope the satisfaction of having fulfilled your nature compensates you for your misery and ours. If I seem harsh to you, Oscar, you must forgive me but I have had a great deal to bear in this past year.

OSCAR:   (*Cries*) Oh, Constance, you are an angel and my conduct surely deserves the reproach—no, the condemnation—of angels. I hope a time will come when I shall be worthy of your kindness.

CONSTANCE:   Do you think that time will come? Have we any hope of ever being together again? Will you be different when you leave this place?

OSCAR:   I think there is a very real chance of us being together again, but our future depends upon you more than me. Of course, I shall be different. I shall be humbler, more compassionate. But not better—prison does not ennoble.

CONSTANCE:   You don't answer my question. Are you afraid? Will . . . will you live as you did before? Will you be like that again? If so, then . . .

OSCAR:   How can I tell? It is like asking me how I shall conduct myself in the Hereafter?

CONSTANCE:   Answer me! (*She rises*) How are you resolved to live when you leave this place?

OSCAR:   As best I can. I ask myself your questions, Constance, and the answers I get are never the same—which suggests that I am a vacillating creature. This much I know: I have been true to my nature and for that I am being cruelly punished. In another time and another country, I would not have merited punishment.

CONSTANCE:   It seems to me, Oscar, that you are almost beyond help. If you cannot see that you have done wrong and need to amend, then I can see no hope for us.

OSCAR:   My dear, I am what I am. I shall try to be what you wish, but I fear there will be times . . .

CONSTANCE:   Oh, no! If there was only myself to consider . . . (*She sits*) But there are the boys . . .

OSCAR:   The boys . . .

CONSTANCE:   You ask too much, Oscar. You must see that I could not possibly subject myself and the boys to the furtive horror of such an existence. Either you break completely with the past . . .

OSCAR:   (*Rising*) Or else? No need to complete the sentence. The verdict is in your face.

MARTIN:   The prisoner will remain seated.

OSCAR:   Of course. (*He sits again*) You are judge and jury, and you have condemned me before I have committed any crime.

CONSTANCE: You are right to describe yourself as a lord of language. You can make words mean anything you choose. But the spell has ceased to work with me. You have had your chance, Oscar.

OSCAR: Chance? It does not seem so to me. I have been condemned.

CONSTANCE: If you have, it is on your own evidence. I wonder if I have been wrong about you—if I have always been wrong. Because I know what they say about me is true.

OSCAR: What do they say?

CONSTANCE: That I am soft-hearted, stubborn, hopelessly sentimental, reluctant to see what is before my face, unwilling to face things as they are.

OSCAR: Who says this? Who?

CONSTANCE: My relatives, my advisers. They are clearly right about me. They may be right, too, when they say you must serve a probationary period before we can live together again.

OSCAR: You cannot possibly agree with them. (*He watches her face for some sign that she will relent. There is none*) But you do. Perhaps you will be kind enough to explain to me the terms of this probationary period.

CONSTANCE: Yes. A Deed has been drawn up. You are to receive £150 per annum as life interest in my marriage settlement. I'm sorry it is so little but we are not rich . . . and there are the boys.

OSCAR: I understand. In my situation, I must be grateful for any mercies—however small. But I detect a certain hesitancy. The allowance is, perhaps, conditional?

CONSTANCE: Indeed it is. The Deed becomes void if you should be involved in any scandal or if it is proved that you are consorting with any notoriously disreputable persons. I have been asked to emphasize that Lord Alfred Douglas is certainly regarded as "a notoriously disreputable person."

OSCAR: These advisers of yours don't believe in mincing their words, do they, Constance. Is there more?

CONSTANCE: Yes, Oscar. (*She takes a document from the brief-case she is carrying, rises, crosses to Martin, and gives him the document*) Would you give this document to Mr. Wilde, please?

MARTIN: (*After a quick glance at the paper*) Certainly, madam.

(*He goes over to Oscar and hands him the document. Oscar studies it and, while he does so, Constance sits again and Martin resumes his former position. At length, Oscar looks up from the paper in bewilderment*)

OSCAR: Do they really mean all this—that I am to sign away all rights to my children, that I am to lose my sole income if I as much as write to Bosie?

CONSTANCE: Yes, Oscar.

OSCAR: Who is responsible for drawing up this . . . this infamous document?

CONSTANCE: Oscar, my advisers have given instructions . . .

OSCAR: Your advisers!

CONSTANCE: They stipulate a period of probation . . .

OSCAR: A period of probation! Who do they think I am? Probationary period!

(*Constance makes a sign to Martin who goes to her and guides her to the limit of the light. From there, she looks back at Oscar who rises when he sees that Constance is about to leave*)

OSCAR: Constance! Constance! Don't go! Come back! What do they think I am? You cannot mean . . . Who do they think I am? (*But Constance and Martin have gone from the office and Oscar shrieks the last question after them. He crumples the document in his hand and, infinitely dejected, he sits again in the chair. Then he smooths out the document and reads*) "A Deed of Arrangement . . ." (*Then he reads on*) Clauses . . . sub-clauses . . . provisions . . . prohibitions . . . threats . . . punishments and all in the name of justice and conformity. (*He has fallen silent again when Martin returns and comes over to him*)

MARTIN: Mr. Wilde, I am a family man myself and I do understand what this means to you. (*He rummages briefly in his pocket and produces a small object*) Here, take this. (*He thrusts the object into Oscar's hand*)

OSCAR: What is it?

MARTIN: A piece of chocolate. I'll leave you for a minute to two. (*As Oscar regards the chocolate dubiously*) Go on, eat it. It'll . . . it'll comfort you. (*Obediently, Oscar puts the chocolate in his mouth, Mechanically, he munches it. Martin exits. Oscar shakes his head in bleak denial—there is no comfort, no solace to be found anywhere. Light out on the office and up on the neutral area where Nelson is joined by the Chief who salutes*)

NELSON:   At ease, Chief. (*The Chief relaxes*) Is all well?

CHIEF:   No, sir.

NELSON:   What's the trouble?

CHIEF:   It's Wilde, sir. I've been talking to Martin. He has just been present at an interview between Wilde and his wife.

NELSON:   He's not called upon to take note of what is said as long as security is not involved.

CHIEF:   Martin could hardly help himself, sir. Mrs. Wilde asked him to pass a paper to the prisoner.

NELSON:   A paper? He shouldn't have . . .

CHIEF:   Oh, it was a legal document—a Deed of Separation or something of the sort. It seems she agrees to pay him an income if he'll sign away all rights in his children.

NELSON:   You mean he's not to see them? (*The Chief nods*) These sweet, gentle women can be so bloody cruel, Chief.

CHIEF:   They can that, sir.

NELSON:   I'll take a look at him. See you later, Chief.

(*The Chief exits. Light out on neutral area and up on office where Oscar is still sitting in his chair. Nelson enters, goes to his side of the desk, and stands regarding Oscar*)

NELSON:   I heard what happened. How are you?

OSCAR:   As well as can be expected in the circumstances. I have been sitting here endeavouring to adjust to the knowledge that I am considered unfit company for my own children. I have been trying to take in the import of this. (*He waves the Deed in his hand*)

NELSON:   With what result?

OSCAR:   I realize that I have already lived several lives, having been a student, poet, editor, playwright, and prisoner. I have also been a son, a husband, and a father. Each life ends in a little death and all these lives are behind me now. The life I have now to lead is that of an outcast, a pariah.

NELSON:   Understandably, you exaggerate. You need time. Other men have adjusted to your situation.

OSCAR:   With respect, they were not circumstanced as I am. I am shocked to discover that I do not wish to leave this place.

NELSON:   In one way or another, you will survive. A year from now, you will marvel that you ever doubted.

OSCAR:   Let us hope you are right. A year from now, I see myself as shunned by all except my closest friends, dragging out my existence with no means, no urge to write . . . sponging on friends . . . begging from acquaintances. I see myself as becoming demanding, querulous, foolishly extravagant.

NELSON:    But if you see this . . .

OSCAR:    I see and am powerless in the knowledge of my own nature, for I have learned a good deal about myself in this place. In addition, I know myself to be unstable and totally amoral.

NELSON:    If you know this, you can prepare safeguards, erect defences. You have remarkable qualities.

OSCAR:    At the risk of embarrassing me, enumerate them.

NELSON:    I'm not sure that I could offhand . . .

OSCAR:    Oh, come! You underrate yourself.

NELSON:    (*Considering*) Let me see. You are capable of considerable application . . . you are enormously eloquent, wonderfully witty, kind, generous, and loyal to friends.

OSCAR:    My dear sir! What an end-of-term report! Oh, if I could only be accepted again.

NELSON:    You can be. You know you can. And you feel better now? Easier in your mind?

OSCAR:    When you are here, I am appreciably easier in my mind. It is when I am alone . . .

NELSON:    Then you must remember my catalogue of your qualities and my predictions for your future.

OSCAR:    Oh, believe me, I am greatly comforted . . .

NELSON:    There!

OSCAR:    . . . but not entirely convinced.

(*Nelson picks up the handbell and rings it. Martin enters and salutes*)

NELSON:    Conduct the prisoner to his cell. Goodnight.

OSCAR:    Goodnight, sir. And thank you.

(*Light up on the neutral area where the Chief is still waiting*)

NELSON:    Give me the Deed. I'll return it when you leave.

(*Oscar passes the Deed to him and, with Martin leading, they pass through the neutral area. Martin salutes as they pass the Chief and he reciprocates. Martin and Oscar exit. Light goes out on the office as Nelson leaves, enters the neutral area and encounters the Chief who salutes*)

NELSON:    Ah, Chief. You waited. I'm afraid I've been rather a long time.

CHIEF:    How is he, sir? Is he any better?

NELSON:    I'd like to think so. I've helped him to put his fears in perspective.

CHIEF:   And is that a good thing, sir?

NELSON:   A good question, Chief. All I am sure of is that an imagination such as his is not an asset at this time.

CHIEF:   I'm sure you're right, sir. Were you able to help him?

NELSON:   No, I wasn't. Nobody can help him. Nobody. But don't tell him so.

(*He goes out in the direction of the office. The Chief remains and stands looking after him. Light out on the neutral area. Light comes up slowly on the office. Nelson goes to the desk and takes a brown paper parcel and an envelope from a drawer. He is looking at these when the Chief enters and salutes*)

CHIEF:   Good morning, sir.

NELSON:   Good morning, Chief. Is all well?

CHIEF:   Yes, sir. He was fast asleep when Martin called him. I wouldn't have expected that. There's the other prisoner for release this morning, sir.

NELSON:   Oh, yes. C—Seven—Seven. The . . . er . . . the . . . er . . .

CHIEF:   The simple one, sir. I thought you'd like to get him out of the way.

NELSON:   Good idea. Let's have him in. (*The Chief goes to the limit of the lit area and calls*)

CHIEF:   Come in, Davey. (*Light comes up on the neutral area as Davey enters the office. From now until the end of the play, both areas remain lit. Davey is dressed in ragged clothes and carries a brown paper parcel. He is awed by the occasion and looks from one to the other*)

DAVEY:   I'm going out today.

NELSON:   That is what I want to talk to you about. First of all, there's your money.

DAVEY:   (*Smiling*) Yes, they said I'm to have half a sovereign.

NELSON:   That's right. For the work you did while you were here. Sit down. (*Davey sits uncomfortably on the edge of the visitor's chair. Nelson produces a bag from a drawer in the desk from which he takes a coin*)

NELSON:   Here you are.

DAVEY:   Thank you, sir.

NELSON:   (*Pushing across a piece of paper and offering a pen*) Now if you'll just sign there (*He indicates*) that you've received the money.

DAVEY: Sign? (*Doubtfully, he takes the pen*)

NELSON: Can't you write, Davey?

DAVEY: Yes. Leastways, I can write my name. (*Watched by the Chief and Nelson, he makes with some difficulty, two hieroglyphics on the page. Doubtfully, Nelson studies the result*)

NELSON: What is this?

DAVEY: (*Pointing*) That's "D" for Davey and that's a cross for "Cross"—my name. Is it all right?

NELSON: (*Nodding*) Yes . . . yes, I think so. If you'll just witness it, Chief. (*He passes the paper to the Chief who signs it*) As you are being released today, it is my duty as Governor of this prison to have a few words with you. (*He opens a file on the desk*) This is the fifth time you've been in prison, Davey.

DAVEY: (*Nodding*) You've got it right, sir. Been in five times.

NELSON: (*Severely*) And each time for the same offence? Shouldn't you have learned a lesson? What have you to say for yourself?

DAVEY: (*Earnestly*) It's not my fault, sir. It's them—it's the women.

NELSON: The women? (*He looks up at the Chief as if seeking enlightenment*)

DAVEY: (*Increasingly confidential*) They keep after me . . . and after me. They keep on asting me to do it . . . and I don't want to . . . but they keep on and on, and it's the only way to shut them up. So I does it in the end. Then they tells on me and the coppers come and take me away.

NELSON: I see. Well, I want you to promise me that you won't do it again.

DAVEY: Not if they was to ast' me? And keep on asting me?

NELSON: Not even then.

DAVEY: (*Davey considers*) All right. I promise you. (*He holds out his hand to Nelson who, after a momentary hesitation, shakes hands. Davey settles back in his chair*)

DAVEY: But they'll be terrible upset.

NELSON: They must learn that this life is full of disappointments. (*Suddenly, Davey begins to squirm in his chair. He looks acutely uncomfortable, gazes wildly around, rises, and rushes up to the Chief. He whispers in his ear*)

CHIEF: Emergency, sir. Back in a minute.

(*The chief seizes Davey by the arm and hurries him out. Nelson busies himself with papers on his desk. Martin comes in, escorting Fingers)*

MARTIN:   Wait here.

*(Fingers halts at the edge of the lighted area. Martin continues on his way to the desk where he halts and salutes. Nelson looks up and obviously gives permission for Martin to stand at ease. They converse but we do not hear them, for our attention is engaged by Fingers who addresses us directly)*

FINGERS:   Still here, are you? Did you hear that? "Wait here," he said. Why is it always an order and never a request?
What is your verdict now that you've seen
The stupefying and the obscene
Sameness of the prison routine?
Shouldn't all of you thank your lucky stars
That you're there *(Pointing)* and not here
*(Jerking his thumb over his shoulder)* behind bars?
Before you go hence, you should testify:
"There, but for the grace of God, go I."
Wilde leaves here today. What will he find?
That he'll be branded in a world unkind—
An outcast, a criminal, a liar,
Pederast, monster, and pariah.
In a sad situation such as his,
You'd feel the world's against you *(He nods soberly)* . . .
And it is.

*(Now we can hear the exchanges between Nelson and Martin)*

NELSON:   You say I agreed that C—Three—Nine should be present this morning?

MARTIN:   That's what the Chief said, sir.

NELSON:   If he says so, then I must have done, but I have no recollection . . . You'd better bring him in.

*(Martin comes to attention and salutes)*

MARTIN:   Yes, sir.

*(He goes over to Fingers who has relapsed into a trancelike state and who gives a great start when the Warder taps him on the arm. Martin indicates that Fingers is to follow him and the two move toward the desk)*

NELSON:   *(Nelson glances up and, pointing, says to Fingers)* Wait there.

*(Fingers grimaces to draw our attention to this dismissive order and takes up a position behind the desk. Martin goes out and Nelson writes busily. Fingers edges stealthily toward the desk until*

*he is in a position to read what Nelson is writing but, at the sound of approaching footsteps, he moves quickly back to his former position. Escorted by Martin, Oscar enters. He is resplendent in tall hat, frock coat, and patent leather boots. He pauses and Nelson looks up)*

NELSON: You look very smart.

OSCAR: *(Running a hand down his sleeve)* Yes, not too bad. Ah. Fingers . . .

FINGERS: I've got permission to say goodbye, Oscar.

OSCAR: And I'm very glad you have. *(He goes over to him with hand outstretched)* Very glad. *(They shake hands. Fingers makes a brushing movement on Oscar's coat as he says)*

FINGERS: Very nice bit of stuff. You're a credit to us.

OSCAR: *(Smiling, Oscar turns to Nelson who has risen)* What is to be done?

NELSON: If I could just tell you the arrangements . . . *(He sits and his gesture invites Oscar to do likewise)*

OSCAR: By all means. *(He has removed his hat and now places it carefully on the desk)*

NELSON: You will leave presently with the Chief and Martin, and they will escort you to Pentonville where you will be officially released tomorrow. *(He produces a paper from the file on his desk)* Would you please sign this as a receipt for money paid for work done while you have been here? *(He passes a pen to Oscar)*

OSCAR: Most certainly.

NELSON: *(Indicating)* And, while you are about it, kindly sign lower down the page for the Deed and the manuscript which we recently discussed.

OSCAR: *(Signing)* There you are. *(He throws down the pen)*

NELSON: *(Taking a coin from the bag and passing it to Oscar)* And here you are.

OSCAR: *(Contemplating the coin in the palm of his hand)* Thank you. I can justly claim that I have never worked so hard and so long for so little. *(He pockets the coin and rises, Nelson produces the brown paper parcel and the envelope. He passes the envelope to Oscar)*

NELSON: Here is the Deed. *(Oscar stows it in an inner pocket. Then Nelson passes him the parcel)* You know my views on this manuscript. It can only cause trouble, distress, enmity. You know how I think you should dispose of it.

OSCAR: *(Weighing the parcel in his hand)* If anybody could

persuade me, it is you. But I must hold to my purpose or I shall always regret it. (*He places the parcel beside his hat and pauses, struck by a new thought*) I shall see him soon. I shall see Bosie.

DAVEY: (*An obviously relieved Davey precedes the Chief into the lighted area. He halts in surprise on seeing Oscar*) Why, it's Oscar! I wouldn't have known you! (*He walks around Oscar surveying him with admiration*) My, you are a toff! I wouldn't dare to speak to you outside!

OSCAR: I should be most offended if you didn't. I didn't know you were due for release today.

DAVEY: Oh, I got . . . I got . . . (*Defeated, he turns to the Chief*) What was it I got?

CHIEF: Remission. You got remission for good conduct.

OSCAR: I see. Remission. You did well, Davey.

CHIEF: (*Indicating*) If you'll just sign here, Davey . . .

(*Davey goes to the desk and, as before, signs laboriously. The Chief makes a sign to Martin*)

CHIEF: Take him to Reception. Goodbye, Davey.

(*Davey puts down the pen when he has completed his signature. Nelson shakes hands with him, and the Chief does likewise*)

NELSON: Remember what I said.

DAVEY: Yes, I'll remember. (*He glances up and sees Fingers*) Why, Fingers! You going out today?

FINGERS: Not me. I've still got two years to serve. I'll be here when you come back.

DAVEY: I'm not coming back. Not never no more!

FINGERS: You want to bet?

CHIEF: (*Sharply*) We'll have no more of that!

OSCAR: (*Oscar goes over to Davey*) Here, Davey. Please take this as a remembrance. (*He shakes hands with Davey who looks down at the coin in his hand*)

DAVEY: Why, it's a half sovereign! But I have one. I have one already.

OSCAR: Have another and promise me to spend it on drink or some other simple pleasure.

DAVEY: (*Fervently*) I will! Oh, I will!

OSCAR: There's no enjoyment to be had from money spent sensibly. Good luck, Davey.

DAVEY: Good luck, Oscar.

(*Martin leads Davey to the fringe of the lighted area where he looks back*)

DAVEY: I won't do it no more—not even if they was to go down on their bended knees. (*He goes out with Martin following*)

NELSON: If there is one thing certain, it is that he'll be back.

OSCAR: (*Oscar goes over to Fingers*) So good of you to come and see me off.

FINGERS: I hadn't any other pressing engagement.

OSCAR: (*Laughing*) It's still very good of you. (*He claps him on the shoulder*)

FINGERS: And you'll need this when you get outside. (*He hands Oscar a wallet*)

OSCAR: (*Clapping a hand to his pocket*) Good Heavens, my wallet! When did you . . . (*He restores the wallet to his pocket*)

FINGERS: When I was brushing you off. (*He demonstrates*) Remember? You've got to watch out all the time. (*He is suddenly aware that Nelson, the Chief and Martin are all regarding him stonily*) Sorry, gents. Just keeping my hand in. (*He turns back to Oscar. Nelson and the Chief look at each other and shrug helplessly*) Now I'll give you a bit of advice.

OSCAR: I'm all attention.

FINGERS: Don't expect anything from anybody. That way you won't be disappointed.

OSCAR: I'll bear it in mind. The best of luck, Fingers.

FINGERS: And to you, Oscar.

OSCAR: (*Turning back to Nelson*) What now, Major Nelson?

NELSON: That's all. That's all the formalities.

OSCAR: Then I leave you with my thanks for all your forbearance and for your many kindnesses. My imprisonment would have been infinitely more bearable if you had been in charge when I first came here. I shall remember you with gratitude all my life. (*He shakes hands with Nelson*)

NELSON: Take care of yourself and let me have a line when you get to the Continent.

OSCAR: I most certainly will. (*He turns to the Chief*) And you are coming with me . . .

CHIEF: I asked to come. I hope you don't mind.

OSCAR: My dear fellow. I am moved. Quite moved.

CHIEF: Just think of those still inside every now and then.

OSCAR: I will, I promise you. (*Martin returns and takes Oscar's proffered hand*) Thank you for all you have done for me. Think of me sometimes.

MARTIN: I shall never forget you.

*(Oscar goes to the desk where he picks up his hat and the parcel. His expression is thoughtful)*

NELSON:  Are you all right?

OSCAR:  Oh, yes. I was just thinking that there is no justice. In Heaven, perhaps. Not here.

NELSON:  Do you mean because Cross was given remission and you were not?

OSCAR:  *(Dismissive)* Oh, that? No, no. There is something else. I've just realized that I, a self-confessed lord of language, have been ruined for life by a foul-mouthed marquis whose conversation is a social disaster, who has only a nodding acquaintance with grammar and can't even spell! *(Clearly, he is ready to depart but still lingers. As if to bridge an apparent awkwardness, Nelson says:)*

NELSON:  Well there, Mr. Wilde! It is finished. Your punishment is over!

OSCAR:  *(Smiling)* Oh no, Major Nelson. Now it begins.

*(He claps his hat on his head, briefly surveys the others and then his nod beckons the Chief and Martin. They follow him from the lighted area. Nelson stands gazing after him without moving, but Fingers is nodding agreement as the light on the two areas gradually dims until the darkness is as complete as it was when the play began)*

Curtain

*Saul Zachary*

# THE COLOR OF HEAT

# Saul Zachary

Though Saul Zachary completed the first draft of *The Color of Heat* in 1966, it remained unproduced until 1975, when the Playwrights Platform gave it a production in Boston. Four years later, the Impossible Ragtime Theatre in Manhattan gave the script a showcase production, followed by a reading at The Whole Theatre Company in Montclair, New Jersey, in 1980. Additional presentations were made at Manhattan's Circle Rep and San Francisco's One Act Theatre Company in 1981. That same year, the play won the Dubuque Fine Arts Society National One-Act Playwriting Contest, and together with another of Mr. Zachary's one-act plays *Shapes of Midnight* (under the collective title *Lost Love*) won a 1982 grant in playwriting from the Creative Artists Program Service (CAPS).

In *The Color of Heat*, a middle-aged husband, trapped in a marriage mired with ennui, while sunning on the beach with his wife, attempts to revive their relationship by a titillating voyeuristic report on the activities of a romantic couple in the nearby dunes. But beneath the surface humor, there is a wrenching sadness. As John S. Patterson observes, reporting in the *Villager* on the Impossible Ragtime Theatre's production, "It is pathetic, touching, horrifying, and wretched all at once and the author's insightfulness leaves us with a sense of lives lost though still occupied by warm bodies."

Mr. Zachary was born in Brooklyn in 1934. He received a B.A. from Brooklyn College and an M.A. in Theatre from Smith College. After receiving his degrees, he directed productions and taught theatre at Smith and at the University of South Florida.

Active in organizing groups to showcase fledgling playwrights, Mr. Zachary served as co-founder of both the Playwrights Platform in Boston and the Manhattan Playwrights Unit. He has also been active in the Directors/Playwrights Unit of The Actors Studio in New York City.

In addition to the awards mentioned above for *The Color of Heat*, Mr. Zachary has received grants from the National Endowment for the Arts, the Massachusetts Arts and Humanities Foundation, P.E.N. American Center, and the Music Corporation of America.

Most recently his play *Letter to the World* received a presentation by the Manhattan Playwrights Unit.

## Characters:

SIMON DUFFNEY, *a man who has a public life, a private life, and a very private life, with a moat between each. He loves his wife in the encrusted manner of the long married, but has made a habit of protesting the fact.*

JANICE DUFFNEY, *his wife, is an inquisitive, materialistic, gentle woman with a sometimes rough delivery. She feels constantly on one foot with her husband, but has developed her powers of balance so that only a little of what he says throws her off anymore, or so she thinks.*

## Scene:

*A gently rounded hill, well outside the city limits. Young, green grass festooned with daisies and an occasional dandelion—an ideal spot for a picnic but for the lack of shade. It is two o'clock on a brilliantly hot afternoon in May, and the full power of the sun makes the air ripple upward like a scene witnessed underwater.*

*Simon Duffney and his wife, Janice, lie on two aluminum beach chairs parallel to each other, their faces raised to the sun. They have come with all the paraphernalia of city folk armed to storm health in a hurry—sun reflectors, lotions, eye protectors, etc. On the grass near them is a blanket.*

*They are in their late forties, similar in coloring, not unduly attractive. Simon is relaxed, appears to be asleep; Janice is restless. She scratches her calf, then a moment later it is her shoulder blade, can't reach the itch, moves her back across her chair sideways, then she slaps at something buzzing near her face. Finally, she opens her eyes, winces at the sun's glare, and covers her eyes with her hand.*

JANICE:  I'm dying . . .
SIMON:  (*Not moving*) Mmm-m . . . what's that, dear?
JANICE:  (*Relieved*) Oh, you're awake. I thought you were asleep.
SIMON:  (*Drowsily*) I thought so too. (*Pause*) I was . . . and I wasn't.
JANICE:  Simon.
SIMON:  (*Stretching*) What a beautiful . . . (*Stifling a*

*yawn*) . . . day. Someone ought to bottle days like this for December. They'd make a fortune.

JANICE: Simon, can we go? I'm so bored.

SIMON: Go?

JANICE: Besides, I'm broiling. I feel like I'm on a spit.

SIMON: Really? I hardly feel the sun.

JANICE: Your thermostat needs adjusting. Must be close to one hundred degrees here.

SIMON: Nonsense. The weather forecast said eighty to eighty-five. Can you reach over and get me the suntan lotion?

JANICE: (*Handing it to him*) Please, Simon. I'd like to leave. This heat's impossible.

SIMON: (*Looking down abstractedly at a palmful of suntan lotion*) Suppose we stay another half hour?

JANICE: And if I get sunstroke?

SIMON: That would be . . . unfortunate.

JANICE: All right—fifteen minutes.

SIMON: (*Rubbing the lotion on his chest*) . . . Sun's good for you, Janice. Brings out the poisons.

JANICE: Fifteen more minutes and we go?

SIMON: Go where, dear?

JANICE: . . . Home, I guess.

SIMON: What are we going to do home?

(*No answer. Janice falls back in her chair. Pause*)

JANICE: If only there were some shade here.

SIMON: If you close your . . . eyes, you'll be in the shade.

JANICE: (*The implication of his remark going right by*) That's no protection against permanent eye damage.

SIMON: Very true.

JANICE: You think I'm being difficult, don't you?

SIMON: No.

JANICE: I wish this pest would stop bothering me . . . isn't that what you're thinking?

SIMON: Don't be silly. No one is asking you to feel guilty if you're uncomfortable. I understand.

JANICE: That's a relief.

SIMON: Just so long as you recognize it wasn't *my* idea to drive all the way out here, that's all.

JANICE: You've made your point, Simon.

SIMON: Fine.

JANICE: It's sticking in right . . . (*She twists in her chair, indicates the area between her shoulder blades*) . . . here.

SIMON: (*Smiles weakly, kisses his fingers, puts his hand on her back*) There. First aid. Better?

JANICE: (*Thinking about it, then allowing the mood to lift*) Yep.

SIMON: Look, if you're that unhappy we can leave now.

JANICE: (*Lightly*) You know, it's really amazing. I used to love the sun.

SIMON: S'all the same to me, Janice.

JANICE: Now I can't stand it.

SIMON: She didn't hear a word I said. I asked you . . .

JANICE: She heard you, she heard you, she heard every participle and pronoun. Who said I'm unhappy? I'm very happy, just . . . a little restless. You took a day off for me; the least I can do is give you fifteen more minutes.

SIMON: Thank you, Janice.

JANICE: Don't mention it. (*She leans back, closes her eyes, and starts to sing in a low and surprisingly pleasant voice*)

> "You are not my first love,
> I've known other charms,
> But I've just been rehearsing
> In those other arms . . .
>
> My heart is second-hand,
> Yes, my heart is second-hand,
> But there aren't many scratches
> And you hardly see the patches.
>
> You are not my first love . . . *

SIMON: Can you sing something else?

JANICE: You don't like? I find it cooling. (*Pause*) Speaking of air-conditioners, let's get one for the kitchen. They're having a sale at Korvette's.

SIMON: We've got six air-conditioners in the house now.

JANICE: But we don't have one in the kitchen. You know what they say: "If you can't stand the heat, stay out of the kitchen." Watch out, Simon. I may just do that.

SIMON: Threats now. Every time you're upset about something you buy an air-conditioner. Hats are cheaper, Janice. And they don't burn up as much energy.

---

*"You Are Not My First Love," by Bart Howard & Peter Windsor. Copyright © 1953 Walden Music, Inc. All Rights Reserved. Lyrics reprinted with permission of Walden Music, Inc.

JANICE:  Oh, don't be such a cheapskate. I'll get a small unit—if they're really marked down, that is. ". . . You are not my first love—" Oops, excuse me. The whole thing started the summer I was pregnant with Louise. I was so hot. Even at night I felt like the sun was sitting on my head. All I wanted was an air-conditioner. I don't think I ever wanted anything so badly. And I remember . . . we couldn't afford it.

SIMON:  It wasn't a question of money. In that little apartment we had, an air-conditioner would have blown every fuse. Anyway, now you've got enough of 'em to start your own sale.

JANICE:  Not in the kitchen we don't. It's true, though; we've come a long way.

SIMON:  . . . Have we?

JANICE:  Of course! Bank statements don't lie. Give or take a few dollars, we're worth at least . . .

SIMON:  Somehow I'm not interested in how much we're worth, not on a day like this. Why don't you . . . Why don't you read your book?

(*Janice looks at him for a moment, picks up her book, puts it on her lap, picks up her handbag, starts going through it*)

JANICE:  Guess what?

SIMON:  What?

JANICE:  Guess what Mrs. Coleman said about you yesterday.

SIMON:  I give up . . . Who's Mrs. Coleman?

JANICE:  You know, she lives on the corner. Mrs. Coleman. The one whose kids are all in therapy.

SIMON:  Oh, yeah.

JANICE:  She said you were very good looking. (*No response. Janice purses her lips as if to say, "She has no taste anyway"*) . . . I can't seem to find my glasses. Simon, did you see . . .

SIMON:  (*Concentrating on the sun*) No.

(*Janice looks perfunctorily through the collection of beach accessories, finally giving up*)

JANICE:  Where could I have left them? Nothing's going right today, nothing. (*She falls back in her chair, disgusted*) A penny for your thoughts.

SIMON:  (*Inert*) My thoughts don't come that cheap.

JANICE:  Just using a figure of speech, Simon.

SIMON:  (*Sarcastically*) I see . . . Besides, I'd have to give you change if I told you.

JANICE:  Tell me anyway.

SIMON:    . . . Just then?

JANICE:    Yes.

SIMON:    Or before then?

JANICE:    (*Confused*) I don't know; take your pick.

SIMON:    Well, if you're not that interested in what I'm thinking . . .

JANICE:    Simon, talking to you is like trying to pick a lock. I'm your wife, not a stranger, you know.

SIMON:    (*Quietly*) Is there a difference?

JANICE:    . . . There used to be.

SIMON:    Used to be—eggs used to be twenty-two cents a dozen. But you can't make an omelette with ancient history. . . . I'm sorry, Janice. Too nice a day for squabbling. (*Smiling*) Since you're so persistent, I was thinking of . . .

JANICE:    On the bureau! *That's* where I left my glasses!

SIMON:    (*Limply*) Spots.

JANICE:    What did you say?

SIMON:    (*Deflated*) Nothing, it's not worth repeating . . . (*Suddenly bursting out*) SPOTS! I . . . I was thinking of spots. (*Closing his eyes*) I wasn't so much thinking about them as I was watching them. (*Scrutinizing closely under his eyelids*) They look a little like . . . doughnuts, some of them. Once in a while you get one that looks like a water lily or a jellyfish. Pinkish and gray and blue and iridescent. Pretty little things. I haven't seen 'em in years.

JANICE:    (*Looking at him oddly*) You're whacko.

SIMON:    (*With relish*) The way it works is you close your eyes tight and wait. Before you know it, your head turns into a glass-bottomed boat with all sorts of little squiggly spots swimming from . . . (*Following their path with his arm, still with his eyes closed*) . . . upper right—it seems—to lower left. Sort of a private aquarium. And with a small amount of practice, you can train them to change direction. Oops, there's one that got away! It's really quite a sight. See for yourself, Janice.

JANICE:    Are you joshing?

SIMON:    I've never been more serious.

JANICE:    How could I see anything with my eyes shut?

SIMON:    Ah-ha, you may be in for surprise. Close your eyes.

JANICE:    (*Gently admonishing him*) You sneak.

SIMON:    Sneak  . . how so sneak?

JANICE:    I've been complaining about this sunny pizza oven;

meanwhile *you've* gotten the sunstroke.

SIMON: Just close your eyes, Janice. Trust me.

JANICE: (*She closes her eyes again. Pause*) . . . Nope, don't see a thing.

SIMON: Be patient. You wouldn't expect to see a fish as soon as you drop your hook in the water.

JANICE: What hook? What water? Would somebody tell me what I'm supposed to be fishing for?

SIMON: (*Watching her expectantly*) Keep looking.

JANICE: I am, I am, but my eyelids get in the way. This is ridic . . .

SIMON: Don't open!

JANICE: (*Turning to face him with her eyes screwed shut*) You trying to make a fool of me?

SIMON: DAMN IT, IT'S IMPORTANT, JANICE!

JANICE: (*Quelled momentarily*) . . . It's either sunstroke or . . . You haven't been taking LSD, I hope. (*Snapping her eyes open*) No spots today. (*Blinking rapidly*) Isn't this a riot . . . now *all* I can see is spots! (*Laughing*) Where . . . Where are you, Simon? (*She extends her arm, groping blindly for him. Simon looks at it for a second too long, an oddly contracted expression on his face, then he takes her hand diffidently*) I must say, you're still full of nonsense, Simon. Even after sixteen years. I certainly hope you never talk like that to your clients. Spots . . . half the time I never know whether you're kidding or not.

SIMON: (*He pats her hand and drops it*) Only because half the time you're not really listening, dear.

JANICE: What?

SIMON: (*Chuckling*) Forget it. (*He leans back and looks up very high*) Blue . . . innocent, innocuous blue. Funny, I always thought the color of heat was red. It's blue.

JANICE: Speaking of colors, I mentioned the house painters are coming next week, didn't I? What color would you like for your room? You still haven't told me.

SIMON: Decisions, decisions . . . (*Suddenly looking off*) Janice, didn't you say this was to be a private party? Seems we have company.

JANICE: Company . . . where?

SIMON: (*Pointing*) Hand-in-hand midst the daisies. How sweet.

JANICE: (*Squinting*) . . . I don't see anybody. What are they, Simon, more of your spots?

SIMON: If they are, they're the first I've seen carrying a picnic basket.

JANICE: Show me.

SIMON: No, no, not there. Look where I'm pointing. To the left of that tree, the left!

JANICE: You know I can't see that far without my glasses. *Wait*, wait, wait, wait . . . oh yes, you're right. I see them now. It's a . . . boy and a girl.

SIMON: Congratulations.

JANICE: I don't mind that other people are here, do you? Makes this place seem . . . hard to explain . . .

SIMON: Of more value?

JANICE: That's it, yes. Of more value. I'm beginning to think like a real estate broker's wife, aren't I? Judging a place by the amount of people attracted to it isn't right though.

SIMON: (*Shrugging*) It may simply have something to do with not wanting to be alone . . .

JANICE: (*Reaches over for her handbag, takes out compact and lipstick, and starts applying it*) Simon, am I getting fat?

SIMON: (*Gazing off*) Not that I noticed.

JANICE: How could you tell when you're not even looking?

SIMON: Do I have to look at my hand to know how many fingers I've got?

JANICE: Might not be a bad idea from time to time. Just to be on the safe side. Well, what's happening over there? All I can see is a blur.

SIMON: Nothing's happening. (*A quick thought*) Did you bring something to drink?

JANICE: You shouldn't stare so obviously at them, Simon.

SIMON: I asked, is there anything to drink? You brought the thermos, I hope.

JANICE: (*Her eyes widening*) Forgot that too!

(*Simon shakes his head ruefully, then turns back to his study*)

JANICE: . . . Simon, stop it! You'll make them feel uncomfortable.

SIMON: Not those two. They have this day unto themselves. I don't think they'd notice if a flying saucer landed next to them.

JANICE: How marvelous. (*Sighing*) . . . God, I feel a hundred years old.

SIMON:   It's not you, Janice. It's just the first warm day in
May. Makes everything that's not as young as itself feel old.

JANICE:   Simon, that's the nicest thing you've said to me in
a long, long time. Even if . . .

SIMON:   Even if what?

JANICE:   Even if you didn't mean it.

SIMON:   (*Averting his eyes*) Of course I meant it.

JANICE:   (*The lie transparent to her*) Yes, of course you did . . . If
nothing's happening over there, what are you staring at?

SIMON:   I didn't say nothing's happening *now*.

JANICE:   Oh!

SIMON:   It's really none of our business, Janice. I'm surprised at you.

JANICE:   Well, you're the one that's looking, not me. I'm
only asking because I can't see as far as you.

SIMON:   All right, fellow voyeur—they're kissing. Sit down,
Janice, please. You're going to embarrass us both.

JANICE:   (*Low*) Hypocrite. (*She sits*)

SIMON:   (*Preoccupied*) What did you say?

JANICE:   Nothing.

SIMON:   (*Suddenly*) Let's go.

(*He gets up, starts folding his beach chair*)

JANICE:   Go . . . now?

SIMON:   You were anxious to go a little while ago. So we're
going. We'll just throw this stuff into the blanket; we can sort
it out later. Can you manage? I'll carry the chairs to the car.

JANICE:   Would you mind telling me what this flurry of
activity is all about? I appreciate the breeze you're making
but . . .

SIMON:   I just told you.

JANICE:   You should see your face . . . it's white as a mum-
mer. What's wrong, Simon?

SIMON:   We'll discuss it in the car.

JANICE:   No, I think we should discuss it . . .

SIMON:   Oh, stop acting so damn coy! You know what they're
doing . . . for God knows what purpose, I don't . . . you
keep asking!

JANICE:   You mean . . . they're making love?

SIMON:   In large quantities.

JANICE:   (*Delighted*) No kidding!

SIMON:   As if you didn't know.

JANICE:   Well, are they doing a good job of it?

SIMON:   Neither one seems to be complaining. Want me to go ask them for a candid appraisal?

JANICE:   What a disgusting idea! But you've got your hands full, let me. (*She starts to scamper off, singing to herself*) "You are not my first love, I've known other . . .*

SIMON:   Janice, come back here!

JANICE:   (*Ambling back*) Shame on you, Simon. For a man who's always playing jokes on other people, you've got no sense of humor. I wouldn't dream of trespassing on their privacy. (*Pulling up a handful of grass*) I just sort of wish . . .

SIMON:   You could see them?

JANICE:   (*Cocking her head*) Hmmm . . . I don't know. Maybe.

SIMON:   Why?

JANICE:   Why not? Why must there always be a "why" pinned to everything? You know women are naturally snoopy. I'm entitled.

SIMON:   Okay.

JANICE:   Speaking of "whys," why are you so upset about it?

SIMON:   Who's upset? I just don't like exhibitionism.

JANICE:   He said in a hard, executive manner, slamming the subject closed.

SIMON:   Exactly.

JANICE:   On his own pinky.

SIMON:   (*Slowly and evenly*) Seems to me you're the last person in the world who should want to keep the subject open. Unless you like the taste of your own blood, that is.

JANICE:   Old grudges never die, do they?

SIMON:   Nope, they just hibernate till May.

JANICE:    . . . Sounds like we're going to have an argument, doesn't it?

SIMON:   I'm afraid so.

JANICE:   At least if it were fun. We haven't had a really *good* argument in years.

SIMON:   That's true. Perhaps you ought to try throwing things.

JANICE:   At *you?*

SIMON:   I don't mean at *them.*

---

JANICE: (*Giggling a little*) I . . . I couldn't do that. Too late to change my style.

SIMON: Pity not to try. Might make the situation much better.

JANICE: You think it would improve?

SIMON: No, it would only make it worse.

JANICE: Then why do it?

SIMON: Because it would make it worse.

JANICE: That's sick.

SIMON: Now you've hit it! As an ancient philosopher once said on his deathbed: Sickness is to truth what poodle shit is to shoes.

JANICE: (*Nodding gravely*) Ah-so! Meanwhile, what's new with-uh . . . (*Indicating the couple*) Are they still . . . ?

SIMON: (*Looking off*) Well, now it seems he's made some sort of awning out of part of their blanket.

JANICE: Then they must know we're watching them, Simon.

SIMON: Relax. They're trying to hide from the sun, not from us.

JANICE: What else can you see?

SIMON: I can see they're breaking a half dozen ordinances.

JANICE: Listen to the outraged citizen! You were in love once . . . I hope . . . weren't you?

SIMON: Never publicly.

JANICE: (*Smirking*) As another ancient philosopher once said: Man with tall forehead have short memory. (*Softly*) Don't you remember our third date?

SIMON: Sometimes. Mostly at night when I wake up screaming. Oh, yes . . . wasn't that the time I decided to splurge and take you out to dinner at the Automat? You kept throwing nickels in a slot marked "Quarters Only," and I ended up fighting with the manager.

JANICE: Typical Simon! For your information, we spent it just like those two . . . horizontally.

SIMON: Us! (*Appealing to the sun*) Your Honor, I hardly know this woman!

JANICE: On an empty beach on Long Island it was. Bayshore, Long Island. The same sort of day as today. The sun was hot but the water was still too cold for swimming.

SIMON: (*Sharing her memory, but reluctant to give up the inertia of his last remark*) . . . Lies, pack of lies.

JANICE: We stayed until it was dark. And we got lost trying

to find the way back to the railroad station. Simon, don't you recall it? (*Simon nods slowly*) I'm glad you do. Because if you forgot, there'd be only me to remember . . . then it would be that much closer to never having happened at all. Am I making any sense to you?

SIMON: The best kind. But applicable to each in his own way.

JANICE: I . . . I don't follow you, dear.

SIMON: (*Taking a deep breath before plunging into the exertion of verbalizing*) If somebody snaps his fingers, let's say, our heads will turn in the same direction. But whether we see the same things is anybody's guess. You're you, and I'm me. So why should our memories be the same? Because we've been married for sixteen years? Makes no sense. Even Siamese twins don't share everything in common. And *we're* not even in each other's skins.

JANICE: (*Stung, her eyes starting to brim*) You say that now, but we were . . . that day on the beach.

SIMON: (*Wryly*) In a way. I suppose. Don't start crying. I haven't got any tissues.

JANICE: I'm not crying . . . Were you very disappointed?

SIMON: Disappointed? I was relieved, oh, was I relieved! I was no more disappointed than you were, I guess. When your expectations get out of hand, the real thing is bound to be a bit of a letdown, I suppose . . .

JANICE: I wonder how it is with them.

(*Simon turns and looks down the hill. Without breaking his gaze he places the folded beach chairs he has been holding on the ground and stands motionless for a long moment, transfixed*)

SIMON: . . . Who knows? I'm . . . I'm out of my element here. Ask me about plant sites, mortgages, commission checks . . . I can talk faster than you can listen. But something happening in a field three hundred feet away that has nothing to do with me . . . What can I say? For all I know they might be little, naked dolls some kid left behind. Who knows? In heat like this you don't know what you're seeing. So a couple of juvenile delinquents are belly to belly in the clover . . . why should it get me riled up? None of my business. . . . How quiet it is! Why isn't anything moving out there? Everything looks like it's pressed behind glass . . . notice? (*Pointing upward*) Even that one little cloud . . . look how confused it looks. Poor thing, what are you waiting for? Move!

JANICE:   Maybe the cloud wants to watch them too. (*Pause*)
I'm sorry; what did you say?

SIMON:   I didn't say anything.

JANICE:   Simon.

SIMON:   Yes, dear?

JANICE:   (*Timidly*) Would you believe it, I have never seen
another couple . . . doing it. Of course this is going to sound
foolish any way I put it, so if you want to be sarcastic, here's
your chance. Had I remembered my glasses . . . (*She stops, at
a loss as to how to continue*)

SIMON:   (*Coaxingly, a faint smile on his lips*) Come on, come
on.

JANICE:   Could you be my eyes, Simon, and tell me what
you see?

(*He looks at her penetratingly, though what she says seems to come
as no surprise. When he speaks, his voice is softer than it has been*)

SIMON:   Be happy to . . . I see a tangle of arms and legs.
First glance you'd think you're seeing some sort of sea plant,
all wavery and underwater-looking 'cause of the heat lines
coming off the grass. (*He rubs his eyes to get a better focus*) They're
both very dark, very sunburnt, about twenty, I'd say. Looks
as if they're wearing white bathing suits, but it's just the distance. The boy's lying across her; she's pretending to be asleep,
got one arm flung out on the grass . . . Not moving at all,
maybe they are asleep. No, I didn't think so . . . What's he up
to?

(*He chuckles. Little by little Janice gets drawn into the scene Simon
describes. As she listens she grows calmer, her movements less random and self-conscious until she is herself watching the couple in
her mind's eye, her frozen posture barely suggestive of her involve-
ment and a complete confirmation of it*)

SIMON:   He's tickling her shoulder with a blade of grass.
She's not going to be bothered, brushes it away; she thinks
it's a fly . . . Ah, he's doing it again. He's got her scratching
now. Oh-oh! She's opened her eyes, grabbed some grass of
her own, she's tickling *him*! They're rolling over, he's got her
wrist. They're laughing . . . Do you hear?

JANICE:   I hear.

SIMON:   (*Laughing contagiously*) Who's boss now? Now she's
got you, Mister. You should see—she's bouncing up and down
on his chest, tickling him to pieces. That's it, girl! Give him a
taste of his own medicine. Oh, he finally got her wrists pinned

to the grass; I think the bout's over. Oops . . . wrong again! The girl is wild; she's biting his chest—not hard—little nips to make him let go. (*More subdued*) . . . He's wrapped his arms around her back. Now she's slid down his body; she's lying full-face on top of him. They're kissing. Hardly moving except for his hands making figure-eights on her back . . . She seems a trifle uncomfortable, lifts her upper body, kind of flinches. She's opening her legs . . . I think they've begun. Her legs are spread like a starfish; she's settling again on him. Oh yes, they've begun. Slowly, ever so slowly, taking their pleasure in small sips . . . there's a squirrel! It's standing upright about five feet away from them, watching. Absolutely fascinated. Strange creatures, these human beings. They don't see it, of course. They're dead to everything, everything except each other and a few indelible facts, like maybe her lips are dry and there's a lady bug in her hair and her body has a mind of its own . . .

JANICE:    Simon.
SIMON:    (*Hoarsely*) A mind of its own.
(*Pause*)
JANICE:    (*Sitting on the grass*) Simon?
SIMON:    (*Turning to her*) Yes, dear?
JANICE:    Simon, how is it with us?
SIMON:    What do you mean?
JANICE:    Can't we . . . do the same?
SIMON:    Here?
JANICE:    Yes.
SIMON:    Now?
JANICE:    Yes. If you'd like to, I would. Very much.
SIMON:    (*Ambivalently*) All right.
(*He goes to her, drops to his knees and kisses her, somewhat hesitantly. Their kiss becomes more passionate and they sink into the grass, still embracing*)
JANICE:    (*Touching his face*) . . . I see myself in your eyes. Two of me.
SIMON:    Guess I'll just have to make love to both of you. (*They kiss*) What are we whispering for?
JANICE:    My husband is around here someplace.
SIMON:    So's my wife.
JANICE:    I didn't know you were married. (*Sighing "The Heroine"*) Oh, dear, I've been led astray again.

SIMON: (*And he "The Villian"*) My intention exactly. (*A long kiss*) . . . Lady, where'd you get the freckles?

JANICE: Supermarket. They were on "Special."

SIMON: Very becoming . . .

JANICE: Simon, do you love me?

(*Taken off-guard by her question, Simon does not answer immediately. When he does, it is with the grinding shyness of a man long unaccustomed to expressing such thoughts*)

SIMON: . . . Cuts and bruises not withstanding, I . . . I'm afraid I love you with all my heart.

JANICE: Afraid?

SIMON: (*Nodding*) A *little* afraid. Don't ask me why . . .

JANICE: Let's not talk anymore.

(*She offers her lips. He kisses her quickly, ardently, pressing her down*)

JANICE: (*Squirming*) Excuse me. Something . . . What . . . What's sticking me in the back? (*She sits up and starts fumbling around behind her*) It's probably a rock. (*She produces a pair of eyeglasses*) Look! Look what I found, Simon! My glasses! They were probably under the blanket all along. I had a *feeling* I took them along with me this morning.

SIMON: (*Trying to draw her back to the previous moment*) That's wonderful.

JANICE: (*Puts on her glasses and jumping to her feet*) Now I can see 'em for myself!

SIMON: Janice! (*He stands up*)

JANICE: (*Scampering off a few feet*) I'll only be a minute. (*Giggling*) Besides, maybe I can learn something. Kindly remove yourself, Simon. You're blocking my view.

SIMON: Janice, will you please stop.

JANICE: Such an impatient man! (*She darts playfully out to the side*) Now I've got 'em in my sights. (*Pause*) . . . WHAT IS THIS? WHAT KIND OF A STORY HAVE YOU BEEN FEEDING ME, SIMON?

SIMON: I don't understand.

JANICE: The hell you don't! They're not making love; they're not even touching each other. They're *reading magazines*! Like two goddamn strangers in the subway reading magazines!

SIMON: You shouldn't have looked. (*Wearily turning back to the beach chairs again*) Take the blanket, will you.

JANICE: Take it yourself. (*Looking at him with newfound curiosity and wariness*) I want to know why you ran off this—

this porno movie for me. I'm your wife, you don't have to seduce *me*. You have your rights. Just ask.

SIMON:   (*Mumbling to the ground*) Had nothing to do with my "rights."

JANICE:   Then what, then? If I had any brains I wouldn't ask—God knows what you'll come out with next! Once in a while you read stories in the paper about women who find out their husbands are killers or spies or have five mistresses. I never could believe they were as dumb as all that. Now I'm not so sure! You never know, not even after sixteen years. *Mister, what is your name? Who are you?* 'Cause anybody who could dream up such a story—don't look at me! (*Crossing her arms over her bathing suit*) I feel like a sinkful of dirty dishes. Why'd you do it? WHY?

SIMON:   (*Woodenly*) . . . I . . . I just wanted to see if we were still alive. If we had something besides a house with six air-conditioners. It gives me no joy to say it, Janice, but we are dull people. Dull and predictable. Our ears close as soon as the other opens his mouth to speak—happens all in one motion. And with good reason . . . There was once a time we would have laughed at people like us, right in our faces we would have laughed because we knew in our snotty young way we could never become such . . . zombies. Here's an irony for you, Janice—we managed.

JANICE:   So I'm a zombie. Nobody's perfect. Is there a point to all this?

SIMON:   (*Eagerly*) The point is when those two came along, we became alive! All the static disappeared. You listened to me. Really listened. And I could hear your heart beating . . . (*Pointing off*) "That's us! That's us! That's us!"

JANICE:   (*Pulling away from him*) Bullshit! You lied, and I caught you.

SIMON:   It wasn't a lie! We were like them once. We made love out of love, not because there was nothing to watch on TV. You're the one with the memory—what about our third date, Janice? Bayshore, the empty beach? Aren't we the same people we were then?

JANICE:   No, we're supposed to be mature adults now. Stop trying to change the subject. How many times have I asked you what you're thinking? Never once in sixteen years did you tell me the truth, huh? *Huh?* But today I found out . . . by a fluke.

SIMON:   (*Shaking his head*) Static . . .

JANICE:   Men like you should be very carefully watched. From this day on, I promise you, you will be.

SIMON:   All I'm getting is static.

JANICE:   (*Secure now behind an emotional wall*) You're a dirty old man, my husband!

(*Simon takes the beach chairs and starts to leave*)

SIMON:   I'll wait for you in the car.

JANICE:   Only one thing in your head . . .

SIMON:   (*Almost sorrowfully, but with a mechanical smile*) Spots . . . I told you, Janice. Pinkish and gray and blue spots. That's all.

(*Simon leaves. Janice starts collecting their things, angrily brushes off some grass still adhering to her, glances down the hill at the couple. Her face softens for a moment and she unconsciously runs the tip of a last blade of grass down her shoulder and arm, shivers suddenly at the contact and begins to scratch her arm. She scratches harder and harder until she is raking her skin with her fingernails, choking back her tears and uncontrollably scratching as the curtain falls*)

*Arthur Laurents*
# LOSS OF MEMORY

# Arthur Laurents

Playwright, librettist, screenwriter, and director, Arthur Laurents has forged a distinguished and versatile contribution to the performing arts. Among his many achievements for the stage are *Home of the Brave* (1945), *Time of the Cuckoo* (1952), *A Clearing in the Woods* (1957), *Invitation to a March* (1960), and *The Enclave* (1973), as well as the librettos for *West Side Story* (1957), *Gypsy* (1959), *Anyone Can Whistle* (1964), *Do I Hear A Waltz* (1965), and *Hallelujah Baby*, which won the Antoinette Perry Award in 1967.

His screenplay credits include *Rope* (1948), *The Snake Pit* (1948), *Anastasia* (1956), *The Way We Were* (1973), and *The Turning Point* (1977), which received the Screen Writers' Guild award for best original screenplay. Mr. Laurents also wrote the novelization of *The Way We Were* and *The Turning Point*.

Turning his hand to directing, Mr. Laurents staged both plays and musicals for the theatre including *I Can Get It For You Wholesale*; the highly acclaimed production of *Gypsy* starring Angela Lansbury; his own play, *The Enclave*; his newest play, *Passion Play*, produced at the Alley Theatre in Houston: and *The Madwoman of Central Park West*, co-authored with Phyllis Newman, who starred in the production.

Mr. Laurents also is a member of the Council of the Dramatists Guild, the association which serves both professional and amateur playwrights as a source of information and advice.

In *A Loss of Memory*, his first contribution to this series, Mr. Laurents offers a bittersweet portrait of a lonely American in a chance encounter with an Israeli officer. The play appears here in print for the first time.

## Characters:

NARRATOR, *about fifty*
MAN (AMERICAN), *about thirty-five*
YOUNGER MAN (ISRAELI), *about twenty-eight*

## Scene:

*A pool of light stage left on a chair with arms. The NARRATOR enters above it, carrying a slim manuscript in a folder.*

NARRATOR:   There is no moon. (*He sits as he continues to speak, referring to his manuscript for a second*) And the vague lights behind a few of the curtained windows in the hotel from which the man comes are not much help. (*A slight dark blue washes the rear wall*) Still, a sky filled with as many stars as this one has a glow: pale but warm as the night air.
　　(*The Man enters upstage right, behind the Narrator. He, too, is attractive and wears a seersucker suit, shirt, tie, and loafers*)
The man—about 35 and probably a week-end tennis player from the way he has moved across the terrace from the rear lobby door—the man hesitates a moment, trying to accustom his eyes to the pale dark. The hotel behind him is fairly new: a proud if not quite successful attempt at modern luxury. (*Light begins to glow down front center on two wooden chairs with moderately high backs. The chairs touch. During the next, the Man walks to the chairs, using their backs as a ledge*) He tries to appear confident should there be someone watching in the night. A few feet ahead is the dim outline of what might be a wall. He touches it: a stone balustrade. He leans against it, remembering now the bathing beach that must be down below.
　　(*The Man takes out a pack of cigarettes and fishes one out as:*)
At that time—the mid-sixties—almost everyone smoked. It had a certain advantage.
　　(*A Younger Man in sports shirt and slacks, has entered right, and as the Man fishes for a match, flicks a cigarette lighter for him*)
MAN:   Oh. Thanks. (*A quick look, then lights his cigarette*)
NARRATOR:   He is too startled to get a good look at the

younger man: high cheek bones, strange blue eyes, strong fingers.

MAN:   Would you like one?

YOUNGER MAN:   (*Oxford English with a slight, odd accent*) I do not smoke. (*Puts his lighter back in his pocket; stares front*)

MAN:   Nice night . . . Warm, though . . . Much warmer than I thought it would be.

(*The light grows brighter on the two men, dims on the Narrator*)

YOUNGER MAN:   (*Pointing out front*) That is the Mediterranean.

MAN:   I know, but it's November.

YOUNGER MAN:   Are you English?

MAN:   No, American.

YOUNGER MAN:   Good. The English, they are cold.

AMERICAN [The Man]:   Oh. Well, I'm not!

YOUNGER MAN:   Also, they are shits.

AMERICAN:   Why?

YOUNGER MAN:   Americans are quite ignorant of anybody else's history.

AMERICAN:   Oh, not all Americans. Have you met many?

YOUNGER MAN:   No. But I have been told. And the English *are* shits. During the war, they would not allow Jews in here. And in '48, they did their best to help the Arabs kick us out.

AMERICAN:   You're an Israeli.

YOUNGER MAN:   Of course.

AMERICAN:   I mean you were born here, you're a . . . Sabra.

ISRAELI [The Younger Man]:   Wrong.

NARRATOR:   The American shifts his position so that his right hand dangles from the balustrade, close to the bare elbow of the Israeli leaning against it. Close, but not quite touching.

AMERICAN:   It really is warm. My room's so cool, I didn't realize. I'm staying at the hotel there.

ISRAELI:   Yes, I saw you come out. Quite elegant. The hotel, that is.

AMERICAN:   Not really.

ISRAELI:   You don't like it?

AMERICAN:   Oh, yes, it's fine! My room's very comfortable . . . The bed's big and not too soft . . . I like hard beds.

ISRAELI:   *I* have no trouble sleeping.

AMERICAN:   Well, I'm sure I won't. I'm on the top floor and there's a breeze. From a balcony that overlooks all this.

NARRATOR:   As he gestures, his fingers lightly brush that bare elbow. But now the Israeli shifts *his* position so that he is hugging his elbows to him.

ISRAELI:   This beach is superb. Much superior to the Riviera.

AMERICAN:   Oh, do you go there often?

ISRAELI:   Never. But I have been told.

AMERICAN:   Well, from the brief look I got, this beach is certainly wider and the sand is whiter. And Israelis are friendlier.

ISRAELI:   Oh, do you know many?

AMERICAN:   (*Grins*) None. But I have been told. (*No reaction*) I just arrived this afternoon.

ISRAELI:   And you like it.

AMERICAN:   Well ... it's ... strange. I got off the plane and the attendant said "Welcome home"; I walked into the hotel and the doorman said "Welcome home"; I went up in the lift and the operator said "Welcome home." I don't feel I'm home.

ISRAELI:   Americans do, and I'm trying.

AMERICAN:   Israelis do, and I'm trying.

ISRAELI:   Try harder ... You would if you were a Jew.

AMERICAN:   I am. I can't speak Hebrew and I wasn't bar mitzvahed, but if they heat up the ovens again, in I go.

ISRAELI:   And your parents?

AMERICAN:   I'm afraid they don't even speak Yiddish.

ISRAELI:   Of which you are proud.

AMERICAN:   No.

ISRAELI:   No; just a real American.

AMERICAN:   O.K. But I'll tell you something funny—no, marvelous! I took a little walk down I don't know what street—it doesn't matter. But it suddenly struck me: for the first time in my life, I am part of the majority.

NARRATOR:   The Israeli turns and looks at him as though those brilliantly dark blue eyes could see in the darkness.

ISRAELI:   You are a writer.

AMERICAN:   How did you know?!

ISRAELI:   You are a romantic, not a realist. You write novels.

AMERICAN:   Sorry. Children's books.

ISRAELI:   Even more romantic. Israelis are realistic.

AMERICAN:   Nevertheless, one of my books sold quite well here.

ISRAELI: Which?

AMERICAN: You wouldn't have heard of it.

ISRAELI: Which?

AMERICAN: In English, it's called "A Country Made of Ice Cream".

ISRAELI: That is not a children's book.

AMERICAN: It certainly is.

ISRAELI: It is not. I read it. Many here have read it. To find out about America. It is quite good.

AMERICAN: Thank you, but don't spoil me.

ISRAELI: You are a personage.

AMERICAN: A very warm one at the moment.

NARRATOR: Once again, he lets his hand dangle from the balustrade close to the Israeli.

ISRAELI: Then you are here to write about our children.

AMERICAN: Well, I have an advance from my publisher to look around and see what life is like for children on a kibbutz. Anything about a kibbutz is fashionable right now.

ISRAELI: I was brought up on one. You won't get a book.

AMERICAN: Why not?

ISRAELI: Our children are too healthy.

AMERICAN: Well, God knows the weather doesn't seem to affect them when they grow up. (*He claps the Israeli on the shoulder*)

NARRATOR: The shoulder is broad, firm, muscular.

AMERICAN: I'm really very warm. Why don't we have a drink?

ISRAELI: Israelis do not drink.

AMERICAN: A soft drink.

ISRAELI: . . . Where?

AMERICAN: Oh—the bar in my hotel.

ISRAELI: Many officers in the army frequent that bar. I myself am a Major.

AMERICAN: Well, we could have the drinks sent up to my room.

ISRAELI: There is no room service at this hour.

AMERICAN: O.K., I'll be room service.

ISRAELI: Pardon?

MERICAN: Bring 'em up myself. It's really very pleasant out on my balcony.

ISRAELI: . . . I would prefer ice cream.

AMERICAN:   O.K., ice cream. (*Starts in the direction of the hotel, but:*)

ISRAELI:   There is a little Italian cafe farther along the croisette which has superb gelati.

AMERICAN:   (*Glumly*) Better than in Italy.

ISRAELI:   So I have been told. (*Starts to walk, the American following; the light spreads*) And by now, there will not be any decadent Europeans around.

AMERICAN:   (*Stops*) What do you mean—'decadent'?

ISRAELI:   Are you not a writer?

AMERICAN:   Different people have different definitions.

ISRAELI:   I mean those French, Italians, English with the gold medallions. They holiday here because it is so cheap. And Israelis are so innocent and sweet. They approach me because they find me exceptionally attractive, of course. But whatever language they speak, I pretend I do not understand. Even Hebrew.

AMERICAN:   . . . Why do you speak to me?

ISRAELI:   . . . What were you doing there?

AMERICAN:   Where?

ISRAELI:   Leaning against the wall in the dark.

AMERICAN:   I'm alone; I wandered out after dinner.

ISRAELI:   So I thought. Well, that might be why I speak to you. Come: gelati!

(*The light goes out on them, but they can be seen silhouetted against the dark blue wash across the back wall as they each take one of the two chairs, place them as though on opposite sides of a little table and sit, facing one another. During this, the light has brightened on the Narrator*)

NARRATOR:   At the little Italian cafe, they eat ice cream outside in the night. A spray of tiny colored bulbs is merely festive decor, but the light streaming through the wide front window enables them to see one another. The lean . . . (*Slowly, light comes up on the two men*) . . . suntanned American is attractive, particularly his smile which is not limited to his mouth. But the Israeli, who apparently has no smile—well, small wonder the decadent Europeans approach him. His forearms are a preview of the whole body; the deep sea blue of his eyes is almost an invented color; and the way he spoons ice cream into his mouth is a sexual metaphor. The American tries desperately to concentrate on hard facts.

AMERICAN:   And how many languages *do* you speak?

ISRAELI: 8, 9. Russian, German, Hebrew fluently. And English?

AMERICAN: Also fluently.

ISRAELI: So I have been told. To learn is not difficult when one is very young. The ice cream is good?

AMERICAN: Very. How young?

ISRAELI: Well, I was not quite 7 when the Germans came to the Ukraine. That is where I was born. After a time, they hanged my father, machine-gunned my mother, and did what they did to my baby brother. My two sisters were most clever: they got me away and together, we ran all over Europe picking up languages. My oldest sister, I lost somewhere between Austria and Yugoslavia. My next oldest, I lost in Greece while we were waiting to be smuggled onto a boat for here.

NARRATOR: As the Israeli calmly supplies details between mouthfuls of the very good ice cream, the American listens, the anger that is always deep within him because of the casual bigotry encountered at home, rising closer to the surface. *Yet . . .* yet, at the same time, a part of his mind is trying to calculate that if the Israeli was 7 in nineteen-forty-what and since this is nineteen-sixty-five, then how young is he now? Boy or man? And how old does he himself seem? (*The American turns sharply to the Narrator, and looks at him as though he is being betrayed. The Narrator looks right at him*) And if the Israeli went through all that horror as a tough little child and was such a healthy youngster on a kibbutz and is now a Major in the virile army with such disgust for decadent Europeans . . .

ISRAELI: Well, that was quite delicious. Shall we go to my flat?

(*The startled American swivels back to him, almost blushing*)

AMERICAN: (*So nonchalant*) Uh . . . yes, sure. Why not?

ISRAELI: (*Gets up*) It is not far. (*The American gets up. And now the Israeli does smile, charmingly*) And the bed is quite hard. (*The lights go out on them, but again they are silhouetted against light on the back wall, now a deep red. The Israeli gets a third matching chair from up right, then lines all three together front center—they will be a "bed." He then stands behind it, watching the American examine the flat. During this:*)

NARRATOR: The flat is really one modest, very neat room. Most of the color is in the thin, handwoven Moroccan spread on the large bed. The rest is very sparse except for photographs and framed blueprints and records and books—one of which is "A Country Made of Ice Cream." The author graciously autographs it, but his hands are trembling, for the Major is removing the Moroccan bedspread and folding it neatly. (*Light comes up fast on the "bed" area*)

ISRAELI:　You know that place behind your hotel where we met? That is the cruising place in Tel Aviv.

AMERICAN:　Oh, Jesus.

ISRAELI:　Never do I permit an Israeli to pick me up. Nor to see *me* pick up someone.

AMERICAN:　I thought I picked you up.

ISRAELI:　Certainly not.

AMERICAN:　Well, I tried, you succeeded.

ISRAELI:　Of course. No one picks *me* up. I do the picking.

NARRATOR:　He is undressing now.

AMERICAN:　But no Israelis.

ISRAELI:　Oh, never.

AMERICAN:　Don't you like Jews?

ISRAELI:　Are you not a Jew?

AMERICAN:　That was a joke.

ISRAELI:　Explain. (*Helps the American out of his jacket*)

AMERICAN:　Well . . . oh, forget it.

NARRATOR:　He is undressing now.

AMERICAN:　(*Back turned to the Israeli*) It was just my impression that you were very proud of being Israeli.

ISRAELI:　(*Hangs the jacket on the stage left chair*) I am. But gossip is a national characteristic. And this is not only a very small country but also a very anti-homosexual one. I must think of my sister who lives nearby in Ramat Gan, and my other sister in Herzliya.

AMERICAN:　I thought you lost your sisters.

ISRAELI:　In Europe, yes.

NARRATOR:　(*As the two men take in each other's body with their eyes*) Wearing the briefest of briefs, arranging the lighting, he relates how one day, when he was 12, a woman appeared at his kibbutz. He didn't recognize her: she was 20 but her hair was white. She burst into quiet tears and swept him into her thin arms. His oldest sister. The other sister turned up only 3 years ago, with a child of her own.

ISRAELI:　They love me very much, and of course are very proud of me. I have been decorated in the army several times, and I am quite well known as a civil engineer. However, my sisters do not know that I am homosexual and they never shall.

AMERICAN:  How can you be sure?

ISRAELI:  I am making sure. I am leaving Israel.

NARRATOR:  He points to a silver framed photograph.

ISRAELI:  That is my lover.

AMERICAN:  . . . Does he know?

ISRAELI:  Of course. Oh, that is another joke.

AMERICAN:  No; I meant about me. And, I assume, others.

ISRAELI:  What matter? He is not here. Certainly he takes care of his needs as I do. It is only natural.

NARRATOR:  His shorts are off and he is nude.

AMERICAN:  Is it?

ISRAELI:  Do you not have a lover in America?

AMERICAN:  Yes.

NARRATOR:  His shorts are off and he is nude.

AMERICAN:  But I feel guilty.

ISRAELI:  Stupid. Quite unnecessary.

AMERICAN:  What happens when your lover is here?

ISRAELI:  Oh, he is now finished with coming here. I am going to live with him.

AMERICAN:  Where?

ISRAELI:  Where he lives. In West Germany.

NARRATOR:  He has a partial erection.

ISRAELI:  He came here with the West German Trade Commission. That is how we met. You have a very good body. (*The Israeli sits on the stage right chair*)

NARRATOR:  He lies down on the bed.

AMERICAN:  He's not a Jew.

ISRAELI:  (*Laughs*) On the West German Trade Commission? Hardly.

AMERICAN:  . . . How can you?!

ISRAELI:  How can I what?

AMERICAN:  How can you have a lover who is German? How can you live in Germany? How can you forget?

ISRAELI:  (*Getting up*) How do you dare? I think it is you who forgets! My parents, my brother were murdered by the Nazis—yes, Germans! My house was burned down, my country was bombed out! Your parents are alive, you were untouched, your country was untouched. Oh, Americans and

Jews are so relentlessly moral! And you—an American *and* a
Jew! You *should* write children's books! You do not understand
why I am going to live in Germany? Very simple. I am going
to live in Germany because I want to be with my own kind.

AMERICAN:   . . . Your own kind. Basic common denomi-
nator.

NARRATOR:   (*To the American*) Is it?

ISRAELI:   (*To the American; tears glisten*) It is nice that you
had your little moment of feeling you are part of the majority.
But you aren't, you know. We are not wanted here. Perhaps
we are in America, but Americans are quite nervous on that
subject. Anyway, my lover is German—and there, I know I
*am* wanted. (*He curls up on his chair, facing away*)

NARRATOR:   He adjusts the pillows on the bed and curls
on his side, as though he is ready for sleep.

AMERICAN:   . . . I think I'd better go.

ISRAELI:   As you wish.

AMERICAN:   I've made you angry.

ISRAELI:   No. It is I who have made you angry. I think you
do not like me now. That is O.K.

AMERICAN:   No, it isn't.

ISRAELI:   Is, isn't. Why don't you stop thinking? This has
nothing to do with the brain. Listen: you like my face, you
like my body. (*Slowly, he stretches his legs out*) You want to
touch . . . to kiss . . . to hold . . . You want me.

NARRATOR:   He rolls over on his back, his hands clasped
behind his head, his legs apart.

ISRAELI:   Here I am . . . So do you come to bed and be
satisfied? Or do you go back to your hotel and be frustrated?
(*A pause. The American is frozen, unable to move. The Narrator
looks at his manuscript, then at the audience. With charm:*)

NARRATOR:   I've told this story before—several times, but
I have varied the ending—by suiting it to the morality of the
listener. (*Slightly angry*) No, no, wait. It actually happened. But
it was so long ago, and now—as with so many stories, with so
much of history, I suppose—I no longer remember how it
really did end.

AMERICAN:   (*To the Narrator*) Oh, come on. You're just
ashamed.

NARRATOR:   Of what?

AMERICAN:   Of me.

NARRATOR: Well, a moment ago, you were so moral! And you always carry on so about principles.

AMERICAN: Have you held on to them? (*A beat, then the Narrator looks away*)

ISRAELI: Why not do what you really want and come lie here?

AMERICAN: (*Turns to him*) You think I find you so attractive.

ISRAELI: Yes.

AMERICAN: (*Indicating his crotch*) Look.

ISRAELI: Oh, that is just fear; nerves. Look at me. No: here . . . And I look at you—there . . . Now: in just two minutes—

NARRATOR: (*To the American*) Put your clothes on!

ISRAELI: (*Triumphantly*) *One* minute! . . . You see? Now: come to me.

AMERICAN: No.

ISRAELI: You want to.

AMERICAN: No! You're too fucking sure of yourself!

ISRAELI: Ah! So *that's* what it is really all about! (*Gets up*)

NARRATOR AND AMERICAN: What?

ISRAELI: (*To the American*) Not morality.

NARRATOR: Oh, yes!

ISRAELI: No: masculinity! Your masculinity is threatened. Oh, you *are* American!

NARRATOR: (*To the American*) Balls! Tell him!

AMERICAN: (*Mildly*) Balls.

ISRAELI: No. *I* picked you. *I* chose ice cream. I took *you* to *my* house. I dominated, and you are afraid that in bed, I will also dominate. Well—I shall.

AMERICAN: You're a German already.

ISRAELI: (*Genially, as he returns to his chair*) Oh, I dominate my German, also. But I am adaptable. I have made him adaptable and I shall make you adaptable. You know, it is really time you learned. It makes it all so much more exciting.

AMERICAN: Animal.

ISRAELI: Of course . . . Well?

NARRATOR: (*To the American*) Well? . . .

AMERICAN: (*To the Narrator*) See him on that bed.

NARRATOR: Walk out.

AMERICAN: *See him!*

NARRATOR: You animal!

AMERICAN:   And you?

(*The American turns back to the Israeli who holds out his hand. Gingerly, the American sits at the edge of the left chair. Slowly, he takes the Israeli's hand. Slowly, the Israeli pulls him close. Then embraces him, kisses him fully. The American's arm goes around the Israeli's neck, but his hand doesn't quite touch the Israeli's back. The Israeli kisses him harder; the American's fingers stiffen, stretched out; the Israeli kisses his face; but those stiff, tense fingers remain outstretched. And very, very slowly, the American's hand comes down until it lies limply on his own knee. A moment, then the Israeli cups the American's neck, a little regretful pat. Then he gets up and swinging his chair over his shoulder, slowly walks off stage right. The American sits huddled, both hands between his crunched up knees*)

NARRATOR:   (*Sharp sarcasm*) Well, did he dominate? Were you adaptable? Was it marvelous?

AMERICAN:   (*Not looking at him*) Don't you remember?

NARRATOR:   No.

AMERICAN:   Don't you know why you don't remember?

NARRATOR:   No.

AMERICAN:   Because it wasn't any good.

NARRATOR:   Then it wasn't worth it.

AMERICAN:   (*Gets up, wheels on him*) So you *are* ashamed!

NARRATOR:   At least if you had walked out!

AMERICAN:   But I didn't!

NARRATOR:   Why?! . . . (*Needing to understand*) Why?

AMERICAN:   (*Looking front*) Because . . . it might have been marvelous.

NARRATOR:   But it wasn't.

AMERICAN:   (*Ruefully*) No; it wasn't. (*Picks up his jacket, swings it over his shoulder as he starts to walk off. He stops just behind the Narrator; the "bed" area light has faded out*) Still—which memory would you rather have?

NARRATOR:   Now?

AMERICAN:   Yes: now.

NARRATOR:   . . . Either. But a memory of *something*.

AMERICAN:   Sorry. Really. (*He puts his hand on the Narrator's shoulder. The Narrator covers it with his hand*)

NARRATOR:   As I said, I've told this tale many times over the years and varied the ending—(*The American withdraws his hand and walks off*) to suit my audience. They usually were pleased. Fantasy is usually more pleasing than truth. And there was—there is pleasure for me simply in the telling of the tale. But nothing . . . *nothing* comparable to the pleasure I would have now from the memory of having done—what I *really* wanted to do. (*A moment, then he closes his manuscript folder and the light goes out*)

*Jonathan Levy*

# CHARLIE THE CHICKEN

# Jonathan Levy

In his fanciful tragicomedy of a woebegone vaudevillian and his trained chicken, *Charlie the Chicken*, playwright and educator Jonathan Levy provides a meaningful glimpse into the master–slave relationship. A production in 1973 by the Manhattan Theatre Club, directed by Ronald Frazier, starring Philip Kerr, David Darlow, and Camela Ashland, received a warm reception. Recognizing the depth beneath the surface humor, Dick Brukenfeld, reviewing the production for the *Village Voice*, wrote, "The poignancy of Levy's play lies in this chicken's efforts to break away from his animal qualities—which are being shaped and exploited—and to become more human. It's a most effective dramatic metaphor, and not a word is wasted in this imaginative, witty script." Premiered at the American Shakespeare Festival in Stratford, Connecticut, in 1972, the play has had numerous productions in regional and community theatres, yet this publication marks its debut in print, making it available to many other performing groups as well as the reading public. The play has also been adapted as an opera with music by Quenten Doolittle. The opera premiered in Toronto in 1975.

Jonathan Levy is the author of more than two dozen plays which have been produced Off-Broadway by such distinguished groups as The Impossible Ragtime Theatre, the Manhattan Theatre Club, and the HB Studio. A nationally recognized authority on children's theatre, Dr. Levy also has written a half dozen children's plays, notably *Marco Polo*, *The Marvellous Adventures of Tyl*, *The Play of Innocence and Change*, and *The Little Green Bird*. His many playwriting honors include playwright-in-residences with the Albee-Barr Playwrights Unit, the Manhattan Theatre Club, and the Eugene O'Neill Playwrights Conference. He has also received a playwriting grant from the Creative Artists Public Service (CAPS). Among his recent productions have been *Master Class*, a companion piece to *Charlie the Chicken*, presented at the Aspen Music Festival in Colorado, in 1980, and *Arts and Letters* at the New York Stageworks in 1981.

Dr. Levy received his A.B. cum laude from Harvard College in 1956, an M.A. from Columbia University in 1959, with additional studies in Italy at L'Università di Roma and L'Università di Ca' Foscari under a Fulbright Fellowship Grant. His Ph.D. was awarded by Columbia University in 1966, after he completed his dissertation on Italian playwright Carlo Gozzi.

Presently Chairman of the Department of Theatre Arts, State University of New York at Stony Brook, Dr. Levy has been active in the New England Theatre Conference and the American Theatre Association. Prior to teaching at Stony Brook, Dr. Levy taught at the Julliard School of Music, the University of California at Berkeley, Columbia College, and Brandeis University. Dr. Levy also serves as consultant to the National Endowment for the Arts on the Theatre Policy Panel.

# Characters:

FERENC HORVATH, *a seedy Hungarian entertainer, forties*
CHARLIE, *a large chicken*
DOROTHEA LONG, *a member of the public, fifty-eight*

# Scene:

*The play takes place on the stage of a small, run-down theatre and in a dressing room backstage at the same theatre. The set should represent both. There is no interruption in the action of the play.*
    NOTE: *Charlie's costume should be simple—yellow leotards, yellow top, feet, and perhaps a crest. Under no circumstances should he be dressed in a full chicken costume.*
    *A pianist and a drummer provide the music for the act. If live musicians are unavailable, taped music can be used.*


*Music is heard in the dark. It is loud and gay, but amplified tinily. Ferenc Horvath's recorded voice is singing:*
VOICE:    "CH-CH-CH-CHARLIE, THE CHICKEN,
            YES, INDEED,
            CH-CH-CH-CHARLIE, THE CHICKEN,
            HE'S JUST WHAT YOU NEED,
            CH-CH-CH-CHARLIE, THE CHICKEN,
            WAY-O-WAY—
            O, SURE HE'S A CHICKEN,
            BUT HE'S O.K."
*(Part-way through the song, a spotlight comes up on Horvath, entering. He is gay and smiling. He hops and drag-steps. He wears rumpled tails. He may sing a few words along with the recording; or he may just smile, nod, and flash his eyes. He has a long leash in his hand.*
    *At the end of the leash is Charlie, a large, doleful chicken. He has bad-looking plucked skin, big thighs, and large yellow feet. His eyes are sad. He comes on reluctantly, surreptitiously counting the house.*
    *They are center stage as the song ends. Horvath smiles and bows. Minimal applause)*
HORVATH:    Thank you, ladies and gentlemen. Thank you

for that gratifyingly warm welcome. Thank you for myself, Ferenc Horvath (*He waits. There is no applause*), and for someone who I am sure needs no introduction. I mean no other than our finely fettled friend, that fabulous feathered phenomenon—Charlie the Chicken. Take a bow, Charles. (*Horvath tugs lightly on the leash. Charlie half bows, half curtseys*) Good. Charles, I have a problem and I believe you can help me with it. (*Charlie turns and looks alert*) If I should have five apples, and some kind gentleman or lady should give me three apples more, how many apples would then I have? Can you help me, Charles? (*Charlie pretends to think. He then taps his foot eight times, like a show horse. Horvath whispers "addition" to the audience, then counts the last few numbers*) . . . six . . . seven . . . eight! I would have eight apples? Indeed I would. Thank you very much, Charles. (*Horvath looks at the audience for a reaction. There is none*) You ain't seen nothin' yet. (*Horvath is proud of his colloquial English, and pronounces slang expressions as if they were italicized*) Now suppose, Charlie, I were to lose one apple. (*Charlie looks sad*) Supposing it were to slip out through a hole in these ancient trousers. (*Horvath performs a pathetic bit of business, losing an apple through a hole in his pocket, etc. Charlie acts amused*) And then, Charlie, I were to give *you* three apples. (*Charlie nods and smiles*) But I discover one is rotted, so I must throw it away. (*Horvath throws away the imaginary apple. Charlie sulks and acts glum*) How many apples would then I have, Charlie? (*Charlie pretends to think. The he taps his foot twice*) No, Charlie, not how many apples would *you* then have. (*Aside*) Such a greedy bird. How many apples would then *I* have. (*Charlie thinks, then taps his foot four times. Horvath whispers "subtraction" at the audience*) . . . three . . . four! I would have four apples? That is absolutely *correct*, Charles. (*Horvath waits for applause. There is none*) It is marvellous, isn't it, for an ordinary sixty-nine-cents-a-pound commercial chicken. (*Charlie gives Horvath a dirty look*) Look, folks, I've hurt his feelings. (*Charlie and Horvath stare at one another for a moment*) Charles, I have one or two more questions for you, if you have no objections. (*Charlie cocks his head to one side*) Good. Now, then, Charles, tell me. What do you call a person who by profession sorts papers, who types, who files papers away. That person is called a . . . a . . .

CHARLIE: (*After a big preparation*) Cluck.
HORVATH: That's right. That person is called a *clerk*. And

what do you call that dial with the numbers on his face from which you tell the time. It is a . . . a . . .

CHARLIE:   (*Louder*) Cluck.

HORVATH:   That's right. A *clock*. And lastly, what is the name of that silk garment you sling over your shoulders when you go off to the opera—as you do so often, you elegant bird? That garment is called an opera . . . an opera . . .

CHARLIE:   (*After a big preparation, still louder*) CLUCK.

HORVATH:   Yes it is. An opera *cloak*. Thank you very much, Charles. (*Horvath waits for the audience's reaction. There is none*) Enough of these weighty matters. This is an evening for gaiety. Show the good people your terpsichorean talents, won't you, Charles? Music, please. (*"Charlie the Chicken," without words, is played in a Dixieland arrangement*) Do your stuff, Charles. Let them see you shake a leg. (*Horvath tugs on the leash. Charlie, reluctantly at first, does an awkward solo dance to the music. Horvath stands aside and encourages him*) Oh, that Charlie! Go, Charles, go. Stomp them big yellow feet, Charles. Watch this closely, now. A fabulous finish.

(*Charlie, sweating and puffing, uses all the dancer's tricks to milk applause. Horvath, smiling, assists him. There is little or no applause. Charlie bucks and wings offstage. Horvath joins him, singing the last words of the song: "O, sure he's a chicken, but he's O.K." Horvath exits, smiling, begging for applause, not getting any. The curtain comes down. The music ends. Charlie stops dancing. Horvath stops smiling. He takes out a large handkerchief and wipes his face. Then as if to himself*)

HORVATH:   Well. Not so terrible for a Tuesday. Slow to start but then I warm them up. By the end there were even bravos. (*He tugs at Charlie's leash*) Come along, Charles.

CHARLIE:   (*Exploding*) What the hell do they want for their money, the savages? (*He goes to the curtain and yells through it*) That's right. Sit on your hands, savages.

HORVATH:   Easy does it, Charlie. Don't exhaust yourself. We have the midnight show still to play.

CHARLIE:   If you think I'm ever going out in front of those savages again, you're crazy. (*Charlie begins to take his makeup off quickly and professionally*)

HORVATH:   Put on your dressing gown, Charlie. You'll catch cold. (*Horvath helps Charlie on with his dressing gown. Charlie takes off more makeup*) And the towel. (*Horvath puts a towel around Charlie's head. Charlie finishes taking off his makeup. It must be*

*clear that when Charlie has his makeup off, he is still a chicken*)
There. (*Charlie and Horvath stand looking at one another*) Charlie?
(*Pause*)
CHARLIE: O.K. O.K.
(*Charlie takes a deep breath, then rushes around the room, performing a familiar routine. He draws the curtains, sets the table for Horvath—tablecloth, napkins, silverware, and candles—and then dusts Horvath's chair with his wings. He then pulls two plastic bowls from under the table and arranges them side by side. While he does this, Horvath opens a bottle of wine, sniffs the cork, swirls the wine around in his glass, tastes it expertly, and approves. He then sets the wine bottle down on the table and lights the candles. Charlie ends up panting and wheezing in front of Horvath, just as Horvath blows out the match*)
HORVATH: Very quick tonight, Charlie. Excellent. Here you are.
(*He takes a piece of candy out of his pocket and holds it in the palm of his hand toward Charlie. Charlie pauses, then pecks the candy out of Horvath's hand, holds it in his beak a moment, then spits it out at Horvath's feet*)
HORVATH: (*Reproachfully*) Tsk, Charlie. Nougat. (*During the next speech, Horvath takes a copper pot off a hot plate, savors the smell, serves himself delicately, and scrapes what is left into Charlie's food dish*)
CHARLIE: Horvath, how do you think I feel, night after night, leaping around the stage like some kind of painted fool? It's humiliating, Horvath. And God knows you're no help. Big yellow feet!
HORVATH: Komm, Sharlie. Ábendessen. Vacsora.
CHARLIE: I'm going to die out there some night, Horvath. I'm going to keel right over and die right in the middle of the finale. My heart was pounding like a drum tonight. Feel, Horvath.
HORVATH: (*Eating*) Getting cold, Charlie.
(*Charlie crosses to the table*)
CHARLIE: Feel. (*He takes Horvath's hand and places it on his chest. He breathes deeply and rhythmically several times, eyes closed. He then opens his eyes and sees his dish. Beat*) Where's my beer? You forgot my beer, Horvath.
(*Horvath sighs, takes a bottle of beer out of a carton under the table, and pours the beer into Charlie's drinking dish*)
HORVATH: Eat, Charlie. You know you get dizzy when you

dance if you don't eat. (*Charlie turns away, sulking*) At least drink your beer.

(*Charlie sighs. He crosses to his dishes. He sighs again, then eats and drinks, bending from the waist and bobbing up and down like a toy penguin. Charlie is downstage of Horvath. The audience can just make out his mutterings. Horvath cannot*)

CHARLIE:   What is this slop?

HORVATH:   (*Of the wine*) Kiváló. Hatvankettes? [Extraordinary. 1962?] (*He sucks in the wine*) Hatvankettes. [1962]

CHARLIE:   This looks like *shit*. (*He bobs*)

HORVATH:   Hmm.

CHARLIE:   It *looks* like shit (*He bobs*), it *smells* like shit (*He bobs*), and it (*He bobs*) *tastes* like shit.

HORVATH:   (*Of the food and wine*) Finom. Jaj de finom. [Exquisite. Truly exquisite]

CHARLIE:   (*After a beat*) Took all the meat for himself and left me the potatoes. Typical, typical.

HORVATH:   What's that, Charlie? You're muttering.

CHARLIE:   I said, why don't you talk English, you Hungarian fuck?

HORVATH:   My, My. We are in a foul mood tonight, aren't we?

CHARLIE:   "Fool moot." You're a joke, Horvath. (*Horvath shakes his head and continues to eat*) Why should you eat off imported china when I eat out of a lousy plastic dish? Answer me, Horvath. And why should you drink imported foreign wine when I drink beer?

HORVATH:   You prefer beer, Charlie.

CHARLIE:   (*Stamping his foot*) *My beer is warm*. It's boiling in the dish. Look at it, Horvath. Boil, boil.

HORVATH:   Charlie, you're being infantile.

(*Pause. Charlie kicks over his dish*)

CHARLIE:   That's it, Horvath. I'm through. Finished.

HORVATH:   Eat your dinner off the floor if you prefer it so, you ridiculous bird.

CHARLIE:   You didn't hear me, did you, Horvath?

(*Pause*)

HORVATH:   I heard you, Charlie. You said you were through. (*Pause*) Again.

CHARLIE:   This time I mean it, Horvath.

HORVATH:   Of course you mean it, Charlie. You always mean it.

CHARLIE:   Stop eating, Horvath. I'm serious.

(*Horvath stops eating and wipes his mouth*)

HORVATH:   All right, Charlie. Then tell me. Explain to me. If you quit me, what will you do?

CHARLIE:   Do? You must be kidding. I'm a goddamn prodigy. I *read*. I'm *literate*. (*He tilts the wine bottle toward him and reads the label*) "Tokay szamorodni. To be drunk at room temperature." How many literate chickens do you think there are in the world . . .

HORVATH:   How many employers in the world do you think are looking for literate chickens, Charlie?

CHARLIE:   . . . in *two languages*. In English perfect, with a smattering of Hungarian?

HORVATH:   Nagyon meglep, hogy beszélsz magyarul, Charlie. [It surprises me to know you speak Hungarian, Charlie.]

CHARLIE:   What's that?

HORVATH:   I said I was delighted to hear you know Hungarian, chicken. (*He laughs*)

CHARLIE:   Horvath, don't laugh at me!

HORVATH:   Excuse me, Charlie. Pardon me for laughing. (*Their eyes meet. Pause*)

CHARLIE:   (*Turning away*) Huh.

HORVATH:   (*Ingratiating*) I often wonder to myself these difficult days, Charlie. What has become of that perky, adorable chick, the sweetest of the litter, who caught my eye in Rahway?

CHARLIE:   None of your tricks now, Horvath.

HORVATH:   So eager was he, so full of wonder. Well I recall his tiny tears of gratitude when I carried him away in a shoebox. Remember your shoebox house, Charlie? The bed I made for you of napkins?

CHARLIE:   (*Moved despite himself*) Horvath . . .

HORVATH:   Remember how I fed you with the eye-dropper, and covered you with my handkerchief when you slept? Such a sweet baby you were, Charlie.

CHARLIE:   But I'm not a baby any more, Horvath. I'm . . . nearly a yearling. And I feel . . . I feel . . . (*He crosses his wings over his heart*)

HORVATH:   (*Softly*) Dishes, Charlie. (*Charlie, still in a reverie, begins to clear the table. He does the reverse of his first routine, now slowly and abstractedly*) How proud was I when you began to count, Charlie. Count everything in sight: the claws on your little feet, the bulbs in the mirror, the steps up to the boarding house. How proud I was and pleased, Charlie. (*Horvath sees that Charlie has been mesmerized back into his routine. Horvath leans back in his chair, puts a napkin over his eyes, and dozes*)

CHARLIE:   (*Clearing*) Yes, Horvath, but that was *then*. Now I feel somehow . . . (*He pauses, holding a dish*) I don't even know the word for it, Horvath. I don't even know the god- damn *word*. I feel as if my . . . (*He touches his belly*) . . . wants to . . . to . . . (*He flings his wings upward*) I feel as if my . . . (*The tips of his wings tremble at his chest*) . . . needs to . . . (*His wings tremble upward. Before they are completely raised, he hears the sound of Horvath's heavy breathing*) Horvath, you incredible bas- tard. WAKE UP. (*He bangs a dish*)

HORVATH:   (*Waking*) Huh? What is it, Charlie? Are we on? (*He quickly begins to tidy himself up*)

CHARLIE:   No, we're not *on*.

HORVATH:   So. (*He settles back*) So then no more outbursts, please, Charlie.

CHARLIE:   Horvath, someday I'm going to kill you.

HORVATH:   You, Charlie? With your heart? That, I'm afraid, is cheap romance.

CHARLIE:   (*Suddenly manic*) Ho. Oh, ho. Look who's telling who about cheap romance? (*Charlie closes his eyes, puts his wings over his heart, and recites sentimentally from memory*) "Dearest Fer- enc: I have neither aten nor slept since Tuesday, two-thirty A.M. Well I recall our tender raptures and in between the sweet song you hummed me."

HORVATH:   Where did you find that letter, Charlie? (*Charlie burlesques a romantic sigh*)

CHARLIE:   "Can you come Sunday between nine forty-five and ten P.M.? I know you do not work. The Newmans go to the balett with freunds and little Douglas sleeps now all through the night after his nine o'clock feeding."

HORVATH:   Stop, Charlie.

CHARLIE:   "I long to hear a thousand more tales of your wonderful life and times . . . "

HORVATH:   Stop, damn you. (*He stalks Charlie around the room, quickening his pace during the following dialogue, so that by the end of it, he is chasing him*)

CHARLIE:   " . . . to gaze on you, nude except for your long socks, to listen once again to your tender humming . . ."

HORVATH:   (*Quiet and deadly serious*) Stop, Charlie.

CHARLIE:  ". . . and kiss a thousand times your dear face."
Horvath, you rogue.

HORVATH:  (*Lunging at him*) Argh.

(*Charlie dodges him*)

CHARLIE:  "Sincerely yours, your Polish rose, Anna." (*Horvath catches Charlie and slaps him hard, twice. They glower at one another*) Bully. I was crazy to listen to you. I should have stayed on the farm.

HORVATH:  If you had stayed on the farm, you would have been sold in parts in March 1982. (*Pause*) Am I right or am I wrong, Charlie?

CHARLIE:  (*Sullenly*) I forget.

HORVATH:  You forget? Reflect, Charlie. You are a reflective bird.

CHARLIE:  I could have talked my way out of it.

HORVATH:  Charlie, are you crazy? Are you cracked? Or are you high? (*Charlie turns away*) How many words could you speak when you lived on the farm? (*Charlie is silent*) You could say "Here, chick, chick, chick. Come get fed, you yellow bastards." And that is absolutely *all*, Charlie.

CHARLIE:  What do you expect, with my upbringing?

HORVATH:  And no one could hear even *that* until I transistorized you. So you owe me, chicken.

CHARLIE:  Listen. I don't have to stand here and take any more of your crap, you dumb Hungari . . .

(*Horvath switches off Charlie's transistor. Charlie continues to mouth words, but only an occasional squawk is heard*)

HORVATH:  Ha ha ha, chicken. (*Charlie squawks and gesticulates*) Do you capitulate, chicken? (*Charlie squawks and gesticulates more frantically*) Acknowledge I am your benefactor, chicken. (*Charlie squawks and points*) Acknowledge, chicken. (*Charlie nods "yes"*) Good. Now finish clearing and (*Clapping his hands*) quick, quick, quick.

(*Charlie goes back to his routine clearing, dejected. Horvath sits. Charlie turns to him and points pitifully at his mouth. He and Horvath stare at one another. Charlie points more pitifully and submissively at his mouth. Pause. Horvath turns on Charlie's transistor. Charlie nods thanks and goes back to clearing. Pause*)

CHARLIE:  (*Pleading*) Horvath, teach me things.

HORVATH:  Teach you, Charlie? I've taught you many things.
(*Charlie turns away*) I have, Charlie. Be fair.

CHARLIE:  *Sure* you have. You taught me (*He sings, exaggerating*)
"CH-CH-CH-CHARLIE, THE CHICKEN,
YES, INDEED,
CH-CH-CH-CHARLIE, THE CHICKEN,
HE'S JUST WHAT YOU NEED . . ."
What does that mean, Horvath, "He's just what you need?"
HORVATH:  That's for the rhyme, Charlie.
CHARLIE:  (*Stopping work*) Rhyme? (*Pause*) What's a "rhyme,"
Horvath. (*Playing with it*) Ry-um. A ry-um.
HORVATH:  A rhyme, Charlie? A rhyme is, for example, a
rhyme is "Szeretlek, megvetlek." Or "odaindult, hozzásimult."
Or . . .
CHARLIE:  Horvath, I don't understand. Tell me in English.
HORVATH:  In English, Charlie, is more difficult to explain.
CHARLIE:  Try, Horvath.
HORVATH:  (*Thinking*) Hm. In English, a rhyme is for example (*Singing loudly right at Charlie*)
"CH-CH-CH-CHARLIE, THE *CHICKEN*
WAY-O-WAY—
O SURE HE'S A *CHICKEN*
BUT HE'S O.K."
(*Pause*)
CHARLIE:  By the way, Horvath, what the hell is that supposed to mean anyway?
HORVATH:  (*Puzzled*) What, Charlie?
CHARLIE:  (*Singing right at Horvath*)
"O, SURE HE'S A CHICKEN
*BUT* HE'S O.K."
Why isn't it, "O, sure he's a chicken *and* he's O.K.?"
HORVATH:  That's the way the song goes, Charlie.
CHARLIE:  You *wrote* the goddamn song, Horvath, you can
change it. Put in more rhymes.
HORVATH:  Careful of the tureen, Charlie.
CHARLIE:  (*Suddenly uncontrolled*) I HATE THAT SONG!
HORVATH:  But it's *your song*, Charlie.
CHARLIE:  Right. That's right. I HATE MY SONG. (*He and
Horvath stare at one another. Pause*)
HORVATH:  Charlie? Why don't you go play with Dolly for
a while? Go, Charlie. Play with nice Dolly.
(*Charlie crosses furiously to a large toy dog. He picks up the dog*

*and squeezes it twice. The dog makes two awful wheezing squeeks.
Charlie drops the dog and glowers at Horvath)*

HORVATH: Here, Charlie. Watch. Watch me, Charlie. I'll
teach you the shuffle-ball-chain.

CHARLIE: I don't want to learn any more of that crap.

HORVATH: Charlie, you have been pestering me for months
to teach you the shuffle-ball-chain. Watch, now. Shuffle-ball-
chain, shuffle-ball-chain . . .

CHARLIE: Horvath, teach me . . . astronomy. *(He crosses to
Horvath, who is doing the step with precision and didactic slowness)*
Teach me welding. Teach me music. Teach me anything but
this . . . this . . . *(Charlie has become fascinated by Horvath's feet.
He falls into step beside him. They are now doing the step side-by-
side, half-speed. Horvath whistles. They come to the hands-out ending.
Charlie breaks away disgusted)* Goddamn it, you tricked me again.
*(Horvath continues the step, whistling)* Horvath, teach me some-
thing hard.

HORVATH: *(Dancing)* No.

CHARLIE: Why?

HORVATH: I can only teach you what I know. And this is
what I know.

CHARLIE: Then turn me loose.

HORVATH: No.

CHARLIE: Please. *(Horvath, smiling broadly, nods his head "no")*
Send me to school, Horvath. It won't cost you a penny. School
is free. I can still dance in the evenings. *(Charlie, smiling, begins
to dance and whistle ingratiatingly)* Pleeease?

HORVATH: No, Charlie. No means no.

CHARLIE: *(Stopping dancing)* Then I'm warning you, Horvath. I'm giving you fair warning. You'd better not ever turn
your head for a second. You'd better not ever blink your eyes,
because when you do I'm going to bash you over the head
with a beer bottle and escape.

HORVATH: You can't *hold* a beer bottle, Charlie.

CHARLIE: I'll find a way. I'm smarter than you are, Horvath, and you know it. I'll poison your wine.

HORVATH: One more word along this line, Charlie, and
I'll switch off your transistor.

CHARLIE: When I kill you, I'll turn it back on.

*(Pause. They glower at one another)*

HORVATH: Suppose—just suppose, Charlie—you did catch

me off my guard. Which you never will, Charlie, I assure you. I am a most wary man. But suppose you did. How do you propose to get out of this theatre?

CHARLIE: I'll *fly*. (*Horvath laughs*) Don't laugh at me, Horvath.

HORVATH: Look at me, chicken. Ha ha ha. I'm laughing. (*Charlie, furious, struts up and down, cursing and squawking*) Here. Look, Charlie. Charlie, Charlie. I'm opening the window. (*He does*) Go, Charlie. Fly away. I won't stop you.

CHARLIE: Chickens can fly. (*Charlie flaps his wings more and takes a few warm-up hops*)

HORVATH: Some chickens can fly, and some chickens can no longer fly. They bred you for meat, Charlie. Look at you. You're all breast and drumstick. (*Charlie is taxiing up and down the room, making ferocious asthmatic noises*) Go. Fly, fly away. Here. I'll open you wider the window. (*He does, then stands back*)

CHARLIE: Here I go. Stand back, Horvath. (*Charlie, racing his feet, judges the distance to the window. He then puffs once or twice and cries "cluck, cluck, cluck" loudly and proudly. He jumps at the window and hits the wall under it hard. He grunts*)

HORVATH: Ah ha, chicken.

CHARLIE: I haven't begun yet, Horvath. (*With more preparation and louder clucking, he tries again, with the same result. He sits for a moment, dazed, shaking his head*)

HORVATH: Rest, Charlie. You are in poor health.

CHARLIE: (*Panting and wheezing*) It's all the beer you give me. (*He pulls himself together for a third try. Louder clucking and more preparations. This time he almost makes it. He tries to scramble out the window, using his wings as hands. Finally, he falls back down heavily*)

CHARLIE: Goddamn, goddamn, goddamn.

HORVATH: Don't cry, Charlie. Drink another beer. (*He begins to go to the refrigerator. As he bends to open it, there is a knock on the door. Pause. Another knock*) Who is it?

MRS. LONG: (*Muffled*) Mrs. Long.

HORVATH: Who?

MRS. LONG: (*Muffled, but louder*) Dorothea Long.

CHARLIE: (*Coming back to himself*) Help. Help me. I'm in here. I'm right in here. Help . . .

HORVATH: (*Over the end of Charlie's line*) Just a moment.

(*Horvath switches off Charlie's transistor. Charlie squawks and gesticulates*) Be sensible, Charlie. I'm warning you now. (*To the door*) Entrez.

(*The door opens tentatively. Enter Dorothea Long, carrying a large bunch of flowers. She takes in the scene*)

MRS. LONG:   I'm sorry. Is this a bad time?

(*Charlie squawks*)

HORVATH:   Well, Madam, to be quite frank . . .

(*Mrs. Long carries a bouquet of flowers and has a small flash camera around her neck*)

MRS. LONG:   I'll just stay a moment. I'm Dorothea Long. I just had to tell you how much I enjoyed you and your remarkable bird. But I suppose everyone tells you that. (*She hands Horvath the flowers*) Here.

HORVATH:   So kind of you, Madam. (*He kisses her hand. Charlie hops around, squawks, and points at himself*)

MRS. LONG:   It took me forever to find a flower shop open at this time of night. My husband thought I was quite mad. May I?

HORVATH:   Of course.

(*She takes a picture*)

MRS. LONG:   I'm afraid they're wilted, but it's the thought that counts, don't you agree? I do hope the bird isn't allergic to roses. (*Charlie squawks and hops in impatience. Mrs. Long claps her hands*) Hop, hop, hop. Tell me, Mr. Horvath, did you train him yourself?

HORVATH:   I did, Madam. From a baby. (*Charlie protests*) You must excuse Charlie. He is always overexcited after a performance.

MRS. LONG:   Oh, yes, I know. Temperament. (*She takes another picture*) I'm quite a connoisseur of professional animals, Mr. Horvath. You might say it's a passion of mine. I've seen them all. I saw Price and his Pandas in their heyday. And mine, and mine. No, now don't be gallant, Mr. Horvath. I'm fifty-eight, and I look it. (*Charlie squawks as if to say: "Pay attention to me."*) Oh, I am quite definitely . . . pre-war, Mr. Horvath. (*She takes another picture*) I go way back. But I declare, I don't think I've been as moved in a theatre as I was tonight since . . . well, let me see . . . since the Prague Circus in 1954. All by you and your marvellous . . . (*She finally turns to Charlie*) . . . Charlie. Is that your name? (*Charlie, with mime and chicken noises, tries to speak to Mrs. Long. Charlie's subtext: "Pay attention.*

*This is important. Watch my mouth. I'll speak slowly"*) He is agitated, isn't he.

HORVATH:  (*Pointing his finger at Charlie*) Bad chicken. Bad chicken.

MRS. LONG:  Mr. Horvath, what kind of a . . . name is "Charlie?"

HORVATH:  Charlie? Charlie is an American name, Madam.

MRS. LONG:  No, what I meant was . . . Would you sign this, please. (*She takes a program out of her bag*)

HORVATH:  Of course.

(*While Horvath is signing the program, Mrs. Long whispers in his ear*)

HORVATH:  Oh. You are wondering what *sex* Charlie is.

MRS. LONG:  I told you I was pre-war, Mr. Horvath.

HORVATH:  *That* question, Madam, is a *very good question.*

(*Charlie, outraged, jumps, squawks, and points at his genitals. Charlie's subtext: "It's not a question at all. That's bullshit. Just look here, for God's sake. Mucho macho." Mrs. Long turns away. Horvath points and shakes his finger at Charlie*)

HORVATH:  Bad chicken. Bad, bad chicken. Czak várj. Jól elbánok majd én veled, Charlie. [You will get it afterward, Charlie. Both the slapping and the beating]

CHARLIE:  (*In chicken language*) [I don't care. Nothing can be worse than this.]

HORVATH:  Nem hiszed. Meglátod majd meglátod, Charlie. [You think not? Just you wait and see]

CHARLIE:  (*In chicken language*) [I'm up on all your sadist's tricks, Horvath. I can take anything you can dish out.]

(*Mrs. Long clears her throat*)

HORVATH:  Ah.

(*Mrs. Long clears her throat again*)

HORVATH:  (*Ignoring her*) Azt hiszed, hogy olyam jól ismersz engem, Charlie, olyan kinzásokat ismerek, amelyekröl még nem is hallottál egész életedben. [You think you know all the punishments, Charlie. But I have punishments you never dreamed of in your strangest dreams.]

CHARLIE:  (*In chicken language*) [Just you try it, bastard. I'll rake out your eyes with my claws.]

MRS. LONG:  Well . . .

HORVATH:  (*Still ignoring her*) Összekötöm a két lábadat, Charlie, és. levágom minden körmödet. [I'll *cut* your claws,

Charlie, with a long, sharp knife. And I'll tie your legs together with wire.]

MRS. LONG:   My husband will be wondering what's become of me.

CHARLIE:   (*In chicken language*) [I'll get an eye before you do, Horvath.]

HORVATH:   Majd meglátjuk, majd meglátjuk. [We shall see what we shall see.]

(*Pause*)

MRS. LONG:   I'll be going now, Mr. Horvath. (*Horvath and Charlie are glaring at one another*) Goodbye, Mr. Horvath.

HORVATH:   (*Turning to her, full of charm*) Goodbye, Madam? So soon? Well, if you must. (*He guides her toward the door, then kisses her hand*) Au revoir, Madam. And thank you again for the flowers. We are *both* so grateful.

MRS. LONG:   Please don't mention it. Au revoir, Mr. Horvath. (*Horvath bows*) And Charlie?

(*She clucks "I'll be seeing you" in a fair approximation of chicken language. Pause. Charlie then launches into an impassioned, bravura aria in chicken language, complete with breast beating and tears*)

CHARLIE:   (*As interpreted into English*) "*Look* at me. *Look*. Do you know what's going on here, between me and that man? He slaps me and beats me. When you leave, he's going to torture me.

You can't believe how awful he is. Oh, I know, he looks dapper, he looks suave, but the truth is he doesn't *bathe*. *Never*. He *never bathes*. Just slaps on more eau de cologne. He doesn't own any underwear. He stuffs newspaper into his pants. And he only has one pair of socks, one pair of *long black socks*. When he gets a hole in one of them he paints over it with shoe polish. That's the kind of man he is underneath. (*Horvath and Mrs. Long exchange a look*) And *me. Me.* I have immortal longings. I want to float, I want to soar. I want to know the most learned men of my time and charm the wittiest and most beautiful women. I know there must be people like that outside. *I can imagine them.* There must be more to life than stupid dancing and nougats and "Ch-Ch-Ch-Charlie, the Chicken, yes indeed . . ." There must be a whole world outside this dressing room. Free me. Please, Missus. Take me with you. Take me away from here. If you're got any charity in

CHARLIE'S SONG

Ch- Ch- Ch- Char-lie, the chick-en, yes in- deed. Ch- Ch- Ch- Char-lie, the chick-en, he's just what you need. Ch-Ch-Ch- Char- lie, the chick- en way-o- way-o- Sure he's a chick- en, but he's O. K.

your heart, please, *please* take me away. (*Charlie breaks down in sobs. Pause*)

MRS. LONG:   Well. What was all *that* about?

HORVATH:   I have no idea, Madam. You seem to have said something that set him off. He is not a stable bird.

MRS. LONG:   *Did* I? You never know, do you, Mr. Horvath. Well, goodbye again, all. (*As she is going, Charlie rushes to her and throws his wings around her knees. Horvath, cursing and muttering, tries to pull him off. Charlie hangs on. Horvath slaps Charlie hard, twice. Mrs. Long pulls away*)

HORVATH:   You must never let them get that close to you,

Madam. Their beaks are sharp like knives. And they'd as soon rake your eyes out as look at you.

(*The first bars of* "CH-CH-CH-CHARLIE, THE CHICKEN" *are heard offstage. Charlie, desperate, feigns a stagey heart attack. He falls to the floor*)

MRS. LONG:  Yes, but goodness, Mr. Horvath. What a talent. (*Exit Mrs. Long. Beat. Charlie raises his head and looks at the door. The music grows louder. Horvath crosses to Charlie, holds his head down cruelly, and fastens his leash around his neck*)

HORVATH:  Come along, you talented chicken. (*He jerks the leash. Charlie is jerked up*) Double dancing for you this show. And no false moves. Agreed? (*He jerks the leash*) Agreed, Charlie? (*Pause. Then Charlie nods his head "yes"*) Good. (*The music is louder. Horvath takes off Charlie's robe. Charlie points pitifully to his mouth*) Oh, no. Oh, no. Come along, Charlie. (*He jerks Charlie to his feet*) Very bright from the beginning. Or else no more beer. Ever. (*The verse begins. Horvath opens the door leading to the stage. Music louder. Horvath turns back and raises his eyebrows. He and Charlie exchange a long look. Slow blackout as the verse continues. The last line of the song is heard in darkness*)

don't go to church . . . the days of the week are all the same to me. I'm not afraid of dying . . . and I'm not tired of living.

I live alone out here on the old home place. And the days of celebration in other peoples' lives means little, or nothing, to me.

Orville understands. Big dummy that he is. Orville understands.

I do not celebrate "public works" holidays.

*(The doll rocks in the chair)*

Not Xmas, New Years, Thanksgiving, Easter, Halloween, Valentines', April Fools', not the Fourth Day of July.

*(Lights begin to fade)*

Not Labor Day, Arbor Day, Memorial Day, Flag Day, nor none of the Presidents' birthdays.

*(Lights to half)*

Not Mothers' Day, nor Fathers' Day, nor May Day, Dog Day, Groundhog Day, Derby Day . . .

*(Lights to black)*

. . . nor Sadie Hawkins' Day.

Curtain

*Ken Jenkins*

# RUPERT'S BIRTHDAY

# Ken Jenkins

In announcing plans for the Sixth Annual Humana Festival of New American Plays at the Actors Theatre of Louisville, director Jon Jory promised an emphasis on the monologue as a viable theatrical form, and produced Ken Jenkins' *Rupert's Birthday* as proof. Thus he affirmed the precedent of the highly successful *Twirler*, the anonymously written monologue hit of the Fifth Festival (published in this series in the 1982 edition).

Ken Jenkins here demonstrates his mastery of the monologue form in *Rupert's Birthday*, a vivid miniature of an eccentric farm woman whose teenage experience of assisting in the delivery of a calf provided her with a transcendental revelation. Writing in the Louisville *Courier-Journal*, William Mootz observes, "*Rupert's Birthday* is a mystical celebration of life, disguised as a rural folktale. It crowds a lifetime of experience into a short span of time, and it does so with an appealing serenity of spirit. Performed by Susan Kingsley with an emotional honesty that stabs the heart, *Rupert's Birthday* is an incandescent theatre piece."

Currently Rockefeller Playwright-In-Residence at Actors Theatre of Louisville, Ken Jenkins demonstrates his versatility as actor and director, as well as playwright. In the 1981 Festival of New Plays at Actors Theatre he wrote, directed and performed *Chug*, a tragicomic monologue about frog farming, government regulations, and man's ambitions attempting to leap beyond his limitations. Among the plays Mr. Jenkins has directed for Actors Theatre are Preston Jones's *The Oldest Living Graduate, The Glass Menagerie, The Lion in Winter*, and *Bus Stop*.

Mr. Jenkins has appeared as an actor with several other nationally recognized regional companies, including Long Wharf Theatre in New Haven, The Hartford Stage Company, The Alley Theatre, and Cincinnati Playhouse in the Park in classical roles such as Hamlet, Cyrano de Bergerac and Petruchio; and in the contemporary roles of Brick in *Cat on a Hot Tin Roof*, Starbuck in *Rainmaker*, and McMurphy in *One Flew Over the Cuckoo's Nest*.

*Rupert's Birthday* appears here in print for the first time.

# Character:

THE WOMAN

# Scene:

*A rocking chair without arms. A woman sits sewing blue ribbons and white lace on a white cotton nightgown. With her is an old doll dressed in a white nightgown with blue ribbons and white lace.*

THE WOMAN:    Heard it on the news today—183 shopping days left 'til Xmas. Don't mean nothing to me. I don't believe in Santy Claus. Xmas is not my holiday. I don't celebrate Xmas. I don't celebrate any "public works" holidays.

Not Xmas, New Years, Thanksgiving, Easter, Halloween, Valentines', April Fools', nor the Fourth Day of July.

Not Labor Day, Arbor Day, Memorial Day, Flag Day, nor none of the Presidents' birthdays.

Not Mothers' Day, nor Fathers' Day; Not St. Patrick's, St. Mary's, St. Michael's, nor St. Pete's; Not May Day, Dog Day, Groundhog Day, nor Sadie Hawkins' Day.

Not Advent, Pentecost, Good Friday, Ash Wednesday, nor Fat Tuesday; Not the Feasts of the Ascension, the Assumption, the Annunciation, the Apocalypse, nor the Aurora Borealis; Not Passover, Hannukah, Roshashannah, Candlemass Communion, Holy Incarnation, Transubstantiation, nor the Ides of March.

And—not the Annual Pig Roast and Blue Blood-Letting Contest sponsored by the East Tennessee Chapter of the D.A.R.

Rupert's birthday is my holiday.

Rubert was born on the same night as my brother Orville. I named him. Rupert. Saw the name on a sign in a barbershop. Rupert. Prince Rupert. Looked real distinguished. Had a gleam in his eye.

Rupert outweighed Orville at birth. By about 60 lbs

Orville was the baby. Seven girls. And then Orville. Seven girls: Francine (who was supposed to have been a boy), Sheila Leigh (who wasn't), Louisa May (that's me), April (born on December 26th), and the triplets, Faith, Hope, and Charity. And then—Orville. Daddy said he almost named him Despair. Faith, Hope, Charity—and Despair. Seven girls: 17, 15, 13 (that's me), 9, 5, 5, and 5. And Mamma thought she was through. And then—Orville. Orville came backwards. Been that way ever since.

Miranda was my "baby." That's what Daddy always said. She was born on my birthday and her real momma died the next day. So I became her "momma." Daddy showed me how to put milk in a rubber glove and then poke a hole in one of the fingers so she could suck on it. Daddy said, "She's your baby now." So I raised her. She got her milk from that old glove twice a day for weeks. I was her "momma" till she died.

Miranda was born in 1955 on my 11th birthday.

Two years later, on my 13th birthday, she gave birth to Rupert.

And on the same night—Momma had Orville.

May 16, 1957. Miranda had Rupert. Momma had Orville. And I got my first period.

Early that morning Daddy had driven down to East Tennessee to look at some farm equipment being sold at public auction and was not expected back until the following day. I had wanted to go with him, but he convinced me that somebody had to stay behind and look after the stock. I was the best with animals. Still am. Francine never cared about them, and Sheila Leigh made them all nervous. April helped me sometimes, though she could never concentrate, and the triplets were just too little to do anything—except get underfoot.

Momma started labor while she was cooking supper. She wasn't at all worried. She'd been through it all before—including triplets—but, we'd all been small babies. Orville weighed 12 lbs. and 8 oz. And—he came out backwards. Or tried to.

Our neighbor, Mrs. Price, who had 8 kids of her own and had been midwife for lots of births, including the triplets,

came over to help out, but when she saw how Orville was trying to come out, she called Doc Fisher who said, "Bring her to the hospital! Right now!"

So, Mr. Price came over in his station wagon and drove Momma the 14 miles into town to the hospital.

Francine went with them.

Sheila Leigh was having hysterics from all the excitement and finally passed out on the living room couch. I just threw a quilt on her and let her be.

Then I read a story to April and the girls and they went right off to sleep.

I was still wide awake, so I went outside and stood in the middle of the front yard and stared up at the man-in-the-moon. "Mr. Moon," I said, "You look after my Momma. We need her around here." I held my face up to the sky, my head tilted way back—like this—and said, "Please, Mr. Moon. We really do need her."

I listened. The moon didn't answer.

What I heard was: an old hen squawking as she fell off the roost, the creak of the front porch swing, coon dogs barking somewhere off in the woods, and Miranda mooing.

She was standing in a pool of moonlight looking very regal. And very pregnant. She was due in June. Or so we thought.

She mooed again and turned and walked into the barn.

"You smart aleck," I thought, "you've got no business in there." Someone, me probably, had forgotten to latch the gate.

Well, I started to cross the yard to go get her and all of a sudden my head got light and my knees gave out, and I saw the ground come floating up to hit me in the face.

I passed out.

When I came to, I was lying on my back in the front yard looking straight up at the full moon. I felt like I was floating. Being held up by the moon.

Then I saw the blood.

I had started my first period.

I looked down at the dark stain in the center of my clean white nightgown, and I thought of Momma lying on her back on a clean, white sheet with a child struggling to come out through the center of her body.

"Momma and I are both bleeding tonight. I am helping Momma birth that baby. I and the moon. We are helping Momma."

Then I heard Miranda again. She was grunting and groaning as if *she* were in labor.

"Miranda's helping Momma, too," was my first thought. My second thought was, "That's impossible. She's not due 'til June."

I primed the pump and filled a basin with cold water from the well and washed the blood from myself and from my nightgown and hung my nightgown up in the branches of a white ash tree.

And there I stood.

Hard brown body in the silver light of a bright full moon shivering with chill bumps and looking in some wonder at my "new" body.

"This is a woman's body now," I thought, "the blood that has flowed from me tonight has united me for all time to every woman who has ever walked the earth."

"And you've seen it all, haven't you, Mr. Moon."

Miranda groaned again. "She can't be in labor. She's not due 'til June." Or so we thought.

Barefoot and jaybird naked I tiptoed across the white graveled driveway and stood by the barn door.

The wet pump handle sparkled in the moonlight.

My nightgown fluttered in the green leaves of the white ash tree.

"That nightgown belongs to Louisa May the Girl," I thought, "I am Louisa May the Woman now. I need a new nightgown."

Miranda was standing in the small lot in back of the barn where she'd been born two years before. My "baby" Miranda.

"Well, what about it?" I said.

She looked at me and switched her tail, and shook her ears, and bobbed her head up and down, and turned around so I could see her backside.

And there, glistening in the moonlight, were two little feet sticking out about three inches from her swollen vulva.

"For crying out loud, Miranda, you're not supposed to be having that baby *now*! You're not due 'til June!"

Or so we thought.

Miranda lifted her tail, shifted her weight back and forth on her hind legs, and arched her back in a contraction that pushed the calf's feet out of her body clear up to its knees. They were front feet. That was good. At least the calf was going to come out frontwards. Unlike dumb Orville who was trying to come out backside first.

"Oh, my god! Momma! I forgot all about Momma!"

"Well. I can't do anything about Momma. But, I can do something about this."

So I climbed up into the loft and threw down the brightest bale of straw I could find and spread it out in a corner of the lot out of the draft.

Miranda walked over to it, gave it a sniff or two, and lay right down and commenced to have another huge contraction.

The calf's nose had already appeared. I could see its blue tongue spilling over its chin where it rested on the front legs. In good position. Not breathing yet. Not using air. Still attached to its Momma. Breathing through her blood.

I thought, "What if I have to pull it?"

I had watched calves come before, and once or twice I had seen Daddy pull them when the cow was having trouble.

In my mind's eye I saw Daddy's strong hands and arms clasp the slippery legs of the calf and pull out and down, in rhythm with the cow's contractions, until the head and shoulders of the calf were through the narrow opening of the cervix.

I looked down at my own small hands and thought, "These are no good. But, if push comes to shove, I'll try. I'll have to. I'm the one that's here.

I watched Miranda closely for about an hour, stayed right by her side. She'd get up and walk around, and then she'd lay back down and have another series of contractions. And every time she'd get to the point where the broad part of the calf's forehead would almost clear the cervix, she wouldn't be able to get it out any farther. And she would stop pushing, and the calf would slip back inside her womb.

Cows are real strong, but the birthing muscles will wear out, and if the cervix doesn't stretch enough to let the calf through before the cow's muscles are too weak to push, then the cow will quit trying . . . and the calf will die inside her womb. Eventually the cow will die, too.

Well, I was just beginning to realize that I was really going to have to do something when Miranda turned to me and seemed to say, "C'mon you big dummy! I need some help! What are you waiting on? Xmas!"

So, the next time she lay down, I took a couple of burlap feed sacks and got right up close behind her.

She was lying on her right side, with her legs sticking out—like this.

I lay down on my right side, facing her rear end—like this.

Then, I coiled up like a spring, with my knees bent up, and my bare feet flush against the muscles of her back legs.

Then, I wrapped a feed sack around each of the calf's front legs and tied them on with double strands of baling twine.

Then, I looped the strands of twine together between the calf's legs so that there was just enough room for my two hands to grab a hold of. I got a firm hold and waited.

When Miranda pushed—I pulled.

I pulled for all that I was worth.

Every time she'd get the calf's head up in place, she'd have

to stop and rest. And every time she'd stop pushing, the calf would start slipping back inside her.

"C'mon, Miranda, you can do it."

After several series of contractions I was dripping with sweat, and every muscle in my body felt like it was on fire.

"It's now or never, Miranda, you hear? I ain't got much more strength left in me."

She pushed—and I pulled. I held my breath and pulled with all my might. I stretched my body taut like a bow string.

"C'mon, Miranda!"

And just when I thought I was going to explode, Miranda gave a great groan, and out sloshed the calf's head and shoulders and slid right up my naked body and came to rest with its head lying in my lap.

Its body and back legs were still inside Miranda. Umbilical still attached. Half in Miranda—and half lying on top of me.

I looked at the calf's head lying there, wet, between my legs: not yet quite alive, blue tongue lolling sideways out of its mouth, nose still full of birth, ears slicked back against its head, eyes dull and lifeless.

And—as I was looking at the calf's eye—Miranda stood up.

And, as she stood, the rest of the calf's body slipped out, and—the umbilical broke.

And—as the umbilical broke—a *light* switched on in that calf's eye!

I saw it!

It came to life! Life came to it.

As the umbilical broke—it became itself.

It became conscious. It saw.

And the first thing that it saw—was me. Me—looking right at it. Looking right in at it.

I saw the first flash of life come into that calf's eye. Saw it switch on—like a light in a dark room.

It was a bull calf. Dark red with a white star on his forehead. Big framey calf. Distinguished looking.

Well, I stayed there with Miranda and her baby until she'd cleaned him up, and coaxed him up on all four wobbly legs, and helped him find the udder, and he had sucked the first rich colostrum milk, and was ready for a nap, and then I got some soap and a towel and went swimming in the pond.

Floating on my back in the deep water I looked up at the moon and said, "Everything's O.K. on this end, Mr. Moon. I just hope you're taking care of Momma."

The moon did the best he could.

What happened was—Doc Fisher had to open Momma's stomach with a knife and reach in and pull Orville out by the ears. 12 lb. and 8 oz. And tried to come out backwards.

Momma was wore out for a while.

Orville was fine.

May 16, 1957.

Momma had Orville—with no help from him. Miranda had Rupert—with a little help from me.

May 16, 1957.

I turned 13. And my Daddy brought me home a store-bought dolly from East Tennessee for my birthday. I was happy to get it—but, I laughed to myself to think that I was a "woman" now—and here I was—playing with a dolly dressed in a white nightgown trimmed with blue ribbon and white lace.

The next day I made myself a new nightgown. Patterned it after this dolly's dress. First thing I'd ever sewed in my life . . . all by myself. White cotton trimmed with blue ribbons and white lace.

Every year I make myself a new nightgown. White cotton. Blue ribbons. White lace.

(*She puts on the gown*)

Momma and Daddy have long since passed away.

My sisters are all scattered to the winds. Some married. Some not. Some with children. Some not. They all write. And come to "visit" on "holidays."

Orville runs a gas station in town. He comes out. Sometimes. We talk.

May 16, *1958*.

Exactly one year after Orville and Rupert were born. I was 14.

May 16, *1958*.

Rupert's birthday.

Daddy and I loaded Rupert into the truck and carried him into town to be slaughtered for meat.

I didn't cry.

I rode in the back with Rupert and held his huge head in my arms and thought, "One year ago today this big, old head was so small that it could fit between my legs."

At the slaughter house I made Daddy and the butcher be real quiet while I stood in the killing chute with Rupert and rubbed his belly and scratched his neck until he relaxed and lifted up his head and looked me in the eye.

Then, when he was calm and happy, I nodded at the butcher and he shot him in the back of the head. Shot him clean.

He died instantly.

I was looking right in Rupert's eye when the gun went off— and—I saw the light go out in his eye.

I saw it.

I saw the light flash on when he was born. I saw it go out when he was killed.

I was 14.

My sisters all think I'm crazy. I don't send Xmas nor Easter cards. I don't know when any of their children were born. I